LIBERIA

LIBERIA

BLACK AFRICA IN MICROCOSM

Charles Morrow Wilson

Introduction by J. William Fulbright

HARPER & ROW, PUBLISHERS

NEW YORK, EVANSTON, AND LONDON

 For information address Harper & Row, Publishers, Inc., 49 East 33rd Street, New York, N.Y. 10016. Published simultaneously in Canada by Fitzhenry & Whiteside Limited, Toronto.

FIRST EDITION

LIBRARY OF CONGRESS CATALOG CARD NUMBER: 74-123970

CONTENTS

Part III. Yesterday and Tomorrow

A section of illustrations follows page 74.

INTRODUCTION

As most of us will recall, Liberia is the oldest republic in Africa; for more than a century it was the only republic in Africa. The human and historic ties with the United States are especially strong. Most of the first founders of Liberia were freed, or unowned, Negro slaves. Although a few of the founders of Liberia were from the West Indies, and a considerable number were black people rescued from slave ships or slave compounds—from the beginning of the unique colonization, 150 years ago, the majority of the founders were American Negroes.

From that brave beginning by black people who had never before had the opportunity to participate in organized government or to know the privileges and rights of citizenship, Liberia has built its way first to a commonwealth status, then, beginning in 1847, to the continuing status of an independent constitutional republic.

Liberia endures and builds stature as a black nation founded by and perpetuated for black people. Currently the oldest republic in a vast continent which now leads all others in the total number of republics, Liberia holds a position of distinction and influence. It has never suffered a major civil war. It has never taken part in a war of conquest or aggrandizement. At present Liberia leads all countries in the proportion of its national revenues being expended for education. It is a charter member of the United Nations and the first African nation to have been admitted to the Security Council of the

United Nations. Its foreign policy is directed toward peace.

During both the First and Second World Wars, Liberia was an ally of the United States, contributing of its many resources—people, harbors, air bases, strategic minerals, natural rubber, and various other strategic harvests. At present, as throughout the quarter-century just passed, Liberia's most outstanding contributions have been in areas of diplomacy, persuasion, and leadership in behalf of peace—for a turbulent Africa and a turbulent world beyond. In a continuing era of wars, in great part neither formally nor constitutionally declared, a peace-maker nation is a particularly valuable friend.

Liberia, directed by the effective administration of its president, William V. S. Tubman, continues to maintain its role as a dedicated peace maker and peace planner for Africa and to stand as a friend of the United States. Politically, socially, and diplomatically, as the ensuing text points out, this is a historic attainment.

The background here is all the more noteworthy because Liberia is a nation built and perpetuated of and by diverse peoples; it is a significant success story of intra-racial integration. As this book points out, at least nine-tenths of the present census of Liberia is of indigenous Africans, members or descendants of more than twenty long-established tribes, many of strongly contrasting lingual, religious, and ethnic resources or cultures. Through the years the Republic of Liberia has succeeded in bringing these divergent peoples into a nation wherein all find not only acceptance but opportunities to serve as elective officials or otherwise in respected public service.

In all these and many other ways Liberia endures and progresses as an interesting and significant black microcosm. It is a small country; its present area is about that of the state of Ohio and its present census estimate is somewhat less than two million.

Liberia is located on the great western bulge of Equatorial West Africa, where marked contrasts among tribal peoples are traditional. This fact further enhances the significance of Liberia as a microcosm for Africa and its many hundreds of native tribes, native languages, and its diversity of religious faiths. Thus, with English its official language and Christianity its officially accepted religion, Liberia has managed to respect and live in amity with its own and neighboring tribespeople. Liberia has adopted and remained loyal to a national constitution similar to that of the United States, correlating this pivotal document with the ever-contrasting needs of a strongly diverse population.

All the foregoing joins in making Liberia a worthwhile subject for a worthwhile book, a book which necessarily must be validated by the experience and perceptiveness of its author. By this criterion, I believe the author is qualified.

I have known Charles Morrow Wilson practically all my life and his. We are almost exactly the same age. We grew up together in Fayetteville, Arkansas. Charley is a native of this attractive Ozarks town; his great-grandparents were among its first settlers.

Charley and I attended the University of Arkansas together. Subsequently he went into newspaper work, for the *Arkansas Gazette, St. Louis Post-Dispatch,* and, later, the *New York Times.* About the time I joined the law faculty of the University of Arkansas, Charley went to Central and South America for a long stretch of reporting and corporation work. He later put in several years in Liberia and some adjoining areas of tropical Africa. We have remained warm friends through the years, and I have followed his many books with real interest. He regards this book about Liberia as his best, and he may be right. It is sound journalism with an important plus—experienced, sympathetic appreciation.

—J. WILLIAM FULBRIGHT,
Chairman, Foreign Relations Committee,
United States Senate

FOREWORD: Peer Softly Softly

In West African pidgin, sometimes known as tall-bush Esperanto, "peer softly softly" means "look carefully."

Liberia, a little country at the base of the huge western bulge of Africa, justifies and rewards peering softly softly. It is the pioneer republic in that second largest and, as many believe, the most globally decisive of the continents of planet Earth. Liberia remains a Negro nation, with citizenship limited to black people, or, as its Constitution states, to persons of "African descent."

If this is a limitation, Liberia, formally established as a republic in 1847, has overcome it effectively if not always easily. Again and again during the past century and a quarter this distinctive African nation, which free or, better say, unowned American Negroes—in great part former slaves—did most to establish, has been citable as the only black man's republic in all the world.

The name "Liberia," rooted in *libre* (free), even if not apropos of all the historical facts, carries integrity and significance. For the most part the Negro republic was founded and sustained by black people who, either at firsthand or by way of their parents, had suffered and survived enslavement by white people. A majority of the founder pioneers were either so-called free slaves from the United States and the West Indies or fellow Africans who had been rescued or recaptured from the slave traders. But the most decisive founders were a comparative handful of American Negroes, all bearing the scars of enslavement, who returned or were returned to an Africa plagued and tarnished by slavery, which in great part was being perpetuated by black Africans as well as by white slavers.

From this background of multiple afflictions and perilous remoteness, Liberia emerged and endures as a particularly revealing body politic and proving ground for the integration of Negroes with and among other Negroes possessing marked differences of religion, language, places of origin, traditions, degree of skin pigmentation, tribal status or lack of it, and presence or absence of citizenship.

Inevitably the Liberia story is an epic of intraracial dependence and conflicts, an epochal, profoundly human saga of yesterdays meeting tomorrow. It has not been and may never be a smooth, glib success story. It is certainly not a chronicle of geographical bigness; as already suggested, Liberia is a little country—only its significances are big. During the heyday of African empire-snatching, in greatest part between 1870 and 1910, Liberia was reduced to barely one-fourth of its maximum size; more specifically, from about 171,000 square miles to its present area of about 43,000 square miles, and a population currently estimated as between 1.15 million and 1.5 million. Thus in land area present-day Liberia is about as big as Ohio, with no more than one-seventh as many people.

By surface measure the first African republic is describable as a mere dot, even if an exceptionally engaging green-golden and brightly flowered dot or dabble of Equatorial Africa. With most generous diversity Liberia is a beautiful land of beautiful people and many other splendid resources. But these do not include ready accessibility. For the most part the roads are still few and weather-imperiled. To the south and southwest the largely harborless and historically troublesome South Atlantic coast had little to offer except engaging scenery, outrageous tides, ship-buckling rock reefs, sand-littered estuaries, bar-imperiled shipping lanes, and other nautical encouragers of isolation.

As pictured on a map, Liberia now shapes a recognizable image of a Scottish terrier lying on its back, head slightly raised, forepaws folded, and rear legs retracted. Such an image is multiply misleading. Through the years, in all about one hundred and fifty, Liberia has been of necessity standing and moving, intermittently crawling, trudging, trotting, or, as at present, leaping ahead. It follows that

Africa's first republic and only nation with American antecedents can be and deserves to be envisioned not as a comfortably reclining Scotty, but as a capable seeing-eye dog that attends and helps to guide the arousing but still sleep-blinded giantess, Africa.

As one meets and comes to know Liberia, he inevitably reflects on this most unusual heritage of responsibility. As one gains acquaintance with Liberia's special hallmarks, such as the magnificent indigenous vegetation, including the amazingly colorful flowers and the sky-crowding trees that sparkle in the sun like the armor of ancient knights, and as one begins to anticipate and return in kind the engaging, finger-snapping Liberian handshakes, he gains the absolute awareness that Liberia is indeed a very special land with very special destinies.

Sometimes even before one hears the drum songs of line-dance chants or grows accustomed to the vast sweeping breath of Africa, he recognizes that Liberians are very much more than transplanted black Americans. Actually, somewhat fewer than one-tenth of the estimated 1.3 million present Liberians are descendants of American Negro immigrants. The preponderance is still of indigenous tribespeople, and this erases any lucid concept of Liberia as being merely a small black satellite of the United States. In fact, Liberia is a kind of confederation of strongly contrasting, principally indigenous Negro bodies politic, for the most part listable as tribes, with such distinctive and pleasant-sounding names as Bassa, Belle, Buzzi, Chien, Dey, Gbandi, Gio, Gola, Grebo, Guzzie, Kpelle, Mano, Mendi, Vai. There are currently twenty-three of these tribes or remnants of tribes. For the most part they are recognizably different from each other; certainly tribal Liberia is not of look-alikes, do-alikes, or speak-alikes. There are currently twenty-eight native languages and dialects, in addition to English, the nation's "official" language. Similarly, Christianity is the "official" religion, but Liberia has at least a dozen distinctive and living tribal religions, all coexistent with both the Christian and the Mohammedan faiths.

Many students, including this writer, see this enduring cornucopia of distinctive religions as both a symbolic and a practical proof of and a way opener for other Liberian vantages of integration, attained and attainable. Included here are now far-influencing social and economic factors. To take the worst first, one might as well grant that if tagged by routine statistics, Liberia is still a comparatively poor country. Its offical motto, "The Love of Liberty Brought Us Here," continues to endure the flippant and not necessarily truthful supplement, "The Lack of Money Keeps Us Here."

Even so, the average per capita income is still less than $170 a year, and the gross national product ranges from one two-hundredths to one three-hundredths that of the United States. But this somewhat lackluster gem of year-book revelation tends to bypass the fact that several oustandingly useful Liberian resources, such as the superlatively rich iron ores, the largest and best developed source of natural rubber (which about 10,000 Liberian growers now help supply), and, at Monrovia, Africa's most effective and widely used free port, are increasingly consequential to the Americas, Europe, and the Western world at large. One after another, the tangible resources of Liberia are contributing to building industries in both hemispheres.

The increasingly crucial industry of diplomacy finds Liberians gaining effectiveness and prominence as most trusted arbiters and as inter-African peacemakers extraordinary. Meanwhile, the largest enduring Negro republic continues to build and sustain international stature by means of growth and more consistent nurture of black-with-black integration within its home boundaries. There are noteworthy sustaining advances. These do not as yet include agriculture. Proportionately Liberia remains one of the most agrarian of nations; currently about 70 percent of its people are farmers. But by totals the agriculture is not yet good enough. Despite some recent and impressive improvement of specific crops, such as rice and oil palms, Liberia remains far short of being self-sufficient in terms of food production. In Liberia as elsewhere, the presence or even the lurking threat of famine is a prime impediment or discourager of integration.

By heartening contrast Liberia's current and almost unbelievable advances in public education are proving to be an Open Sesame, an almost magical expediter of black man's integration with black man.

In appraising this most promising truth, old-time observers, among whom this writer has to be counted, find their own best-confirmed recollections extremely hard to believe. Back in 1944–

45–46, when I first worked in Liberia, the nation's literacy rate in its official language, English, was being guessed as from 5 to 7 percent. At a fairly well-confirmed 45 percent it is now one of the highest in contemporary Africa, and if the written tribal languages were included as literacy qualifiers, the percentage would be somewhat higher. With school attendance for all children between six and sixteen made compulsory by national law, Liberia now leads most of Africa and, according to United Nations estimates, most other sovereign nations, in prevailing rate of gains in public education. Granted there is still cause for improvement, since fewer than 100,000 Liberian children of primary-school age attend school.

Within a single medium lifetime—in Liberia about thirty-six years—public education in the predominantly tribal hinterlands has advanced from scatterings of the traditional tribal initiation schools, the "Poro" for boys and the "Sande" for girls, and a valiant but feeble scattering of mission schools and one-room manacca-thatched grade schools, to a still hard-up but steadily gaining national public school system in which somewhere near half of the eligible tribal children are enrolled. Granted that this is not adequate and that the high schools and colleges are as yet not meeting minimal needs, there is good hope for improvement. The hope is strengthened by the fact that Liberia is now spending more than 30 percent of its national budget for public education, one of the highest proportions on record. Liberian government expenditures for college fellowships alone exceed the total defense budget by about 25 percent, and the republic is rapidly developing its own indigenous teacher force.

In 1945 Liberia had a total of 251 public and mission schools, with about 19,000 pupils intermittently enrolled for school terms averaging about four months of the year. Only sixteen of the available schools were listable as high schools; in all there were barely five hundred licensed teachers and fewer than one in ten had college degrees. The government's total appropriation for public education in 1945 amounted to $845,000.

As the 1960s ended, the teacher force had increased sevenfold, public school enrollments had grown ninefold, government appropriations for education seventyfold, and the number of functioning schools had increased to 889—more than threefold. For good measure, Liberia now has 180 church schools, of which 22 are accredited as secondary; also a national university and two church-sponsored colleges which concentrate on teacher training. Meanwhile, about nine-tenths of the mission or church schools and most of the U.S. Peace Corps school enterprises in the country are being supported at least in part by the Liberian government. For the first time school textbooks are being written by Liberians.

The government's foreign scholarship program opened in 1945 with four; the present list of government-financed fellowships for studies in American and European universities is above 600. In these young-adult study grants the science of government is but one of the ten areas of scholarship; the others are medicine, dentistry, nursing, teaching, mathematics, geology, business administration, engineering, and agriculture. But the fact is already established that former scholarship holders now include about half of all senior government employees.

Vocational and teacher-training schools are distinctively of homeland vintage. The pivotal trade school is still the Booker T. Washington Agricultural and Industrial Institute, but its refurbishment is especially revelatory. The Institute was founded in 1929 as an elementary trade school, primarily for young male tribe members. The Liberian government's act of increasing its contribution from $5,000 to $750,000 per year has made possible the accommodation of 900 students instead of the initial 100, and expansion of the teaching from farming, carpentry, and blacksmithing to include auto mechanics, masonry, pottery making, weaving, and other traditional skills or artcrafts.

The acceptance that integration is an implicit phase of education, and vice versa, takes account of the continuing (and increasing) plurality of the tribespeople, and rather particularly the tribeswomen. The latter, along with the men, are now lawfully franchised and participating in national as well as local government. As this is written twenty-one of the forty members of the national legislature are tribespeople and four are women. Forty-four other Liberian women hold senior government posts, including crucial diplomatic assignments; proportionately to total populations, this is probably the world's highest rate of female participation in government.

Openly and without ambivalence Liberia moves to build and

perpetuate integration as a peace-seeking, peace-practicing nation. It maintains no regular army, navy, or air corps. Its armed services are limited to a very small Coast Guard, a National Guard force of about 2,500, and a voluntary militia of about 4,000. Liberia as a nation is conspicuously allergic to militarism as such, prefers hand-shaking to saluting, civilian politics to the Pentagon kind, and the quest of peace to the rationalization of war.

Liberia's secretary of state, J. Rudolph Grimes, explains matter-of-factly:

> Liberia's basic foreign policy remains essentially the same after a century and a quarter of independence. . . .
>
> It is a policy of respect for the sovereignty of every state; a policy of regard for the fundamental principle of human dignity and the inherent right of self-determination of all peoples . . . a policy based on justice and morality. . . .
>
> Liberia advocates and supports disarmament and urges that modern techniques and inventions be devoted primarily to peaceful purposes and the overall and consistent improvement of human kind.

As any African historian knows, the foregoing is well substantiated. The Organization of African Unity is a fairly typical Liberian creation. So are Liberia's persistent, Africa-influencing stands against the perpetuation of South Africa's apartheid, its condemnation of Portuguese "unrevisable" colonialism, and its championing of human rights in the Congo and, more recently, in Biafran Nigeria.

Back in 1825 James Monroe, retiring from his brilliantly successful eight years as the fifth president of the United States, described Liberia as a "little black America destined to shine gemlike in the darkness of vast Africa." Monroe, usually sincere and sometimes eloquent, had proved himself a compassionate friend of the then courageous, perennially pauperized settler groups of unowned and transplanted Negroes, mostly from the United States, but in some part from the West Indies or newly rescued from slavers and slave traders. Feeble as its beginnings were, the refuge colony never was a "little black America," and it would never be merely a distant "reservation" for the dumpage of unwanted colored minorities. Nor were the "Pepper Coast settlements," which would presently grow together as Liberia, ever permitted the privileged status of being a theorist's dream.

From the beginning and without sustained alleviation, the extremely remote colony of no more than partially free Negroes was obliged to fend for itself against relentless endemic diseases, wholly unconquered shoreline jungles, incipient famine, unrelenting isolation, and confrontation of a numerically overwhelming and sometimes hostile indigenous black minority.

Some seven decades earlier the United States had been founded by and provided a constitution for an already present white majority with already materialized numbers and means sufficient to stand against and eventually overwhelm the indigenous nations or tribes of Indian aborigines. The first American republic was not obliged or committed to effect integration by process of laws or government. As the United States Supreme Court had ruled or interpreted more or less consistently throughout its first sixty-five years of adjudgments, the original Constitution of the United States did not grant franchise or assurance of civil rights or accreditation of citizenship to Indians or to Negroes, whether owned as chattels or nominally free. As recently as 1857–58 the historic Dred Scott decision (and opinion) had denied the right for redress in any federal court to a former Negro slave, and further declared unconstitutional the Missouri Compromise which sought to balance the admission of slave states and free states to the Union.

Liberia had no such prerogatives or precedences for segregation. True, its original constitution, as adopted in 1847, limited citizenship, including the right of owning land, to "persons of African descent," presumably Negroes. But it established no overt barriers to civil or political integration of and with any group, kind, source of origin, or primacy of Negroes. A century before resident American Indians were granted United States citizenship, aborigines and other black peoples participated in the earliest elections of the Commonwealth of Liberia, and, beginning with its founding in 1847, of the Republic of Liberia. Although Liberia was never a union of states (currently the federal confederation includes five counties, three provinces, and one territory), its recognition of citizenship has never been denied or limited by rulings or opinions of its courts. Intermittently and in specific areas its political integration has been regrettably delayed, but aborigine (tribal) representatives have served in the national legislature by virtue of regular and constitutional election since 1851.

In 1944 the national government enacted and won final passage of a constitutional amendment to remove any and all statutory impediments to voting rights and to fully assure representation of tribespeople in the national government. The farther backwoods or hinterland provinces were one group of principal gainers; another was Liberian women, both tribal and nontribal—"all female citizens of twenty-one and over . . . shall be accorded the rights and privileges identical to those which by national law are duly accorded to men. . . ."

The aftermaths and better than incidental results swept through the nation and reached far beyond its boundaries. One after another, lingering statutes that had impeded the integration of the descendants of "Americo-Liberians" and the tribespeople were repealed or otherwise dropped. Typical of the unmourned passings were the century-old Port and Harbor Laws, which had sought to limit areas in which foreign merchants could locate stores or trading posts and to prohibit travel into the interior provinces except by hard-to-obtain government permits; also moldering remnants of statutes that sought to restrain tribespeople from dealing with post-boundary traders or seeking the overthrow of the government at Monrovia.

During the 1940s the Liberian government, long resigned to isolationism and to enduring diplomatic peonage, began to advocate and effect "Open Doorism" as a foreign policy. The basic premise accepted Liberia's *status quo* as a developing nation, its need of foreign capital and technical skills for attaining common-benefit development of certain of its resources, and its willingness to establish a "climate of amiability" toward bona fide foreign investors.

The inaugural address of the then new and still incumbent president, William Vacanarat Shadrach Tubman, turned out to be what may well be the most definitive policy document in Liberian history. Its prime thesis was that compatibility and sincere integration at home is prerequisite for harmony abroad:

We must now destroy and abandon all ideologies that tend to divide us. . . . All of us must register a new era of justice, fair dealing and equal opportunity for every part of the country regardless of tribe, clan, element, creed, or economic status. . . . In foreign affairs and domestic administration alike we must strive for the assimilation and unification of our various populations. . . . To this end we shall honor and respect the working man and woman . . . those who use the plough, the hatchet, the cutlass, the hoe, the axe, the saw, the brush, the machine, and other tools of the farm and of the artisan, who are the bulwark of the nation. . . . Liberia must be a place for all Liberians to live in alike—all to stand equally privileged, responsible and protected by like administration of the law. . . . We must here guarantee freedom of the press, the conscience, of speech and religion, the right of trial by jury, the protection of the person by writ of Habeas Corpus, supremacy of the civil over the military authority . . .

The speaker, who as this is written is still the president of Liberia, is regarded by friends, foes, and neutral appraisers as a durable personification of the integrated Liberian.

William Vacanarat Shadrach Tubman (back in 1910 when he was twenty-one, he added the "Vacanarat" by his own choice) is a grandson of a free-slave immigrant from Maryland County, Liberia. Nicholas Tubman, the president's father, was a diligent resident of downcoast Harper Village in Maryland County, a stonemason who labored mightily to earn a living for himself, his wife, their two daughters, and three sons. The second son was christened William Shadrach and known as Shad.

Nicholas Tubman was a family head who proudly admitted that he lived by faith, prayer, and the sweat of his face. He was the kind of believing Methodist who roused his family around four every morning for an hour of household prayer; permitted neither smoking nor drinking; sternly forbade the wearing of belts, as disfiguring, and the practice of sleeping on mattresses, as decadently softening: all the Tubmans slept on floor pallets home-woven of home-grown cotton.

At eight Shad was enrolled in the one-room, palm-thatched mission school in Harper Village. On completing its final fifth grade, he won admission at thirteen to the two-room Methodist Seminary at nearby Cape Palmas. Graduated at eighteen, he returned to his native village and read for three years in the only local law office. At twenty-one Shad passed the bar examination and began a career in public office that has continued for more than half a century. From a clerkship for the local Monthly and Probate Court, he won election as the government revenue collector for Maryland County; at twenty-eight he "stood" successfully for election as True Whig Party candidate for the National Senate. During his ensuing fourteen years in that office Tubman gained the then perilous distinction of being the most emphatic champion of what he regarded as Liberia's neglected plurality of tribespeople. His persistence and undeniable effectiveness prompted a group of Americo-Liberians to maneuver to hoist the overly effective young senator into the Liberian Supreme Court—by way of vote of the legislature. Following a six-month tenure as a frequently dissenting associate justice, Shad Tubman resigned to seek the presidential nomination by the True Whigs, previously known as the True- or Pot-Black Party. Despite his skin coloration, which is considerably short of being pot black, the former Mr. Justice Tubman won the nomination with great difficulty and the election and five subsequent reelections with comparative ease.

At seventy-seven and after more than a quarter-century in the presidency, William V. S. Tubman, who hears himself addressed as "Mr. Liberia" and "Mr. Africa," declares that he hopes to be remembered as "Mr. Peace Maker," or "Mr. Open Door," or, for those who might see fit, as "Mr. Integration." The designations, as he ponders and feels them, are synonymous on occasion. President Tubman, the stonemason's son from bejungled Harper Village, solemnly assures one that his opposition's references to him as "the convivial cannibal from Cape Palmas" is tempting but not necessarily of total veracity.

The longest-tenured president of the longest-continuing Negro republic keeps hoping to be remembered as architect for what his son Shad labels as the great black peoples' coming-togetherness.

President Tubman, meanwhile, further appraises that, insofar as he is not and can never be the blackest or the lightest of Negroes (as any observant traveler knows, there are Africans, including Liberians, who are markedly whiter than many white men), he hopes ever so sincerely to prove himself the most color blind (at least in terms of skin pigmentation) and the most Negro-appreciative of Negroes.

Shad Tubman's father could remember a time when most, at times all, of Liberia's senior officials were brown men. His grandfather, Abraham Tubman, the son of a slave, could recall that an actual majority of Liberia's pioneers or first settlers were mulattoes or otherwise racially crossed. Understandably, a great many of the so-called free slaves had white fathers, who were predisposed to "liberate" their own begettings.

During Shad Tubman's own youth the color of a candidate's skin still had much to do with his election or rejection; all the early presidents of Liberia were brown men. But for several decades Mr. Tubman's party had made a virtual fetish of nominating "true black" candidates to offset the Republican Party's conspicuous preference for mulattoes. The True Whig Party gained its earlier victories as the "True Black Man's Party for Serving in True Black Africa."

Liberia's prevailing and increasingly successful quest is for a black leadership which holds with and demonstrates in practice two unchanging premises: (1) the denial of justice to any person by any government is condemnatory of that government; (2) regardless of race, place, creed, pigmentation, or politics, where *any* person stays enslaved, no man or body politic can possibly be free.

I. In the Beginning

1

THE AMERICAN COLONIZATION SOCIETY

AMERICAN HISTORY and African history have many traits in common; one is that both abound in prophets and prophetic phenomena. Liberia began as such a phenomenon; for good or bad it was conceived by white theorists who pondered and dreamed of black peoples' future.

In keeping with an already determined and vigorous American custom, these theorists formed a society, originally named the Society for Colonizing Free People of Colour in the United States, but mercifully shortened to the American Colonization Society. The founding date was December 28, 1816. But the traceable precept of the American Colonization Society dips back to pre-Revolutionary times, at least as far back as 1773.

During that year Samuel Adams, occasionally remembered as an astute governor of Massachusetts as well as a signer of the Declaration of Independence, devised and published a pamphlet entitled "A Plan For Training Freed Negroes in the American Colonies As Colonizers and Missionaries." His companion in uplifting thought and planning was the Reverend Dr. Ezra Stiles, who presently became a distinguished president of Yale College.

Adams, originally of the Cape Cod Adamses, and a descendant of a member of the Mayflower Company, pointed out in 1773, and again in 1779, that colonial America was already "sorely burthened" with former slaves who were no longer "chattels"—he estimated there were no fewer than 60,000 such "black souls" living in "British America." Samuel Adams held with the studied opinion that Negroes had souls. He was convinced, too, that the number of unowned black people in America would continue to increase. By 1779 Adams was thoughtfully suggesting that the unowned Negroes, in greater part freed slaves, were the most rapidly increasing of American population sectors. By 1810 Governor Adams had pointed out that the "American counting" of free Negroes was not far from a third of a million and that these unowned black people, who according to the Constitution of the United States were not citizens as then interpreted by the U.S. Supreme Court, were a multiplying peril to the profitable and lawful commerce in slaves, to the already burdened public charities, and to the "tranquillity" of the new American nation. Granted that eminent American clergymen still denied that Negroes have souls, nobody could deny that they had stomachs, and, as the Massachusettsan deftly stated, "inalienable mortal needs."

And, none could deny that the unowned blacks were most definitely a burden on the American conscience—such as it was. Slaveowner Thomas Jefferson kept with a course of wonderful paradoxes regarding the abolition of slavery. Decades earlier, while a member of the Virginia Assembly, Jefferson had introduced without success a bill requiring that Virginia's adult slaves be "liberated systematically," and that all young Negroes be freed on reaching the age of twenty-one. Jefferson, then of Albemarle, also revealed that he favored the removal of black people not only from enslavement but from the visible American scene. As a Virginia legislator he had also advocated, again with more eloquence than success, a plan for what he abstractly termed the subsidized colonization of already freed blacks in "a far away place selected as the circumstances of the time should render most proper."

There was no immediate fruition. The American Revolution had effected a conspicuous waning of interest in freeing slaves and the advocacy of public sponsorship of Negro colonies either within or beyond hoped-for national boundaries. There is reason to believe that this demise of interest was augmented by the fact that both British troops and territorial officials had repeatedly responded to arbitrary urges to unofficially "liberate" American-owned slaves and, in more than a few instances, to dispatch them to the British Isles or release them in the vastnesses of the large sector of British North America which would presently be known as Canada.

By the middle 1780s Thomas Jefferson had returned to and amplified his advocacy of systematic termination of slavery and the distant colonization of Americans of African descent. During 1790 he found his views being strongly echoed by a fellow Virginian, Ferdinando Fairfax, a gentleman of means, talent for gaining repeated election to the Congress of the United States, and devotion to the case for the establishment, preferably by the federal government, of a free-slave colony, perhaps in Africa, but in any case a long way off.

Although the earlier efforts to convert the Congress had not succeeded, the cause for colonizing or otherwise exporting unowned black Americans gained strength and vigor with the advent or resumption of "Abolitionism" in the United States, particularly in New England of the 1790s. One of the most effective proponents was a moving spirit of the British Abolitionist movement which was even then on the up and up. He was Dr. William Thornton, a revered London physician who had migrated to Boston, where he began proselytizing for "human and Christian emancipation."

Dr. Thornton did not advocate the use of government funds for attaining what he termed the good conscience colonization of black people. He submitted that this could be best attained by sincere missionary efforts by the "morally committed" churches and all true Christian believers. The crusading physician was confident that the enlightened redemption of unowned Negroes was both attainable and predestined. Back in London a vivid and respected "society" of abolitionists, including philanthropists, churchmen, public officials, and others of good will, had already moved to found a first refuge colony in Africa. The society was even then founded on a charitable, British-government approved "African Institution." This quasi-public trust was actively projecting the establishment of a free-Negro "refuge station" in Sierra Leone in West Coast Africa, where five European powers were already occupied in seeking out or snatching up colonies. By then, too, the British government was turning against the inequities of the slave trade and confronting the need for resettling victims of this traffic.

By 1810 the Sierra Leone refuge site, in the area of Freetown, was taking form and showing tangible progress. But public acceptance of the goals of the station had reached far beyond London and the British Isles; it had already touched most of the European capitals and was gaining strongly in the United States, particularly New England, then commonly designated as the Beehive of American Population.

This metaphor, of course, was somewhat ludicrous in terms of the lingering sparsity of U.S. population. As the census of 1810 would eventually reveal, the United States then had barely 10.3 million people. But somewhere near a third of the total were Negro slaves, and the increase of unowned Negroes was proportionately greater than that of any comparably sized population group. More relevantly, as the most direly impoverished of minorities, and one very widely scattered through the then sixteen states and seven territories, the unowned black people were increasingly feared as potential "mass criminals" or revoltists.

The "Christian Charity Approach," which Dr. Thornton had evangelized in Boston, was presently resuscitated by an exceptionally energetic small-town pastor, the Reverend Mr. Robert Finley of Basking Ridge, New Jersey. Finley recognized the black American's profoundly tragic plight as a basis and cause for interdenominational evangelism. The New Jersey clergyman believed and ably presented the case that American Negroes, both owned and unowned, were not being served religiously, were not being "saved" or competently schooled in God's Scriptures; he therefore recommended resettling American Negroes in "religious colonies." Following his marriage to Esther Boudinot, a foster daughter of one of Alexander Hamilton's wealthy colleagues, the no longer poor village pastor from New Jersey boldly assumed the mission of founding a suitable benevolent society for advancing the cause of "religious colonization" of American Negroes beyond national boundaries.

Finley was a white man but his first disciple turned out to be a man doubly of color. Paul Cuffee was a seafaring resident of Cuttyhunk Island (Massachusetts), a devout Quaker, a successful merchant-sailor, and the son of an Indian mother and a Negro father.

With his own means the engaging Indian-Negro during 1811 visited the then British colony called Sierra Leone, and its materializing free-slave refuge near its coastal capital. Cuffee liked what he saw and promptly advised Finley and others of his willingness to pay ship's passage and other necessary costs to enable a test group of American freed slaves, preferably farmers and artisans, to establish themselves in the refuge back of Freetown.

When the London-based directors of the Africa Institution agreed, Cuffee proceeded to recruit and see delivered to Sierra Leone a pioneer party of thirty-eight free Negroes, mostly from New England.

The venture turned out to be a historic overture, but in several respects a tragic one. Within the year Cuffee was striken with "African fevers"—presumably a virulent malaria—and died. But his devoted conviction that people of color can indeed help people of color in gaining "Christian establishment" was sustained by a leadership team that Cuffee had also recruited. All three—Daniel Coker of Baltimore, James Forten of Philadelphia, and the Reverend Mr. Peter Williams of New York—were unowned Negroes who were eager and willing to carry the torch.

By no means surprisingly the War of 1812 brought about a two-year delay of the resettlement efforts, but by 1815 the Negro colonization crusade was clearly revived. Pastor Finley resumed his proselytizings for church participation in free-slave colonization in Africa. Negro churchmen and others indicated their eagerness to join in the cause. White churchmen followed suit. One item of proof was the founding in New York (during 1815) of the African Education Society. This was headed by Presbyterian Synods of New York and New Jersey, which undertook to establish training schools or seminars for Negro teachers and preachers, for the most part former slaves.

Robert Finley meanwhile moved adroitly from church folds to national politics and active association with some of the most prominent political advocates of Negro colonization.

The cause was aided by a most astonishing turn of weather; 1816 emerged very dramatically as the "year without a summer," or, as some termed it, "Eighteen Hundred and Froze to Death." Throughout more than two-thirds of what was then the United

States, from the highland Carolinas to Maine (then an oversize northern county or department of Massachusetts), every month of that year brought killing frosts that decimated or totally ruined harvests and left the predominantly rural nation at the brink of famine. The two previous years had gone in the almanacs as cold dry "Napoleonic" years, but 1816 was the leaves-blackening, crop-killing year of berserk weather.

One result was the intensified renewal of the "Second Great American Religious Awakening," which had actually begun with the remarkable epoch of frontier camp meetings which followed Jim McGready's meetings in Logan County, Kentucky, during the summer of 1800. The great American religious revival boomed across the nation. In normally agnostic Vermont, which was ground zero for the catastrophic weather, church membership increased more than fiftyfold. Along with the most intensive revival "moment" the nation had ever known came the founding, also in 1816, of the American Bible Society, the American Peace Society, and, more immediate to our subject, the American Colonization Society.

The year of stark-mad weather and unprecedented reaches of religious revival also brought epochal political upsets. These included the virtual demise of the Federalist Party, the landslide victory of the refurbished Democratic-Republicans led by Virginia's brilliant and, at times, rabblerousing governor, James Monroe, who found himself almost catapulted into the presidency, where he would presently win reelection by the greatest plurality ever received by any American president. The kinky-headed, homely and freckled Virginia patriot, one of the "wounded heroes" of the Battle of Trenton, saw 1816 as a way marker for an unprecedented American era of good feelings and soul-saving repentance. God and Monroe apparently agreed that America had a great deal to be repentant about. Included, of course, was the increasing painfulness of the still out-of-control slave trade and the "Afro-Americans," both enslaved and nominally free. With cautious astuteness the president-elect looked favorably on what he termed "federal provisions for Africa resettlement by American Africans."

Alertly aware of this, Robert Finley leaped boldly into the higher political ramparts of the still smoldering national capital, where the chars and embers of recent British invasion were merged with encroaching swamps, outrageously muddy streets, and virulent rashes of whorehouses and saloons.

Along with letters of introduction to both the outgoing and the incoming presidents, the former New Jersey pastor was able to recruit two exceptionally able counselors. These were his foster brother-in-law, Elias Caldwell, by then Clerk of the United States Supreme Court, and the passionate abolitionist and lobbyist-extraordinary, Francis Scott Key, author of the horrendous verses of "The Star-Spangled Banner," which would shortly be set to the music, to use the term loosely, of a decidedly bleary but still popular English drinking song.

Lawyer Key's penchant for evangelism extended into churches as well as lobbies, and much the same held for his good friend, Supreme Court Clerk Caldwell. Accordingly, while Caldwell made a beeline for his favorite dinner-party guest, Henry Clay of Kentucky, Key went for his revered elderly acquaintance, Bushrod Washington, a nephew of the first president and an attention-claiming associate justice of the Supreme Court. Slaveowners Clay and Washington had their own vested motivations for feeling deeply about nonslave Negroes, and were more than casually interested in helping with the founding of an "agency" for colonizing nominally free Negroes in a suitably distant place such as Equatorial Africa.

Thus when the first organizational meeting took place at the then élite Davis Hotel on December 21 (1816), Henry Clay presided and Massachusetts' Daniel Webster was present, along with Maryland's Senator Robert Goldsboro, and an impressive group of Virginians including John Randolph, John Stull, Ferdinando Fairfax, Richard and Edmund Lee (elder brothers of General-to-be Robert E. Lee), and several front-pew standouts including Presbyterian Elder Stephen Balch, the irrepressible Bishop Mead of the Virginia Episcopalians, and the Reverend W. H. Wilmer, a founder of the Virginia Theological Seminary.

Mr. Clay opened with approximately thirty thousand mellifluous words in which he clarified the fact that he was a slaveowner without chagrin; that he cherished the humble, hard-working darkies who made the Clay plantation and cattle farms an internationally revered success. Three years earlier Marse Henry had imported the first registry of English Durham (Shorthorn) cattle to reach the

United States; he had his darkies drive the herd overland some five hundred miles. Henry Clay was tolerant of obedient, hard-working blacks who knew their place, but as for the liberated, unowned black creatures, hell or back to Africa for them. Supreme Court Clerk Caldwell spoke next and in changed tenor branded prevailing abuse and evasion of the unowned Negroes an American "monument of reproach." Mr. Caldwell implored the distinguished company to adopt a resolution for seeking the active assistance of the United States government for establishing a colony of free Negroes somewhere in Africa.

A week later (on December 28), in the temporarily untenanted House of Representatives, a gathering of about fifty white Americans formally established the American Society for Colonizing Free People of Colour, and elected Bushrod Washington first president and Caldwell first secretary of the Society. The list of thirteen vice presidents included Henry Clay, General Andrew Jackson, and the incoming Secretary of the Treasury, William Crawford. On the board of governors were Francis Scott Key, Edmund Lee, and several renowned churchmen. From highly vocal retirement Thomas Jefferson extended his endorsement and indicated his willingness to recommend the creation favorably to the president-elect.

Monroe meanwhile waited for a public reaction, which turned out to be notably negative. Several principal newspapers criticized the professed goals as partisan and hypocritical; the Boston press tended to agree that dispatching people to Dark Africa was little better than arbitrarily condemning them to hell. A Philadelphia gathering of free Negroes at the Bethel Church deplored the proposed African colonization as gross political evasion of the nation's responsibilities to free people of color and flayed what it termed the cruel and shoddy stratagem of dumping American Negroes into the savage wilds of the Dark Continent. Unowned Negroes in New York reiterated this contention, adding that the proposed colonization was a self-evident hoax designed to deny free black Americans just participation in public education and church life.

The Colonization Society kept with its tall talking. Bushrod Washington accentuated what he termed the astute political foresight and "civil prudence" of the Society's objectives. With a flair for lobbying, which was not entirely alien to Supreme Court members, Washington presently settled on the direly troubled House Committee on the Slave Trade to urge that the committee support the cause of "acquiring" a colony in Africa—in the justice's somewhat gaseous words, "a territory great enough to accommodate the entire Negro race."

The committee's obviously harried reaction was a markedly cautious suggestion that the United States government might best begin experimenting by sponsoring or encouraging the experimental settling of a small, carefully selected group of American free slaves in Britain's newly founded refuge colony in its then newest West African territory, Sierra Leone. The committee's mealy-mouthedness was clearly related to the dismal failure of the two previous administrations to control or even modestly supervise the audaciously evil slave trade. The first "Jefferson Anti-Slavery Act of 1803" had failed wretchedly and the subsequent "Way Showing Act" of 1807 had left the wicked commerce booming along, with the United States clearly marked as the number one slave-trading nation.

As the American slave population continued to multiply, both the number and despair of the unowned Negroes also proliferated. The preponderance of so-called free slaves remained unskilled laborers, and the gain in numbers of owned slaves severely reduced their chances for employment or any dependable vestige of solvency, the more so because no people of color had yet been lawfully accorded citizens' rights, and very few had had opportunity to qualify as skilled workers.

Britain, meanwhile, was pioneering in statutory restrictions and foreplanned prohibition of slavery. By 1815 the British fleet was being used to patrol aggressively against slave trading on the high seas, and the British government was employing firm diplomacy to effect "cease-and-desist" treaties or agreements with several of the more notorious slave-trading nations, including Portugal, Spain, and France. By 1815, in some part by 1810, it was common knowledge that American slave traders were the most pernicious of all, since as much as two-thirds of the expertly estimated total of international slave trading was accredited as American "enterprise."

To his lasting credit James Monroe assumed the presidency with a carefully planned regimen for figuratively lowering the boom on the most evil of American business enterprises; the frequently soft-spoken Virginian was determined to promote federal legislation to define slave trading as piracy. During 1817 the Monroe antislave trade "schedule" emerged as the toughest prohibitory legislation ever introduced in an American Congress. There were protracted delays, and the initial bill was bludgeoned with crippling amendments; the stipulation for making slave running a capital crime was soundly defeated in the distinctly proslavery Senate. Even so, the bill which gained passage on March 3, 1819, was epochal and had very real bearing on our story.

The shall-not clauses were generously supplemented with shall clauses, including a surviving amendment which authorized the president to "effect arrangements" whereby all Negroes captured or otherwise recovered from slave ships would be "safely kept, supported, and removed beyond limits of the United States." The distinctly pitiable sum of $100,000 was appropriated for attaining this end. But the presidential authority as commander-in-chief of the Navy was forcefully accentuated by directives whereby the president would officially order senior officers aboard U.S. Navy or Coast Guard vessels to stand responsible for the recovery of the "slave trade victims" and direct that they "provide accommodations for those victims."

The importance of this, obviously, was the lucid recognition that the previous expedient of merely abandoning recaptured slaves on any convenient alien shores, thereby making them an easy prey of other slavers, could no longer suffice. The same held for the deplorable precedence whereby the United States government had long remained a party to slave trading, with government employees or "agents" permitted to sell contraband slaves at public auctions within the United States. Monroe had openly deplored this practice, but he had no less openly assumed that colonization abroad was the one rational and attainable alternative.

It followed that the "constructive sense" of the Anti-Slavery Trade Act of 1819 which specifically supported a Negro colonization venture turned out to be a principal ground for opposition. Unowned Negroes and increasing numbers of abolitionists joined in branding the colonization scheme as evasive, hypocritical, and otherwise immoral in terms of national responsibilities for or toward the most painfully unprivileged black people. The opponents could and did reiterate and deplore that the most vocal advocates of colonization were slaveowners and/or "nigger haters." The argument that the act of conveniently hauling unowned slaves back to Africa would only serve to revive the foul-smelling slave trade was vigorously renewed. For generations America had also been the black man's homeland. Why should the dark-skinned American be bilked of this inherent right?

James Monroe continued to look and listen. He was well aware that the new colonization society was following a markedly ambivalent course—in one it was an élite lobbying group and a still strongly controversial church front. While using its board members and principal officers, including its host of famous-name vice presidents, for the most part slaveowners, as proselytizing lobbyists, the society was simultaneously seeking and winning entries into church organizations and using sundry pulpits as public forums for promoting the proposed colonization venture. Protests grew more vehement; there were disturbing reports of police or mob brutality toward Negro protesters and public floggings of highly suspect legality. Associate Justice Washington's reiterations that the so-called free slaves were in no legal sense citizens of the United States and should therefore seize the opportunity to "earn citizenship" in Africa or another comparably distant place were less than soothing to the protesters.

Monroe, meanwhile, waited for a propitious time to direct his Minister to Great Britain to investigate the progress of the Negro refuge colony in Sierra Leone and solicit the counsel of the African Institution. An immediate result was the somewhat unctuous recommendation from Thomas Clarkson, a respected British philanthropist, that the American government purchase or "otherwise obtain" a free-slave and recaptured-slave colony site somewhere downcoast from Sierra Leone. Monroe pondered politely while the Reverend Mr. J. Mills of Boston, then a principal of the newly founded American Bible Society, volunteered to make a firsthand investigation of possible sites for an American Negro colony in Africa, with the American Bible Society paying the tab. But Mr. Mills was subsequently chagrined to discover that the Bible Society had no money for that purpose.

Bushrod Washington gallantly offered his illustrious name for use as a magnet for raising the necessary funds, but the magnet failed to draw. Thereupon, Francis Scott Key, then thirty-seven and launching a third career as a public lecturer, undertook a church-based lecture tour to raise the needed exploratory funds. The Star-Spangled Banner man exuded eloquent word pictures of the wonders and beauties of tropical Africa, which by his own admission he had never seen. Even so, the lecturer graced pulpits and other public platforms, charmed crowds, and failed dismally to raise the money.

But the American Bible Society's Mr. Mills eventually succeeded in latching onto sufficient funds for his investigatory tour. He also acquired as travel companion an engaging Vermonter, Ebenezer Burgess, the professor of mathematics and natural philosophy at the then infant University of Vermont. Burgess, who prided himself on being a linguist, took for granted that he could serve as interpreter in multi-language Africa. That assumption turned out to be erroneous. But the two Americans presently arrived at Freetown, the palm-thatched capital of Sierra Leone Colony, and both were very favorably impressed by the resettled Negroes, most of whom had been victims of slave traders and had been duly rescued by British Navy personnel either aboard slave ships or in landside stockades. By 1819 the refuge colony had about 12,000 residents; about half in the new port capital, the rest in nearby farming communities. The investigators noted that the black colony was already developing its own black leadership. An engaging example was John Kizel, a former slave from South Carolina who had been liberated by British troops during the American Revolution, shipped to London, and in due time to Sierra Leone.

Kizel volunteered to serve as escort for the visiting white Americans and recommended that they seek to purchase Sherbro Island, downcoast from Freetown, as a colony site. To that end the former Carolinian arranged for an African-crewed sloop to carry the party downcoast. One gathers that the tour progressed enjoyably. But the native chiefs, although uniformly gracious, politely declined to discuss the possibility of selling or otherwise granting a colony site; they appeared to accept that an American colony would necessarily be a front for grabbing up slaves.

The ensuing Mills-Burgess report conveniently minimized the chiefs' recalcitrance and urged official U.S. government sponsorship of a free-slave colony on Sherbro Island with protection of the U.S. Navy and the preliminary employment of native (tribal) labor for clearing land and building shelters for the forthcoming colonists. The descriptions of the natural resources were glowingly optimistic, but the report carried no mention of the prevalence of lethal diseases. Indeed, the Reverend Mr. Mills had already contracted a baffling and painful illness from which he died aboard ship en route to New York. At that point the first American overtures at African colonizing had scored a casualty rate of exactly 50 percent.

Even so, the Mills-Burgess report was noteworthy; indirectly a revealing testimony of how profoundly the slave trade sapped the very life of West Africa, the principal homeland of enslaved or formerly enslaved Africans then scattered throughout the United States, the West Indies and extensive areas of tropical South America.

Understandably, a great many of the smaller and weaker tribes, including those of the successive Mosquito, Gold, Pepper (now Liberia), and Ivory Coasts, were the worst ravaged by the infamous trade; entire communities had been destroyed. Many others were decimated while entire tribes and once-abundant farming centers had been reduced to scatterings of distressed, harried, and fearful survivors. The travelers were also reminded that in numerous instances the victim slaves or their immediate forebears had earlier been slaves of African masters, or had been betrayed into slavery by vengeful native enemies or corrupt chiefs. But the prime villains had been and still were the slavers; and, alas, the majority of these were known to be Americans.

Vermonter Burgess argued that "legitimate" colonization, directed by the United States government, was the most rational preventive for this first scourge of Africa; a strong and well-protected colony would encourage the natives to resist the slavers and help to replace the infamous traffic with legitimate trade. Vermont-like, the Burgess arguments were a somewhat baffling intermixture of noble sentiments and pragmatic expedience. The same held for the supporting arguments of the renovated board of managers of the Colonization Society. They simultaneously favored saving souls, purifying consciences, and protecting the "property rights" of slave ownership.

When the Society again began deluging the president with self-styled "constitutional lawyers," including the nobly lurking Bushrod Washington and Francis Scott Key, Monroe deferred to his Cabinet. Secretary of State John Quincy Adams opposed "Africa colonization" with vehemence, declaring that the "Act of 1819" did not authorize actual purchase of alien lands, a contention with which Attorney General William Wirt and Secretary of War John C. Calhoun strongly agreed.

The president delayed a final decision and again the Colonization Society returned to soliciting funds for the highly controversial cause. New support was won with the government auction in 1819 of forty Negroes who had been taken during a U.S. Navy interception of a Spanish slave ship. The victims were being sold on public bid at Augusta, Georgia. The Society succeeded in obtaining a court injunction against the auction and permission to buy and liberate the Negroes. All that was lacking was the needed money. Once more the nefarious auction took place; once more the Treasury of the United States took funds from the duress sale of the living flesh of slave victims.

The Colonization Society, still without money, gave its blessings to the proposal of the African Missionary Society of Petersburg, Virginia, for recruiting one hundred free Negroes for resettling in the British refuge colony. The supporting propaganda stressed "respect for property rights," i.e., slave ownership, and restated the intent of helping black people leave their "adopted land" and take "colonial establishment."

The move deeply disturbed and displeased President Monroe, who called on his Cabinet to join him in reconsidering the prime issue. Somewhat begrudgingly Attorney General Wirt modified his earlier opinion to the extent of construing that the president possessed legal authority for establishing an agency or station for free slaves and for providing "support structure" within limits of the $100,000 already appropriated by Congress. Monroe complemented the opinion by restating that the primary goals were limited to retarding the long-illicit but persisting slave trade, and relieving unrest among the unowned black people. He next accepted the proffered "cooperation" of the immensely vocal but still almost moneyless American Colonization Society and confirmed the appointments of a colony director and assistant director whom the Society recommended.

As its first director the Society chose a white man with oddly contrasting talents. The Reverend Mr. Samuel Bacon was an Episcopal pastor, a former missionary, and a recent associate of the American Bible Society. In the War of 1812 he had served as captain of U.S. Marines; after returning to his hometown, Sturbridge, Massachusetts, Sam Bacon had attended Harvard College, and there had joined the Abolitionist Society.

The Reverend Mr. Bacon was an energetic activist. After lengthy and respectful visits with the president and the Washington headquarters of what by then had been officially renamed the American Colonization Society, Sam Bacon moved into action. With frugal respect for government monies he proceeded to charter a merchant brigantine, the *Elizabeth*, to carry the first volunteer group of free Negroes to West Africa. He next employed sixteen free Negroes to serve the expedition as carpenters, storekeeper, blacksmiths, and otherwise useful artisans. He provisioned the *Elizabeth* with food stores—"dry rations" sufficient for supporting three hundred people for an entire year. His supplying clearly suggested plans for permanent colonization; it included farming tools, wagons, carts, wheelbarrows, blacksmith tools, a grist mill, a fishing barge; and, on the grimmer side, several small cannon, a hundred flintlock muskets, and a dozen kegs of gunpowder.

The next serious impediment, which the best persuasive talents of the American Colonization Society could neither bypass nor erase, was the recruitment of colonists. A great many black Americans were interested in the general proposal, but the feat of final acceptance and reporting aboard ship for the admittedly dangerous venture was not easily attained. After six months of recruiting efforts, in great part by way of churches and Abolitionist groups, nowhere near three hundred volunteers had materialized. When the *Elizabeth* finally weighed anchor from New York on January 31, 1820, only eighty-six passenger-colonists were aboard; only twenty-eight of these were men, the rest were women and children.

Samuel Bacon could and did report that all aboard were orderly and hard working. Prophetically, the women passengers served most helpfully as cooks, seamstresses, laundresses, stewardesses, and nurses. They, in particular, were determined to be colonists, come hell or high water. Both came. So, in time, did the transition from a deeply troubled American daydream to a profoundly imperiled African reality.

2

BLACK MAYFLOWER

NEAR NOON on January 31, 1820, the chartered brigantine *Elizabeth*, with the U.S. Navy sloop *Cyane* as escort, sailed from her pier in New York's North River. A local newspaper, reasonably named *The New Yorker*, termed the *Elizabeth* the "Black Mayflower" and described the embarkation as inspiring and warming to the spirits.

One gathers that the "warming" aspects did not survive the ten-week, 6,000-mile voyage across the winter-roughened Atlantic. The brave new venture in African colonization by American Negroes began with adversities that were to linger and multiply. One initial and avoidable cause related to bad timing. The expectable voyage time, about ten weeks, would cause the arrival date to coincide with the onset of the long, dour rainy season which is to be expected in Equatorial West African springs. During the ensuing eight or ten weeks clearing land and planting crops would be greatly impeded or impossible. Furthermore, the "great wetness" could be counted on to begin and end with the usual invasion of African fevers, which included the particularly deadly tertian strains of malaria.

The timing of the voyage could hardly have been worse.

Climatically, 1820 kept closely to West African patterns. The mid-April arrival on Sherbro Island was more or less on prevailing schedule. The ocean-tossed colonists-to-be found themselves treated to at least one unanticipated benevolence, a surprising gift of temporary shelter. This included about two dozen newly raised huts and a small warehouse, all built of logs and mud and roofed with thatch.

The provider and donor was John Kizel, whom we have already glimpsed as the one-time Carolina slave boy who during the previous year had served as interpreter-guide for the Mills-Burgess mission. Subsequently Kizel had learned of the *Elizabeth* and by his own enterprise had acquired a tract of land from the claimant chiefs of the island. That accomplished, he had employed tribesmen to clear land and raise the village of huts, all of which he gave, as he explained, "in community" to the arriving colonists.

The remarkable generosity did not erase or otherwise remove several serious shortcomings. The island lacked drinkable water or any semblance of a harbor, or readily tillable farm lands. The tall forests and lush jungle growths, which included sword grass and thornbush, strongly discouraged land clearing.

Even so, acting as first agent of the colony-to-be and special envoy of the president of the United States, former captain of U.S. Marines and presently the Reverend Mr. Samuel Bacon chose to accept the gift of site and shelter, taking for granted that more favorable lands and a dependable water supply could be subsequently "treatied for" on the nearby mainland.

Unfortunately, that hopeful inference did not materialize. But at least one may reflect that there had been plenty of American precedents for establishing colonies by hopeful inferences, or by guess and by God. In repeated instances this had held for Spanish, French, and British colonization ventures in North America. But for the most part the earlier colonization attempts in which Americans were principals had benefited by some degree of environmental similarities to those of the homelands, whether in the British Isles, France, Spain, Russia, Scandinavia, or elsewhere.

By punitive contrast, this particularly valiant attempt to establish a settlement in the deep tropics of coastal Africa was rife with drastic environmental changeabouts and contrasts. So far as the records show, not one of the volunteer settlers had ever before lived in an equatorial climate. Certainly none previously had been obliged to endure the deadly African hazards of virulent endemic diseases. And none, so far as we know, had had prior experience in living in any comparably remote jungle edge. Inevitably, too, the feat of establishing even a most primitive pioneer community requires shaping a government; none of the Negro colonists came provided with such experience. None had held public office, officially voted, or had other practice in the fundamental rights and obligations of citizenship.

One can hypothesize that the Reverend Mr. Bacon had not sufficiently anticipated the drastic environmental changes and the formidable perils thereof. He, too, was venturing into deep tropics for the first time. In uncompromising reality this determined Massachusettsan was leading a familied group of temperate-zone people, for the most part of the less hardy ages, across more than 6,000 miles of ocean and 30 degrees of latitude for abrupt deposit in what was then one of the least habitable tropic coastlines partly known to man. The *Elizabeth* company included no indigenous Africans, only comparatively distant African descendants who were not only aliens but were wholly lacking the ever-important African heritage of membership or vital association in and with the tribes.

Further, most of the company were farm people who sought to live from subsistence farming. This made the awkward arrival time even more punitive. The long rainy season was already begun and land clearing was virtually impossible. The lack of dependable and safe drinking water was still another aggravant. Others waited precipitously. The resident tribespeople associated the new settlers, particularly their white leaders, with the slave trade. That, of course, was more regrettable than surprising; the Sherbro settlement no doubt looked a great deal like a slavers' Negro trap.

Other adversities were of tragic fact rather than of appearances. Tropical fevers were rife; the settlers had little or no resistance to them. The group's only physician was stricken with "the fevers," presumably malaria, a very few days after the island landing. John Crozier of Norfolk, Virginia, had begun his study of medicine as a slave-boy assistant to a white physician who owned him and eventually set him free. By then Crozier was well on his way to becoming one of the first duly licensed Negro physicians of his state.

Tragically, barely three weeks after his arrival on the wet, green island hill, Dr. Crozier died. During the ensuing May eight more of thc settlers died; the fever casualties included two young children, four young men (probably in their teens) and two mature men, the latter recorded as Bankson and Townsend. During the summer two women and nine children succumbed. By the end of September the death list had grown to an appalling forty-nine—more than half the original company of eighty-six.

Late in September, when the "little rainy season" had slackened, "Senior Agent" Samuel Bacon managed to board a coastal schooner for Freetown, where he hoped to procure emergency supplies of food and medicine. But the "Preacher Marine" did not fulfill his mission. En route he, too, was stricken with the fevers, and landed at an outpost village on Cape Shilling, where he died.

The gallant Mr. Bacon was replaced by Daniel Coker, a dedicated and compassionate Negro preacher who took over as leader of the distressed settlement and worked valiantly to attend the sick, bury the dead, and comfort the survivors. Convinced that the death trap of an island settlement could not possibly endure, Coker arranged ship's passage to Freetown for the survivors. His move was barely in time; by October the natives, astutely aware that the colonists were no longer able to defend themselves, began raiding the perilously diminished food stores and threatening the settlers. Daniel Coker succeeded in placing his charges aboard ship and delivered them to an outpost mission on Fourah Bay, not far from the Sierra Leone capital.

When the distressing news reached its Washington headquarters, the still impoverished American Colonization Society renewed appeals for federal help. President Monroe approved at least in principle the need to select a better colony site, replenish the tragically diminished personnel and provide a new team of "agents." Again accepting the Society's advice, the president appointed a leadership team of two Negroes and two white men; the preacher members included Ephraim Bacon, a brother of Samuel, and the Reverend Mr. Joseph Andrus, a Negro pastor from Baltimore. When the new leadership team reported to the Navy brig *Nautilus* at Hampton Roads, Virginia, another group of thirty-five free slave volunteers waited aboard to join the distressed colony.

Once more the embarkation was badly timed—the *Nautilus* weighed anchor on January 21 (1821) and reached Fourah Bay just as the March deluges were arriving. The two Negro pastors, Andrus and Coker, volunteered to explore downcoast for a more suitable colony site. The gallant Pastor Andrus promptly contracted a fever and died.

Back in Washington, meanwhile, the president appointed as his personal envoy and "medical agent" Eli Ayres, a U.S. Navy surgeon, who was assisted by a Navy line officer, Lieutenant Robert F. Stockton, commanding the Navy schooner *Alligator*.

The schooner reached Fourah Bay in time to meet still another ruinous epidemic of the fevers. Jonathan Winn, one of the assistant agents, had recently died; the younger Bacon was mortally ill, and at least half of the surviving colonists were also fever-stricken.

As soon as the contagion had subsided, the two Navy officers headed another land-locating expedition downcoast and tried to acquire a landing site near the mouth of the St. Paul River. Patrolling tribe warriors, suspecting another slavers' foray, refused to permit them to land. However, a gracious paramount chief presently permitted the envoys to come ashore and persuaded fellow chiefs to allow a temporary rental of Dozoa, a small island directly off Cape Mesurado, not far from the present site of Monrovia.

The Navy officers advanced a payment of $300 worth of barter goods (principally cloth for chiefs' robes), then returned to the Freetown area to effect the ferrying of the unlucky but determined colonists to what promised to be a more tenable living place.

Once more a dour disappointment waited; the colonists were not permitted to land on Dozoa Island, which by then was being picketed by hundreds of Bassa warriors. The spear-bearers had overruled their chiefs and joined in a meaningful refusal to permit the establishment of what they assumed was still another slavers' stratagem.

As a less than welcome alternative the troubled colonists made a landing on the conspicuously misnamed Paradise Island, in the mouth of the Mesurado River (now a waterway of the Liberian capital). Shortly after New Year's, 1822, the surviving colonists again began building huts and clearing garden sites. Again they were penalized by the lack of suitable drinking water. When an exploring party tried to seek a dependable fresh-water source, they were attacked by tribal warriors.

This opened a prolonged nightmare of harassments by the earlier, native settlers. The colonists sought to break free. Using canoes and a ship's dory, they boldly moved across to the heavily forested thirty-mile outjut of Cape Mesurado and again set to building a thatched-hut village and clearing garden-size fields, this time on the protruding mainland. Before another long, dark, rainy season took over, the settlers, still tending their sick and intermittently burying their dead, had managed to clear a public square, place a flagpole, and ceremoniously raise the Stars and Stripes. The apparent reward was a fire of unknown origin that destroyed the lone warehouse and made obligatory the severe rationing of stored food and other supplies.

When another plague of fevers invaded, Surgeon Ayres dispatched an appeal for supplies to the Washington headquarters of the Colonization Society. Long before the ship's mail could reach its destination, Bassa war parties began to harass and threaten the settlement where barely a dozen men were able to bear arms. Surgeon Ayres managed to flag down a passing ship and take passage which eventually delivered him to Washington.

Early in August (1822), desperately needed help arrived. The brigantine *Strong*, chartered on presidential order, arrived with a replacement of foods, medicines, clothing, and hand tools, and a hardly less welcome bonus in the persons of fifty-five additional free-slave volunteers. The *Strong's* company included a young white couple, Jehudi and Mary Ashmun. The twenty-eight-year-old Jehudi, originally of Champlain, New York, had earlier worked his way through Middlebury College (in Vermont), entered the Congregational ministry, then taken over the editorship of the Baltimore *Theological Reporter*, which was ardently proselytizing for free-slave colonization. Ashmun believed what his paper preached including the tenet that slavery is spiritually and morally wrong and ruinously bad business. The preacher-journalist and his attractive young wife had decided to join the Negro colonizing venture with perceptive awareness that the plight of the unowned slaves had grown even more crucial than that of the owned. Free-slave revolts were materializing in principal southern strongholds of slavery.

During 1821 American newspapers had begun reporting the already frightening specifics of free-slave Revolt. Its initial focus was in or near Charleston, South Carolina, and the already rising leader was a courageous and deeply philosophical former slave, Denmark Vesey, a very competent organizer and, not altogether incidentally, a brilliant Bible scholar who preached and persuaded with rare effectiveness in English, Spanish, French, German, and what was disparagingly known as slave gabble.

By the end of 1821 Vesey reportedly had a well-organized, well-disciplined following of at least 9,000 Negroes, including both slaves and former slaves. He had developed his own inner sanctum of "intelligence agents," whose numbers included such artisans as Negro barbers who were expert at devising wigs and false beards used as disguises by Vesey's guerrillas. The well-rehearsed combat techniques accentuated the use of cavalry (Vesey lieutenants were alertly acquainted with all the stables and grazing herds in the greater Charleston area and the five "sub-areas"), and the astute lifting of firearms and ammunition and the amassing of "silent weapons" including daggers, knives, bayonets, and pikes.

During April, 1822, while the fevers-plagued African colonists were struggling for temporary survival, Denmark Vesey completed plans for a six-area revolt to be effected on the second Sunday in July. The black man's revolution did not take place; Vesey was informed on, two of his senior lieutenants were arrested, and the date of the revolt was moved up by a month. That proved to be Vesey's undoing; he and thirty-seven of his followers were arrested, subjected to prejudiced court trial, and very promptly (between June 18 and August 9) hanged.

Despite the brutal suppression of the would-be Negro revolt, many slaveowners were profoundly worried or terrified, and the South in particular was in a mood to support African colonization as a means for getting rid of unowned slaves, although not as anybody's philanthropy. Meanwhile, the so-called Vesey Revolt had nurtured a deplorable rash of outrageously repressive state legislation which included statutes to forbid the "congregating" of Negroes, whether slaves or free; laws making "educating" slaves a criminal offense; laws forbidding employment of unowned Negroes; and so on and on.

What most or all of the vindictive partisans did not realize included the facts that while Denmark Vesey and thirty-seven of his followers were struggling against hangmen's ropes, black compatriots in the dark wet fringes of coastal Africa were struggling against less humiliating but certainly no less painful or ominous forces of destruction. The adversity-dogged Cape Mesurado colony continued to meet one calamity after another.

By August (1822) the lower cape and adjacent mainland were being occupied by increasing throngs of tribal warriors. The senior Bassa chief, King Peter, who had ceded the settlement site, was conspicuously unable to control his own warriors. That was the less than happy situation on August 8 when the *Strong* lowered anchor on the barricading sandbars and began discharging her passengers and supplies on rafts. Among the first newcomers ashore were three unusual missionaries; two were the young Ashmuns whom we have already spoken of briefly; the third was a handsome middle-aged Negro preacher, Lott Carey of Virginia, who had been ordained while still a slave.

During the long rough voyage Carey and the Ashmuns had grown to be friends, and all three clearly indicated leadership qualities. This was fortunate. In the absence of Surgeon Ayres the colony lacked an official leader; the temporary head was Elisha (sometimes spelled Elijah) Johnson, a free Negro and veteran artilleryman of the War of 1812. Johnson urged Ashmun to take over management of the colony so that he could devote his entire time to shaping and leading a defense. The tribal warriors were already grouping as an attack force; their war drums were pounding day and night; colony scouts were bringing back alarming reports. Johnson, the only combat veteran at hand, volunteered to serve as drillmaster.

Jehudi Ashmun had no military experience, but while eagerly taking over as temporary leader, he saw that only thirty-six male colonists, including older boys, were in condition to bear arms. Lott Carey promptly volunteered to serve as Johnson's assistant drillmaster. Ashmun "confirmed" five other volunteer lieutenants, all Negroes. The drilling began while tribal warriors looked on ominously.

Fortunately the original *Elizabeth* equipage of forty muskets was still intact, although the supply of gunpowder and bullet lead was dangerously short. Elisha directed that all muskets be readied and very personally "set" the brass cannon and the smaller field pieces for action. Since armed guards were essential, most of the available manpower had to be used for sentry duty. Ashmun, meanwhile, had made a count of the surviving colonists; he reported 141 present, including women, children, and about forty sick persons. By mid-August, 1822, the total death count stood at fifty-five, approximately 30 percent of all the volunteers then mustered, but at least twenty more deaths were probable or imminent. Understandably, as he watched the developing thirty-six-man army, the newly designated "Prophet Jehudi" was concernedly aware of the increasing throng of excessively watchful enemies.

Ashmun's initiation as a fighting man rather than a "trading missionary" as he had originally planned was intensified when his twenty-one-year-old wife was abruptly stricken with a "fever" (one gathers a typically virulent tertian malaria). Mary Ashmun died on September 5. While the first white woman casualty was being buried in African earth, other tribal warriors, including Deys, Condos, and Gurrahs, began to join with the militant Bassas.

On November 10, following effectively nervewracking delays, the first open assault materialized. An attacking force, which the defenders estimated as no fewer than eight hundred men armed with metal spears and battle axes, began moving in by canoes or log dugouts from what would presently be named Bushrod Island. Daybreak showed precise formations of warriors converging from three sides upon the miniature log stockade that the colonists had painstakingly built. When they encountered no immediate opposition, the attackers began breaking rank to indulge in some easy plundering of the vacated huts or cabins—by then all the colonists were within or near the stockade.

Prophet Ashmun and Parson Carey joined Elisha Johnson in directing the defense which the Negro former artilleryman had pivoted with the two brass cannon mounted in front of the defensive logworks. As the musketeers took places on the firing scaffold with their womenfolk close behind, Johnson and his cannoneers took positions and augmented the musket fire by simultaneously firing both cannon at pointblank range. The attackers wavered, many broke ranks and fled. Without counting their dead, others remustered and charged the stockade, where they met spirited opposition.

But the colonists were also suffering casualties. Of the first four killed, one was a woman, Mary Tewes, and two of the first five wounded were women, Ann Hawkins and Minerva Draper. The first full-scale battle fought by Americans on African soil was a defensive struggle in which women fought bravely beside their men. There was no final victory, but there was restored hope for survival; Jehudi Ashmun proclaimed a day of thanksgiving and prayer.

He and Carey led prayers for a "redeeming miracle." Within a day their prayers found answer in the arrival of a coastal trading sloop, *Counterlane of Liverpool*. Her master, Captain H. Brassey, ordered an offshore landing and contributed all food stores his ship could spare, also several kegs of crucially needed gunpowder. The grateful colonists resumed shaping their defenses.

Elisha Johnson made ready all available artillery pieces. Manning them required practically all the male defenders. Women and girls took over as musketeers.

On the last day of November, colony scouts reported that another and still more formidable attack was in the making. They estimated the strength of the attackers as more than a thousand warriors, including at least thirty native spearmen for every available adult defender. Another daybreak was marred by the approach of another massed assault. This time the attackers faced a kind of checkerboarding of small cannon. The brass cannon were placed well forward. Two of the "light irons" were pulled into picket positions to the south; the other two to the east. The two swivel guns, fixed on wheeled bases, were left for improvised crews to pull to desired positions. As the closely ranked attackers moved within spear-throwing distance, the mounted guns opened concertedly and pointblank. Temporarily the advance wavered as supporting musket fire opened from the stockade's "gun walk."

But the attackers regrouped and again moved forward, walking over their dead. One after another the gun crews were obliged to pull back to reload. Under a shower of thrown spears and axes, one brass cannon, primed for firing, was left behind. Otherwise, the thin defense continued to reload and fire. But the gunpowder supply was melting away and enemy numbers remained overwhelming.

By midmorning it was evident that, barring another miracle, the tribal warriors would triumph and the colonists would meet massacre. But another miracle did indeed appear in the aging, pipe-puffing, generously beskirted person of Matilda Newport, who had been temporarily inactivated for want of powder and bullets. With seeming complacency the bonneted old lady paused to drop a live coal in her pipebowl, then moved deftly outside the protecting logworks of the stockade. She made for the abandoned brass cannon, which a throng of attackers had paused to examine. The matriarch moved casually to the breach of the cannon; with fire-toughened fingers she removed the live coal from her pipe and dropped it into the powder chamber.

There was a shattering roar followed by a bloody splattering of flesh. It was the psychological turn of the valiant defense. Nearby attackers began breaking rank and dropping weapons as the retreat changed to a reverse stampede. The attack was ended. The warriors disappeared into the woods or crowded into their canoes and dugouts, or plunged into the river.

They did not remuster. One of the most decisive battles of the battle-littered nineteenth century had been won by American Negroes, men and women and older children, confronted with overwhelming forces of destruction.

But the decisive battle led to resumption of the age-old struggle against hunger, diseases, remoteness, reenslavement, and neglect. The tiny, direly afflicted black people's settlement on one of the most perilous and forbidding frontiers of a then most perilous and forbidding continent buried its dead and tried to care for its sick and wounded and grieved.

The duly elected but not as yet officially appointed white leader Jehudi Ashmun renamed his Negro lieutenants his "foremen for peace." The designation was well taken. The surviving colonists set to clearing and planting fields and gardens. It was fabulously hard work. Testimony was provided during the following month when the U.S. *Cyane*, which had escorted the *Elizabeth* and subsequently joined in patrolling West Coast Africa to discourage slave traffic, put in for a friendly call—so friendly that the ship's master ordered his company ashore and had all hands aiding the colonists in clearing land, raising shelters, and making first plantings. The "helpful bee" continued for about three weeks; by then, or before, the ship's company of thirty-one men and five officers was suffering "group exhaustion." Dr. B. Dix, the ship's surgeon, recorded that the reasonably healthy and work-hardened crew simply could not keep pace with the black colonists, not even the women and children. Evidently by then the seamen were showing vulnerability to the climate and remorseless disease hazards. As an aftermath of the landside helpfulness, six of the crew, including Surgeon Dix, died of the African fevers.

The then popular and customarily sad song about Africa's being the white man's grave did not preempt the reality that what would presently be named Liberia had already proved a black man's grave. By actual count the *Cyane* had lost fewer than a sixth part of her company. With its battle only begun the colony had already buried more than a third of all its total number.

The first American Negro nation was meeting an exceptionally perilous and painful birth. It was also writing a definitive and strangely magnificent chapter of American history within and beyond American boundaries. As the 1820s sweated along, the United States had proved itself a pennywhistle giver and an oddly ambiguous Samaritan. In greater part the support for this venture in returning black Americans to Africa had been ugly and odorous.

The nobility factor had been supplied preponderantly by the Negro colonists. Undeniably and whether or not God helps those who help themselves, the black colonists of Mesurado were helping themselves and paying dearly for the privilege.

The impoverished, undersize colony had not yet surely emerged as an African phenomenon. Another two years would drag by before it would acquire the name "Liberia," first conceived by a white man, Robert G. Harper of Baltimore.

Yet the diminutive Negro colony in the vast green hell of West Equatorial Africa had begun to show recognizable moves toward Negro-to-Negro integration. One particularly significant evidence was that as the first settlement began taking shape as such, its colonists joined in setting up the first public market to which they and the nearby tribespeople could bring their produce and other goods to sell or swap. In whatever language, first pathways to market promised to change over to first roads to peace.

3

COMMONWEALTH OF LIBERIA

THE *Old New England Farmer's Almanack & Register* had predicted that 1824 would be a year of exceptional revelations. It could be pointed out that the senior Yankee almanac said approximately the same of every year. James Monroe had foreseen 1824 as still another American year of "good feelings." The outgoing fifth president of the United States had indicated, too, that he might look favorably on a "draught" as the next president of the American Colonization Society. But the homely and politically deft Virginian had observed somewhat owlishly that even though he favored the name "Liberia," he could not welcome suggestions for changing the name of the colony's first capital from "Christopolis" to "Monrovia." Monroe could not and did not regard himself as being a proper replacement, even nominally, for Jesus Christ. From afar Jehudi Ashmun showed no disposition to argue about names. He predicted, however, that 1824 would be remembered as the birth year of the first free American commonwealth on a non-American continent.

From Washington, D.C., the American Colonization Society seemed similarly disposed to refrain from controversies regarding names. Possibly one reason for this was that the Society itself was being splattered with unwanted names; it was being labeled a cheap front for vested (and hypocritical) interests, a rendezvous for politicians in quest of noble images, a rallying point for divergent crackpots, ranging from the most wild-eyed abolitionists to the most fishy-eyed proponents of slavery.

In the living language of the times the American Colonization Society had remained as mixed up as a mad-dog's guts. It was attracting public attention accordingly, but it was not attracting monetary gifts. The Society's collections during 1822 had totaled barely $800, the average for all the 1820s would be less than $4,000 per year. Insofar as the Society was obliged to meet its own headquarters expenses, it could not count on spending more than half of its income for advancing the embryo colony in Africa.

Throughout the beginning years most of the very meager funds had come from the U.S. Treasury and had been used in greatest part for chartering and provisioning immigrant ships, supplying intermittent caches of foodstuffs and medical supplies, and maintaining sporadic naval patrol of the West African coastlines for the discouragement of slave running, in greater part American. The fact that the Colonization Society exhorted the Negro pioneers to "attain self-sufficiency" immediately or, preferably, instantly was somewhat ironic. Actually, the tiny, hard-struggling colony was offering a truly remarkable showing of self-sufficiency while the Society continued to make an extremely poor showing at raising funds. As Jehudi Ashmun continued to point out, it was indeed the "living miracle of Africa." The ardent young missionary from upstate New York also reflected that the amazing black colony had no "solid charter" or constitution, no official legislature or judiciary or law-enforcement agency, no public treasury, and no experienced precedents for a free peoples' government by and for Negroes. What had first taken form in 1809 as the first Negro republic was not in position to provide precedents in self-government; by 1824 Haiti was stumbling into virtual anarchy.

What would shortly be known as Liberia remained in the throes of many other fearful odds. It was surviving in a veritable hellhole of disease without even one qualified physician present. Its entire area stayed rife with alien slave traders and their native confederates; the fact that the slave trade was being intermittently reduced had not diminished its arrogance. When Jehudi Ashmun made bold to oppose the slave recruiters, he gained the enduring nickname of "that white American devil."

Jehudi was not especially sensitive to epithets. He was intensely concerned by the conspicuous realities that famine was threatening, that painful death was no farther away than one's shadow, and also that the colony was being used as a handy dumping ground for Negroes recaptured from slavers' stockades or from ships that from time to time were overhauled by patrol craft of both the British and American navies. Noble as the cause was, the hard-used colony lacked shelter, food, medical, and other facilities for receiving the unpredictable delivery of duress settlers, few of whom were disposed to remain in or near the colony any longer than they were obliged to.

The hardly more predictable arrival of colony volunteers was in itself a formidable obligation. During February (1824), for example, the sloop *Cyprus* arrived at Cape Mesurado with a manifest of 105 unowned slaves. On the following May 23, the *Oswego* hove in with a replacement of desperately needed supplies and a passenger list of sixty-six additional volunteer settlers.

And so it went, in all instances with more than half of the immigrants women and children, and most of the able-bodied men either farm workers or other unskilled laborers. The *Oswego* also returned Dr. Eli Ayres, who was no longer a Navy surgeon; this time he came as the official agent of the American Colonization Society. Dr. Ayres was obviously concerned about ways and means for accommodating the new settlers. He firmly reminded all colonists that they were expected to fend for themselves, and further that slothfulness or rebelliousness would not be tolerated. He demonstrated his renewed reach of authority by abruptly terminating Ashmun's leadership and demoting him to the "common ranks."

The settlers protested, but none could deny that Dr. Ayres' services as a physician were desperately needed; the more so because another "sweep" of the fevers had stricken the colony, claiming eight additional lives. Within a few weeks Dr. Ayres himself was on the sick list; he took passage on a trader's ship for London, where he hoped to convalesce. Instead the vehement redhead died of what he had diagnosed as "malignant jaundice with bladder putrification."

Returned to his informal leadership, Jehudi Ashmun set about shaping a plan for colony government. He reassigned his Negro lieutenants for service as congregation leaders and effected a kind of compromise between New England township meetings and African-style bush palavers.

From distant Washington the Colonization Society continued to spout officious advice and little else. When the advice-givers admonished Ashmun to undertake the punishment of troublemakers in the colony, Jehudi replied that he "disfavored" punishing people without benefit of fair and lawful trial, and branded as extreme and unreasonable the Society's directives to effect discipline by withholding food supplies or banishing the troublemakers. While the ship's-mail arguments continued, Ashmun himself was severely stricken with the fevers. He appointed his Negro preacher colleague Lott Carey acting leader and set out to "fever-free country," specifically Cape Verde, off Dakar.

The Negro pastor demonstrated his own superior talents as a leader by making lots or plots of farmable land available to all family heads who would agree to accept "working residence," and persuaded all to contribute proportionate shares to public-benefit labor—such as clearing trails, building shelters, clearing commons—in lieu of taxes paid in money.

From afar the Colonization Society instructed the upcoming secretary, the Reverend Ralph R. Gurley, to board the U.S. Navy's *Porpoise* to supervise the delivery of another cargo of settlers and supplies and to recommend ways and means of "saving" the colony. Gurley responded with a try at saving Jehudi Ashmun. As a first move he directed the Navy brig to call at Puerto Praya, where he met and formed a warm friendship with the White Prophet and joined him in drafting a tentative constitution for the settlement.

When Gurley dispatched a report strongly urging that Ashmun be restored as the official resident agent, the Society declined, but accorded Gurley a vote of confidence that preluded his promotion to the post of secretary-general of the Society. That attained, the Reverend Mr. Gurley accredited the Reverend Mr. Ashmun as the official resident agent in the colony.

Still feeble from his illness, Ashmun joined his new friend for the journey to Mesurado, where about four hundred colonists were at least surviving. The two white men read the draft of the proposed constitution and invited the settlers to vote on it. Having gained approval, the next step was to set up, again by open election, an advisory council made up wholly of Negro colonists (originally of five, then nine, then fifteen, and so on upward) to serve as a facsimile of a legislature.

The most urgent task related to locating and making available better farming lands; the beginning colony site was not even well explored. There were painfully evident reasons for this. The projected colony site included about twenty-five square miles of jungle-strewn ocean front; crossing it afoot required several days. The hot, sandy plain was ill suited to settlement since it was interspersed with mosquito-swarming lagoons and mangrove-crowded backwaters. The adjoining interior plateau, with elevations ranging from 400 to 1,200 feet, was densely forested and intermittently afflicted with swamps. To the north and west waited higher and more arable lands but these had no roads or trails and thus were too remote for immediate settlement.

The more readily reachable coast lands are subjected to excessive rainfall, as much as 200 inches a year, and rarely less than 125 inches, or about three times the average then obtaining in the eastern United States. The need for seeking out areas with lower rainfall did not dispel the threat of intermittent droughts brought on by the harmattans, or dry winds from the Sahara. The seekers of better farm lands were also obliged to avoid the flat lands or valleys where topsoils were leached of soluble plant foods and the so-called red iron areas, some of which would later be identified as sites for surface iron mines.

Lott Carey qualified as an exceptionally astute student of prevailing soils and cultivation methods. He and his fellow colonists heeded many of the land and farming practices of the indigenous tribespeople. These included land clearing. During the late autumn and early season rain lulls the tribespeople chopped out the bush and undergrowth with cutlasses or axes (Africa was already moving into the iron age), and deadened the larger trees by girdling the lower trunks. When the debris was sufficiently dry, they burned it, then used their broad hoes (in some instances made of wood, in others of locally smelted iron beaten out by native blacksmiths), to work the ashes into the soil. Then the tribeswomen and older children took over as principal farmers.

Carey and his fellow searchers for farm sites learned that the indigenous agriculture included two principal grains, rice and millet; two cultivated and highly edible root crops, cassava and eddo (or taro); also yams and sweet potatoes; various peas and beans; both hot and sweet peppers (capsicums); peanuts, okra, and eggplant. The less widely grown food harvests included tropical perennials such as bananas, plantains, avocados, and pineapples, as well as various wild-growing palm kernels.

The native livestock was largely limited to goats, chickens, and guinea fowl. There were very few draft animals since horses, mules, and cattle were victims of various endemic diseases such as sleeping sickness or trypanosomiasis. Wisely, the colonists were adapting their farming efforts to native precedents. This included the harvesting of wild-growing provenders that featured native fruits, palm crops, fish, and forest-edge game. The native game and wild-growing plant harvests provided most of the "trader goods," which included palm oils, dye woods, tortoise shells, elephant ivory, and, particularly, animal pelts—leopard skins would presently emerge as the number one commercial export of the colony.

The colonists agreed in principle to refrain from seeking farm sites near areas already occupied by tribespeople and to respect the rights of "primacy," or first occupancy. The acquisition procedure was to locate favorable sites, then call on the paramount or senior chief in the area and on the village or clan chiefs to seek "settlement rights." These took the form of primitive treaties requiring that the land-seeker(s) pay the tribal claimants in goods or money, preferably barter goods. Equatorial Africa was "swapping country"; land rights were traditionally priced in terms of bolt cloth, hand tools, guns, wives, or other desirable tangibles.

On that basis the colony that would be known as Liberia had grown from about two square miles in 1822 to roughly 150 square miles by the end of 1824. By the end of 1825 the original Cape Mesurado Colony was abutted by five additional communities, including two embryo farm centers located in the valley of Stockton Creek. Typically, one of these, presently renamed New Georgia, was being settled by eleven families of immigrants and nineteen displaced tribesmen whom the Navy patrol had returned from slave ships.

Early in 1825 the colony's advisory council joined in establishing near the New Georgia settlement a first experimental farm, quite possibly the first in Equatorial Africa; its immediate objective was to help feed the recaptured slaves; its long-term goal was to try out possible harvests for the arriving colonists. The proportions of volunteers and newly recaptured slaves during April, 1825 were similar; the U.S. chartered sloop *Hunter* delivered sixty-six American Negro volunteers to Cape Mesurado and naval patrols (mostly British) landed and released sixty-six recaptured slaves.

The colonizing, meanwhile, spread by small plots. The colony provided farms averaging about ten acres each and town lots of about one acre each. Most were located in creek or river valleys. By 1826 the settlers' rosters showed forty families of farmers on or near Cape Mesurado, thirty-three in New Georgia, seventy-seven in the new Caldwell community, and about twenty in the vicinity of Christopolis, now Monrovia, the capital. The land exploration proceeded without benefit of formal engineering. The volunteer location parties, usually six to twelve men, traveled afoot and intermittently by canoe or dugout, blazing first trails, braving unmapped rivers and perilous mud pits. Remarkably, the choice of farm sites was in great part excellent.

That, certainly, was a saver of lives. The still feeble fund-raising efforts of the Colonization Society and the remnants of U.S. Treasury grants were barely sufficient to pay ship's passage for the inflow of pioneers. There were still no local revenues, and the cautiously expanding colony was still lacking physicians, teachers, and other professional workers. Ashmun's appeals for missionaries had not yet proved effective; law enforcement depended mostly on what Lott Carey termed prayerful persuasion. However, churches were beginning to appear. Despite the absence of white man's courts, jails, stocks, and whipping posts, the crime rate was extremely low and "government by good conscience" (again quoting Carey), was succeeding impressively.

Acting leader and migrant pastor Lott Carey thoughtfully pointed out that most of his fellow black Americans were establishing a principal degree of self-sufficiency during their very first year in Africa, something very few white colonists had ever attained. Furthermore, almost all the volunteers were providing their own ways to shipboard in the assigned U.S. port; entire families had walked hundreds of miles to embark. Most were supplying their own clothing and working tools and household goods; practically none was seeking charity.

Understandably, the same did not hold for the recaptured slaves whom the naval patrols continued to bring in. Most of these people sought to return to their tribes. The Ashmun advisory council continued to deplore the slave trade, and during August (1825) Ashmun and five of his Negro lieutenants began organizing and equipping a first volunteer company of arms-bearing "anti-slavers." All were aware that a new slavers' headquarters was being set up at a settlement called Trade Town in the Grand Bassa area. As soon as the "musket company" was organized, Ashmun sent word to the U.S. Navy outpost at Freetown, requesting ship's passage for the volunteers, who would drive out the slave traders. The Navy outpost consented, picked up the volunteers at Mesurado, and assigned a platoon of U.S. Marines to support the "crusade."

As the colony scouts had reported, the slavers, a conglomerate of Spaniards, Frenchmen, and at least six Americans, were well armed and had completed a strong log-built stockade. They met the landing with a fierce cannonade supported by musket fire. The colonists and Marines took shelter in the dense forest, then attacked and burned a succession of thatched villages that the slavers occupied. The fire presently spread to the slavers' store of gunpowder. A tremendous explosion resulted; the surviving slavers and their black accomplices fled into the forest. The colony musketeers recaptured and released the recently enslaved Africans and made a safe return to Mesurado. That was the first Liberian war of liberation.

Ashmun and Carey promptly set about persuading friendly chiefs to join in a boycott of white traders and others suspected of being in collusion with the slavers. Again, early in 1827, the U.S. Navy came to the aid of Liberia with an armed schooner, the *Sharp,* bearing firearms and ammunition and with orders to assist the Negro colony in its opposition to slavers. With the help of about seventy colony volunteers, all Negroes, the *Sharp*'s commander, Lieutenant A. Norris, and the ship's company proceeded to build a coastal rampart, Fort Norris, near Cape Mesurado. The Navy personnel equipped the rampart with a battery of six-inch shore guns and four pieces of light artillery. Volunteer militiamen of the colony, unpaid and without uniforms, took charge of the miniature fort and stood by to fire on any slave ships that succeeded in bypassing the Navy patrols.

Ashmun and Carey and the advisory council moved vigorously to begin building schools and churches. They had already raised a first combination school and church at Christopolis. During 1826 the council opened the institution to the children of tribespeople, who were taken as guests to live in the homes of colonists while attending the school. The colony's first professional schoolteacher, George McGill, a former Virginia slave, who also served as pastor of the colony's first church, opened the latter to tribespeople also. During 1827 the Negro colony also had established a first public library, quite probably the first in Equatorial Africa.

Also during 1827 the colony made a first consistent effort to effect a revenue department. The year's collections totaled $4,700, principally from excises on ivory, dye woods, and leopard pelts.

The council voted to use the first income to make down payments on building a public market, another elementary school, and a "government house" or refuge for the newly arrived immigrants. The year's climaxing advance was a first friendship-and-trade pact with a principal native tribe (the Bosporo).

During the following year the colonial advisory council returned vigorously to the problems and progress of agriculture. A first agricultural society at the Caldwell settlement helped pioneer a seeds and livestock introduction program. The championed crops included American (white) cotton, indigo "bush" (then a source of a principal commercial dye), sugar cane, American corn (which did not thrive), and a grain sorghum, which succeeded. The introduction of horses, sheep, cattle, and hogs shipped from the United States did not work out well, but cattle and sheep subsequently purchased in nearby Sierra Leone colony showed promise. The remarkable truth held that in terms of experimental agriculture the hard-struggling little colony was several decades ahead of the United States.

From Washington the spirited Ralph Gurley succeeded in recruiting a first "team" of five Negro missionaries from the United

States and three white missionaries from the Swiss Evangelical Society. The colonists welcomed the missionaries, but for the most part the tribespeople were not yet receptive to Christian evangelism.

Nevertheless the American Colonization Society shifted its publicity efforts to the quest of church followings, and to that end encouraged the establishment of state auxiliaries. One of the strongest, the Maryland Colonization Society, was already planning its own free-slave settlement in or near Liberia with direct support of the Maryland legislature. Jehudi Ashmun approved the move but found himself obliged to give notice of a change of address. Again seriously ill of the fevers, he returned to Cape Verde to regain his health. He did not succeed. Still seriously ill, the engaging but prematurely aging prophet returned to the United States for treatment. On arrival at New Haven Ashmun was carried to a local "sick home" (or hospital), where a few weeks later he died.

In a final letter to his champion, Ralph Gurley, Jehudi had requested that the Society's secretary-general confirm his volunteer replacement, the Reverend Lott Carey, as permanent agent. Gurley complied. Lott Carey chose the veteran Negro soldier Elisha Johnson as his assistant. Liberia shifted quietly but finally to leadership by black men.

The difficulties were self-evident, but so were the advantages. Liberia was already changing from an experimental refuge colony to a beginning Negro nation in the great Negro continent. An overture to recurring problems thereof was provided when Bassa war parties, early in 1829, began raiding outlying colonial settlements. Carey dispatched three trusted emissaries, including Johnson, to intercede with a paramount chief, King Bristol of the Bassas. Bristol responded by seizing the emissaries and making them prisoners. Lott Carey organized a volunteer relief force to rescue his lieutenants and joined in preparing a supply of cartridges. Somehow a lighted candle came in contact with the supply of gunpowder. The resulting explosion killed eight of the volunteers and fatally wounded Carey.

The captured emissaries managed to break free and Johnson took over as the temporary colony leader. His replacement, Maryland-born Richard Randall, perished of the fevers only four months after arrival in Liberia. Dr. Randall's first move had been to set up an expanded refuge community for Africans recaptured from slavers. Although severe illness persisted among the colonists, the colony continued to grow.

During 1829 it received approximately 600 free slaves from the United States and about 200 Africans rescued from slavers, and finished its first decade with a population of about 1,500. By 1830 six public schools were functioning. Far out in Bassa tribe country the Swiss Evangelical Society was establishing a first school for the children of tribespeople. About 400 farms, for the most part small and jungle crowded, were bearing harvests. The revenue collections had climbed to $6,700 a year, enough to sustain an embryo government so long as practically all who served it were willing to work for love of country rather than money.

There were many other noteworthy items of wall-writing and earth-writing. Most significant was the emergence of a new leadership of young Negroes. These included two young mulattoes, both in their twenties.

One was twenty-seven-year-old Anthony Williams, whom the advisory council in 1829 chose as its "special assistant." Son of South Carolina slaves, Williams had taught himself to read, write, and lead subsequent to his arrival at Cape Mesurado in 1823. Directly after his arrival the youth had cleared his own "plot" in the newly formed Careysburg community and helped establish a farming community for Negroes lately recaptured from slavery. Williams next instigated a colonywide homebuilding program and helped in setting up a succession of public markets for the gratis use of colonists and tribespeople.

Among his close friends was a then twenty-year-old mulatto, Joe Roberts—more formally, Joseph Jenkins Roberts. He, too, was born of slave parents of Petersburg, Virginia, and had grown up as a cabin boy and deck laborer on Appomattox River boats. Like Williams, Roberts had taught himself to read and write, and he had contributed most of his boyhood wages to buying his widowed mother out of slavery. At nineteen, Joseph Roberts "put in" for passage to the free-slave colony and persuaded his mother and his two younger brothers to join him. Seventeen years later he would persuade his fellow colonists to elect him first president of the Republic of Liberia.

Self-evidently that shape of the future, like the Negro colony as a whole, was portentous, and as many recognized, audacious. Liberia was surviving as an extremely small but living dot on the vast western bulge of a huge, mysterious, and in great part still terrifying continent. But the living dot was beginning to show a strange and wonderful light.

4

THE DISTANT MIRROR

NAMING THE STILL TINY COLONY of unowned Negroes "Liberia" was validly motivated, but calling it a commonwealth was still premature. The colony was able to fulfill a basic definition of "commonwealth" in that it was a "body of people constituting a politically organized community," but it was not a sovereign body politic.

Technically Liberia remained a ward of a still highly controversial and alien nonprofit corporation which claimed ownership of all lands of the colony, selected and appointed its senior officials or "agents," and otherwise sought to dominate the colony and direct its destinies.

Liberia remained and gained significance as a most remarkable American phenomenon, but it was not yet an African nation. American Negroes had clashed with the African tribespeople yet had succeeded in establishing friendships and certain correlations of common interest between themselves and the neighboring aborigines. But even while gaining some degree of African rootage, Liberia had not gained convincing status as an African nation. Even more disappointing, despite its valorous stand against the continuing slave trade, Liberia was being used as a ploy and an inexpensive *pièce de resistance* by one of the most blatant and cynical lobby forces that had ever befouled American government.

The secretary-general of the American Colonization Society was striving diligently and sincerely to better its image and project its activities as part and parcel of what was being hopefully designated as the New American Religious Awakening. But the Society could not deny that most of its founders and a majority of its continuing advocates remained slaveowners or steadfast proponents of legalized slavery. This held for many of its church-leading supporters, particularly in the South, and the colony was still openly publicized as a kind of safety valve for the steadily rising antislavery pressures.

The federal government was still strongly in favor of slavery, even though the perceptible tides of history, personified by the powerfully upbound British Empire, were more and more conspicuously against it. Even so, the viewpoint of the American politician, at national levels, was perhaps best exemplified by Congressman Charles Fenton Mercer of Virginia, who by no coincidence remained a founder-director of the American Colonization Society. Representative Mercer stood strongly for outright federal contributions to Liberia as a procedure, so he explained, for saving "black souls." This thesis, which piously supported the continuation and increase of Society efforts to recruit Negro colonists, was showing two widening gaps in factual logic; as yet Black Africa showed no really convincing interest in "Christianization"; and the growth of Liberia was not being sufficiently supported either by American government or by American churches.

Furthermore, the 1830s were evidencing high vocal gains in the popular opposition both to the institution of slavery and to its various subterfuges. In particular, New England of the 1830s was "flowering" much more conspicuously than it had during the 1820s; it was emerging as the schoolground of the nation, and more or less relatedly, the prime bulwark for the Abolitionist "movement" in America. New England's basic economy, agriculture, and beginning industrialization were almost uniformly incompatible with slave ownership and the various strategies and stratagems thereof. More or less inevitably New England participation in the American Colonization Society was affecting the somewhat erratic steering of the Society and its use of Liberia as a front for seeking public sympathy and contributions.

There were other forces of change by way of more localized interpolation of Colonization Society goals, such as they were. The most impressive entry here was that of the Maryland Colonization Society, which had highly vocal assistance from its woman auxiliaries, in a revised championship of the increasing population of unowned Negroes whom Ralph Gurley described as "friendless, bewildered wanderers with liberated bodies but enslaved minds."

Although nominally an auxiliary of the American Colonization Society, the Maryland Society was establishing a three-way action pattern of its own. Its leadership was beginning to set up direct agreements with slaveowners who were willing to liberate slaves who were particularly well qualified to be successful colonists and who agreed to emigrate to Liberia. As already noted, the Maryland Society had committed itself to helping establish a new and independent settlement, tentatively named Maryland in Liberia. And to implement this undertaking the Maryland legislature had been persuaded to appropriate an initial grant of $200,000 to help support its proposed Liberian colony. Moreover, the Marylanders were pioneering effectively with fund-raising efforts by various Masonic and other fraternal groups throughout the state and beyond.

The mood for more extensive support of the African colonization as a whole was being demonstrated further by the move of the aging but enormously popular Marquis de Lafayette, who had earlier (in 1825) accepted an honorary vice-presidency of the Society; and by the spreading rash of Friends of Africa rallies which began during 1830 in New York, Philadelphia, Boston, and other cities and on principal campuses including Yale, Princeton, Columbia, Middlebury, Amherst, Wesleyan, etc.

Although the money gifts remained modest, the range during the 1830s was from $8,000 to $12,000 per year, which was sufficient for recruiting and shipping out a growing roster of volunteer colonists; the 1830 total, for example, was 318—enough to motivate the Philadelphia Colonization Society's gift of a seaworthy sloop, the *Margaret Mercer,* exclusively for carrying colonists to Liberia.

There was, to be sure, continuing and more and more vocal opposition, from both the Abolitionists and free Negro groups, who deplored the entire procedure as a shoddy, hypocritical evasion of American responsibilities to Negro residents none of whom enjoyed "first-class" citizenship.

Despite its clamoring opposition the American Colonization Society continued to gain membership; by 1835 it had "branches" in seventeen states and "auxiliaries" in at least two hundred cities. Some of the associates began to incubate imaginative business schemes; for example, the Latrobe Plan proposed American establishment of a thousand-mile African coastal trading front that would extend along successive river mouths from the Senegal to the Cavalla and include developing "trade rivers" such as the Gambia, Grande, Munez, and Pongos, and make Liberia the "official American outpost."

Most of the plans were hardly more than loquacious pipe dreams. Even so, public interest in Negro colonization was on the rise and the American Colonization Society was inevitably yielding to changing minds and moods of its increasing membership.

As secretary-general of the Society and editor of its official publication, *The African Repository*, Ralph Gurley avidly continued the solicitation of federal aid for Liberia. His efforts were not immediately successful and, apparently to his surprise, Gurley found himself being lambasted by much of the Southern press, which angrily resented the suspected changeabout of the Society's goals. The Richmond, Virginia, *Enquirer*, for example, branded what it termed the "Liberia mess" as a progressive betrayal of the South by undermining "by implication" the "court-affirmed and God-given rights of slaveholding" and "otherwise fanning the perfidious flames of abolitionism."

During his four years as president of the United States, John Quincy Adams had maintained what he termed sympathetic objectivity regarding Liberia. On assuming the presidency in March, 1829, Andrew Jackson took a wait-and-see stand. By 1830 he had indicated his disapproval of appropriation of federal money for sponsoring the black colony; during the following year Old Hickory repeated his wait-and-see routine. The expedience factor began to leak away during August, 1831, which was bloodied by the Nat Turner Insurrection, at the time the most lethal of the slaves' revolts. In Virginia's Southampton County alone, about sixty white people lost their lives; the black casualties were never accurately reported but may have been ten or twenty times as great.

The immediate aftermath included an increased enthusiasm for exporting unowned Negroes. The Virginia legislature, with the strong approval of former President James Monroe, who had accepted the presidency of the American Colonization Society, led the way by voting $12,000 for "helping to resettle" unowned Virginia Negroes in Liberia.

Monroe shortly discovered that his approval of the Virginia legislature's action was unexpectedly productive. Both the proslavery and antislavery press opposed the token action. The most notable exception was the gifted Negro journalist, John Russwurm, who had earlier used his and the nation's first Negro newspaper (*Freedom's Journal* of New York) to oppose colonization. Russwurm changed from nay to aye, loaded his hand press aboard ship, and proceeded to Monrovia, where he founded the *Liberia Herald,* the colony's first newspaper, and devoted the rest of his life to aiding his adopted country.

There were no comparable reactions from Bostonian William Lloyd Garrison, who in 1831 founded the newspaper *The Liberator* as a first voice for the American free Negroes. Garrison bitterly denounced the Colonization Society as a tool of the slave trade, and a dodging of responsibilities for providing American Negroes with basic rights, including schooling and "conscionable treatment."

While directing his printed words to black people, Garrison turned to white people with other of his talents. He led in refurbishing the New England Anti-Slavery Society, which gained telling support from Quakers and other influential church groups, also the more liberal educators and an impressive list of writers, including the budding generation of poets of causes. The Garrison battle cry was "Uncompromising Abolitionism," and on that basis he whacked the American Colonization Society, its slaveowner directors, and "pulpit sycophants" with vigor and effectiveness.

The New England Anti-Slavery Society told its controversial story like it was and like it wasn't. Correctly the Abolitionists reported that more than a few Liberian colonists were returning from the would-be jungle Utopia disgusted and disillusioned; incorrectly they said that the Negro colony was chronically doused and reeking with liquor—"thousands of barrels" of the Devil's Delight.

The Washington headquarters of the American Colonization Society hotly denied the latter charges, insisting that the Negro colonists were almost unanimously sober, God-fearing, and dedicated pioneers who, along with their other noble attainments, were dissuading the tribespeople of Africa from drinking and/or trading in liquor. But anyone who doubted that the New England Anti-Slavery Society was punching effectively had only to note that the collections of the American Colonization Society had begun to drop alarmingly, to $12,000 in 1832, to $4,000 for 1833, and less than $2,000 in 1834. The fact was quite evident that Liberia could not endure by figurative blood transfusions from a vehemently opinionated and habitually stingy all-American public.

This grew alarmingly clear during 1833 when the colony suffered its first prolonged drought. Harvests dwindled, in some communities failed totally; food stores grew dangerously low and, as expectable, sickness flared again. Washington headquarters of the Society temporarily suspended the recruiting of colonists and renewed its demands that the colony make itself "self-sufficient." It could not do as much for itself but it could and did spew advice. The Society also demanded that "Monrovia" build—most economically, of course—a work house for the "improvident and idle," and take over its own governmental expenses. The facts were that the work records of the colonists were superior to American averages and that Liberia had long sustained a very exceptional record for paying its own way.

Meanwhile, dark as the distant African mirror appeared to be, other colony-sponsored groups remained active. Maryland in Liberia and a new Sinoe settlement sponsored by the Pennsylvania and Philadelphia auxiliaries both began to materialize regardless of the delay orders from Washington. The hard-to-believe proposition held that while no area of the slavery or antislavery story was entirely free of controversy and harsh criticism, the acceptance of Negro colonization was beginning to assume a quality of inevitability.

For much of the Western world the 1830s found the outright abolition of slavery a veteran cause, but one which was not being adequately attained in any country. Africans still held fellow black people in slavery. The British Anti-Slavery Society continued to accuse the high command of Her Majesty's Navy of perpetuating slaver patrols as a guise for locating trading beachheads along the potentially rich West African coast. Despite official antislavery pronouncements by "high government sources" in France, Spain, Holland, Portugal, even Brazil, these powers were known to be profiting financially from the perpetuation of slave trading.

But there were also relevant developments that did not admit controversy. Britain was demonstrating that a gaining power and empire can dispense with and firmly prohibit slavery and remain a gaining power and empire. In its comparatively microscopic way the Liberia venture was proving that Negro colonization was attainable and, to a remarkable degree, was being made self-sufficient.

Early in 1833, when the Reverend R. J. B. Pinney went to Liberia as its first Presbyterian missionary and resident general agent for the American Colonization Society, he found the self-providence of the colony "little short of miraculous." This was conspicuously true in the various "splinter" or outlying centers. The new Quaker-sponsored settlement in the valley of the St. John River had only 126 founding settlers, but this number included practitioners of the most needed trades and professions—physicians, pharmacists, carpenters, blacksmiths, shoemakers, potters, and so on. The colonist craftsmen were already establishing an apprentice training system whereby the trades could be taught alike to fellow colonists and young tribesmen. Pinney could and did report the successful introduction of several field crops from the United States. He noted in particular that Maryland in Liberia had almost catapulted into a self-sustaining establishment; in less than two years the settlement showed forty-seven family farms cleared, planted, and bearing. Impressively, too, John Russwurm, the crusading Negro editor, was in the process of gaining election as first governor of Maryland in Liberia.

Unfortunately, the casualties among the Colonization Society's agents were so excessive that reports were frequently left incomplete. Agent Pinney and his missionary successor, W. J. Skinner, were abrupt casualties of the fevers. Negro leadership was resumed in 1835 when Anthony Williams, who had served as Skinner's assistant, took over as acting governor of the original colony. By then the missionary activities were gaining footholds, or, at least, toeholds, with the Baptist Society of Monrovia; the Liberia Society of Friends; an Episcopalian mission led by Dr. R. Thomas Savage, a physician; a Methodist headquarters directed by David James;

and the American Board of Foreign Missions—all present and active. By the middle 1830s first converts were being reported from the tribes, particularly the Veys.

As acting governor of Liberia, Anthony Williams moved boldly to revive colony opposition to the still festering slave trade, thereby doing away with the abject dependence on naval patrols, in greater part, British. Williams had learned at close range that the slave grabbing was a principal cause of feuds, quarrels, and guerrilla-type warfare among the tribes; also that liquor was the most effective bribe material being used by the slave traders or grabbers. As Sir Harry Johnston later pointed out, "The one article for which the black potentate or trader was ready to sell his soul . . . his wife, child, brother, or offending subjects and friends, was distilled spirit. . . ."

It followed that the colony's antiliquor crusade was no whim or quirk of Puritanism; it was prime strategy in the "home mission" of standing against slavery as the prime menace to successful settlement. Williams also expressed the experienced confidence that Negro leadership was the one dependable hope for the survival and growth of what was being called Liberia.

The acting governor could and did take comfort from the materializing fact that Liberia, even though lacking a judiciary system and police force, had already earned recognition as an exceptionally law-abiding group of communities. During its first twenty years only one capital crime, a murder, had been reported. By 1838 the colony's census, including the 300 to 400 "pioneers" of Maryland in Liberia, was being guessed at about 2,500 American Negroes and 28,000 tribespeople who had more or less formally joined them. There was only one jail for the more than 30,000, and it was usually empty.

During 1838 the colony's commerce, which had been principally barter trade slightly augmented by American or British currency, acquired a first facsimile of a monetary specie. The American Colonization Society provided a makeshift currency made up of "fractional notes," in denominations from five cents to one dollar, and at least theoretically redeemable by way of the Society. The "funny money" did not prove successful, but as its second decade neared an end, the remote colony had at least twenty trading firms that owned eight merchant vessels and accounted for exports totaling about $250,000 a year and imports of about $150,000. Liberia's self-engendered favorable trade balance was getting to be traditional.

Appreciatively and by way of its secretary-general, Ralph Gurley, the American Colonization Society instituted a carefully planned effort to make Liberia a unified settlement and a "confirmable" commonwealth. The Maryland Society did not concur, but the other state affiliates were in favor. Simon Greenleaf, a professor at Harvard Law School and president of the Massachusetts Colonization Society, volunteered to draft a basic constitution for the proposed commonwealth. As *the* American authority on the "law of evidence," Mr. Greenleaf, who would later contribute a tentative draft of a constitution for the Republic of Liberia, insisted on abiding the evidence of willingness of citizens-to-be to accept. As Anthony Williams confirmed, with the single exception of Maryland in Liberia, all the communities then, including Monrovia, New Georgia, Caldwell, Millsburg, Marshall, Edina, Bixley, and Buchanan, indicated willingness to join the proposed commonwealth. The Greenleaf proposal of a commonwealth constitution recommended the establishment of a legislature, made up of the governor and one locally elected representative from each member settlement; a popularly elected chief executive who would be known as president of Liberia and governor of Monrovia; also an elective vice president and an ex-officio council to be made up of the president and vice president and the governors of the member communities. There would be a legislature-appointed Supreme Court assisted by "such other courts as the legislature would establish." The public-ballot acceptance of the proposed constitution was substantially matter of course and the ensuing first election, although somewhat fuzzy, marked the election of Thomas Buchanan, a benevolent Quaker formerly of Philadelphia, as president-governor, with the still youthful mulatto Joseph Jenkins Roberts as vice president and vice governor.

Although the first two senior officials were separated by an age difference of at least thirty years, they were both deeply religious men and devout pacifists. Ironically, they had no more than entered office when they confronted one of the most serious tribal wars in the known history of the Pepper Coast. The powerful Golas and the usually compatible Deys were fighting to the death. Sympathies of the outlying communities of colonists had gravitated toward the Deys. Gola war parties countered by punishing the St. Paul Valley colonists, Buchanan's neighbors and homefolks, with raids, arson, and miscellaneous mayhem. The settlers were fighting back with vigor; the total situation was most foreboding.

Could or would the borning commonwealth do anything about it? The answer was an emphatic yes. Buchanan placed Roberts in command of a volunteer muster of 300 colonial militiamen. The unpaid and ununiformed force picked its way through dense jungle to the St. Paul Valley and on the third day closed on the "armed village" of Gatumba, the senior Gola war chief. The volunteers overran his stronghold; Gatumba managed to escape and thereby forfeited his leadership. When the bulk of his fighting force and several of the petty chiefs had surrendered, Roberts commanded that they repair their depredations—which included rebuilding all the cabins or settlers' huts they had burned. That accomplished, he assembled a party of friendly chiefs who joined him in drawing up a series of "friendship treaties." The distinctly bold venture provided the borning government a procedural precedence for formal peace making.

But the tribulations of the new African commonwealth were only beginning. The new government could not claim status as a sovereign state. A first and frustrating acceptance of this lack of status was indicated by the firm and arrogant refusal of British and other foreign traders to pay duties or other taxes to a "state that was not a state."

An even more painful infringement began to materialize to the immediate south and west. By 1841 France was aggressively expanding her proposed West Africa empire by occupying, by force if required, various coastal lands, beginning south of Britain's then new Gambia Colony and extending to the Ivory Coast and including pivotal Grand Bassa, which Liberia had already claimed on the basis of individual treaties. Buchanan appealed to the American Colonization Society and the United States government to take "corrective actions." None were taken. The official U.S. policy was one of no policy and the Colonization Society was suffering severe internal strife and a bleeding away of prestige.

The Liberian president-governor was understandably distressed. His worries further multiplied when the U.S. Navy openly refused to recognize the infant Negro state. Answering the direct complaint of a mission group, the master of the U.S.S. *Vandalia* had led a Marine unit to effect the capture of a tribal chief whom the missionaries had accused of pilfering their supplies. Without consulting any official of the new commonwealth, the shipmaster ordered the accused chief tried by a kangaroo court, known to the Navy as a drumhead court martial, found him guilty and forced him to restore the allegedly stolen goods. The news spread and many of the chiefs interpreted it as an official notice that the Commonwealth of Liberia was not accredited or respected by the United States.

Thomas Buchanan was deeply chagrined. But not for long. During August, 1841, while returning to Monrovia from a visit to the downcoast settlements, his boat capsized. The dedicated Quaker swam ashore, but was stricken with a virulent fever from which he died the following September 3.

Joseph Roberts succeeded as president-governor. The then thirty-year-old Roberts faced a seemingly incessant array of painful and dangerous exigencies. British traders refused to pay duties on which the new nation was abjectly dependent. French territorial infringements, by then at climax in Gabon or the French Congo, began spilling over into Maryland in Liberia.

Following two years of partly fruitful efforts to improve farming practices and expand the building of schools and churches, Joseph Roberts hazarded his first official friendship tour. His rather brief itinerary of appearances in U.S. churches was successful, but he went completely unnoticed in official Washington. His quest for British acceptance of the commonwealth's prerogative for collecting revenues was also disappointing. The commander of the West African squadron of the British Navy flatly denied what he termed the rights of private persons to "constitute themselves as a government with sovereign authority to levy and collect customs duties." Britain's Minister of Foreign Affairs confirmed by describing Liberia as "no more than a commercial experiment of a philanthropic society."

The United States persisted in an austere ignoring of the black commonwealth. Roberts' response was to recommend that Liberia next establish and declare itself a sovereign republic. On that basis the body politic could seek and effect recognition, along with trade treaties and other rights and privileges implicit in sovereign status.

By 1846 the Board of Managers and the secretary-general of the American Colonization Society were in an agreeing mood, even if their motives were strongly at variance with Liberia's. The status of an independent commonwealth was not surely definable in the prevailing diplomacy and, of course, Liberia had never been a colony in the formal sense of being officially listable as subject of a mother country or empire.

The American backgrounds, meanwhile, had grown even more than customarily dissident and partisan. In Washington the proslavery forces were again gaining power and audacity. While antislavery or Abolitionist groups gained numbers and vociferousness, the proslavery blocs in Congress, with strengthening support of the federal courts, took on degrees of authoritarianism that were extraordinary even for congressional politicians from the slave states. The emerging strategy was the militant extension and increase of slave territory and future slave states. Mexico, more properly the United States of Mexico, was already branded as an unwilling provider of proslavery territory.

Texas was the oversize touchstone. During 1836 the so-called Lone Star Republic had declared its independence from Mexico. Late in 1845 the declaration was confirmed by way of congressional legislation that established the quarter-million square miles of controversy as a state of the United States of America. In November, 1845, President James Polk had delegated a diplomatic envoy, John Slidell, to Mexico City to present boundary claims and various grievances held by Texas and to present an offer of U.S. purchase of Mexico's vast frontier territories then designated as New Mexico, and of far California, which for all practical purposes was already lifted away from the second power of North America.

The harassed Mexican government refused to yield. Early in 1846 President Polk had dispatched an army contingent commanded by General Zachary Taylor to the mouth of the Rio Grande, which Texas claimed as its southern boundary. Mexico insisted that the Nueces River was the treaty-established boundary and firmly protested the unwarranted invasion of what it claimed as its sovereign territory. Early in April, 1846, a Mexican patrol force crossed the Rio Grande in the disputed area. Polk responded by declaring the show of protest an "invasion of American soil." The Mexican government responded with the declaration that the lands in question had been claimed by Texas without treaty or other official confirmation.

Early in May, without waiting for a declaration of war, the Taylor invasion forces struck forcefully. Their successful attacks on Palo Alto (May 8) and Resaca de la Palma (May 9) were both consummated prior to the U.S. Congress's formal declaration of war against Mexico on May 12. The prodigious land grab proceeded across northern Mexico and included the occupation of Matamoras and the U.S. Navy's moves to blockade Mexican ports and selected shorelines to the east. Meanwhile, a frontier expedition commanded by Colonel Stephen Kearny moved into New Mexico and headed for California. It was the most formidable land grab of its era and the most vehement puff the institution of slavery had ever received. By September 24 Taylor's invasion force had captured Monterrey, Mexico's defenses were crumbling, and the basis for extending slavery territory by at least half a million square miles was marked in blood.

Blood was not all that was shed. Throughout most of the hemisphere and much of the world beyond, the prestige and the good name of the United States were plummeting. On both sides of the Atlantic protests were multiplying. For the first time since the Jefferson-sponsored founding of the United States Military Academy in 1802 graduates of that academy were resigning their commissions in courageous protest of a most deplorable rape of a sovereign and respected neighbor nation. By epochal contrast, while its homeland was murdering freedom, Liberia was seeking to restore it. While the Taylor forces were moving against Monterrey, the Commonwealth of Liberia legislature convened in Monrovia to weigh the advantages and disadvantages of founding and declaring the Independent Republic of Liberia.

As acting chairman, Joseph Roberts presented a deeply philosophic review of the case. He pointed out that the Mexican war was demonstrating that the United States "policy" was for the expansion and intensification of Negro enslavement. However, the young president-governor held that the intentions of the "principal bodies" of the American Colonization Society were honorable and were so employable by the nation and government of Liberia. He climaxed his argument:

> . . . In my opinion, it only remains for the Government of Liberia, by formal act, to announce her independence—that she is now and has always been a sovereign independent state; and that documents of this proceeding, duly certified by the Colonization Society, should be presented to the British as well as other governments, and by that means obtain from Great Britain and other powers a just and formal recognition of the Government of Liberia. . . . We should remember with feelings of deep gratitude the obligations we are under to the American Colonization Society; they are deeply interested in our welfare, and I firmly believe they will place no obstacles in the way of our future advancement and success. . . .*

Hesitancy was evidenced by representatives of two outlying communities, Sinoe and Bassa, but the majority acceptance was never in serious doubt. There was consensus that the "grand proposal" should and would be referred to the people of Liberia, in the most democratic manner attainable. Roberts admonished that each member return directly to his home community foresworn to explain the entire issue to every family head and other settlers and to as many of the neighboring tribespeople as possible. The dependence on the spoken word was virtually absolute. But at least there was time enough; the special balloting date was set for October 27, 1846, and it would be limited to the majority desire to found a sovereign Negro republic.

The ensuing election, actually a referendum, showed a substantial majority in favor of founding the republic; the *Liberian Freeman* reported the counting of 1,157 ballots, with 801 in favor.

On January 8, 1847, as General Winfield Scott led his forces into Vera Cruz and General Zachary Taylor readied for his decisive clash with Santa Anna's defenders at Buena Vista, the legislature of the Commonwealth of Liberia again convened at Monrovia. The opposition to "sovereignty" had gained during the intervening weeks. At least a few of the representatives regarded the United

**African Repository*, Washington, D.C., X, 13, 1846.

States' seizure of so much additional slave territory as directly imperiling Liberian plans. Others believed that the already endangering French takeovers of Liberian frontiers might be escalated by the proposed quest for sovereignty. Still others viewed with alarm the continued failure of official Washington to provide any vestige of encouragement to the proposed founding of an independent African republic. Even so, President-Governor Roberts was successful in "luring" the passage of a resolution to set up a constitutional convention and provide for the public election of delegates.

The convention was opened in Monrovia on July 3 and remained in session for twenty-one days. In keeping with its earlier offers, the American Colonization Society had commissioned Simon Greenleaf of the Harvard Law School and the continuing president of the Massachusetts Colonization Society to draft a tentative text of a constitution. During May, Professor Greenleaf had delivered his draft. The Washington headquarters of the Society had asked for a clause which would permit the Society to retain title to, or at least nominal proprietorship of, the territory which would comprise the proposed republic. The convention opposed the request as unwarranted, unprecedented, and in terms of accredited government structures, an impediment to the cause at hand. The convention, therefore, denied the Society's request but presently adopted the principal text of the proposed constitution, which included rather extensive similarities to the Constitution of the United States—although these similarities have been considerably reduced by the passage of time and amendments.

When the eleven delegates representing the three counties of the Commonwealth (Maryland in Liberia was still outside the fold) had completed their work, Roberts proclaimed July 26, 1847, as the date for the official pronouncement of the Declaration of Independence for the Republic of Liberia, the public presentation of its proposed constitution, and public and private prayers for the success of the first African republic.

Following a morning of special church services, Jacob Prout of Sinoe settlement, the convention's secretary, read the special prayer and testament of his colleagues and the citizens-to-be of Liberia:

. . . Therefore, in the name of humanity, and virtue and religion, in the name of the great God our Common Creator and our Common Judge, we appeal to the nations of Christendom, and earnestly and respectfully ask of them that they will regard us with the sympathy and friendly consideration to which the peculiarities of our condition entitle us, and to extend to us that comity that marks the friendly intercourse of civilized and independent communities. . . .

Therefore, we the People of the Commonwealth of Liberia in Africa acknowledge with devout gratitude the goodness of God in granting to us the blessings of the Christian religion and political, religious and civil liberty, do, in order to secure these blessings for ourselves and our posterity and to establish justice, insure domestic peace and promote the general welfare, hereby solemnly associate and constitute ourselves a Free and Sovereign and Independent State by the name of the Republic of Liberia. . . .

The convention announced a referendum and general election on the first Tuesday of the following October (1847), the general election date specified in the constitution text. Prior to adjournment it adopted a succession of national emblems. The great seal of the new nation portrayed a dove on the wing with an open scroll held in its claw, an ocean view with a ship under sail and the sun just emerging from the waters, a palm tree with a plow and spade at its base. Above these was the national motto: *The Love of Liberty Brought Us Here*; and at the bottom were the words, *Republic of Liberia*.

The duly adopted national flag has six red and five white stripes representing the eleven signers of the Declaration of Independence and the Constitution. A blue corner square centered with one white star symbolizes Africa with Liberia "lighting its way." (The Constitution text stresses African identity and limits Liberian citizenship to "persons of African descent.")

The first election, with the terms of president, vice president, and representatives limited to two years each, sought to keep as closely as possible with political precedents already established in the United States. Joseph Roberts announced his candidacy and "ticket" for the presidency of the new republic, and he was joined by a first slate of the country's first political party, the Republican. The first nucleus of opposition adopted the party name of Whig, later True Whig. The opening "trend" of the Whigs was conservative; retention of close associations with the American Colonization Society and support of the interests of the more outlying or farther frontier communities. Roberts' prime issue was in favor of "total sovereignty"; he and his colleagues insisted that permitting the Colonization Society to continue to hold title to Liberian land would leave the government in the position of a political tenant.

The initial tickets included candidacies for president and vice president, two senators from each of the three counties (Montserado, including Monrovia, Grand Bassa, and Sinoe), four legislative representatives for Montserado, three for Grand Bassa, and one for Sinoe. All candidates were Negro settlers, for the most part from the United States.

Liberia's first national election recorded the counting of 1,109 ballots. It finally confirmed the acceptance of the duly revised constitution, and declared Joseph Jenkins Roberts the first elected president, with Nathaniel Brander, a previously little-heeded farmer-pastor, his vice president. (Around the time of this first election Commander Charles Hathan of the British Navy had estimated the population of Liberia as being approximately 1,200 emigrants from the United States and 300 from Sierra Leone and the Cape Verde Islands; 1,100 liberated Africans brought to Liberia by the U.S. Navy; and 2,000 educated natives. In addition about 40,000 aborigines were living "under the . . . influence of the Christian peoples. . . .")

The first inauguration, held on January 3, 1848, was a merger of pageant, public prayers, and formal oratory. Samuel Benedict of Monrovia, as Supreme Justice Delegate, administered the oaths of office. The first inaugural address proved itself a gospel of eloquence and enviable humility. The first president paid tribute to the pioneers—"adventurers inspired by the love of liberty and equal rights, supported by industry and protected by Heaven, who became inured to toil, to hardships and war. In spite of every obstacle they obtained a settlement and happily, under God, succeeded in laying here the foundation of a free government. . . ."

The handsome and still youthful mulatto continued,

> . . . I am also persuaded that no magnanimous nation will seek to abridge our rights, or withhold from the Republic those civilities and that comity

which marks the friendly intercourse between civilized and independent communities . . . in consequence of our weakness and present poverty . . . . No people . . . have exhibited greater devotion for their government and institutions and have submitted more readily to lawful authority than the citizens of Liberia. . . . I believe in my soul that the permanency of the government of the Republic of Liberia is now fixed upon as firm a basis as human wisdom is capable of devising. . . .

He closed with an exhortation to benefit and advance Africa and the cause of the black race— ". . . to lay our shoulders to the wheel and manfully resist every obstacle which may oppose our progress in the great work which lies before us. . . ."

Without waste of time the first president of Africa's first republic sought recognition of his country by the principal powers. Number one to respond favorably was Great Britain, through Queen Victoria's revered foreign minister, Lord Palmerston, who recommended immediate recognition of the new Negro nation. On the following March 13, Britain's official recognition was granted. Not long thereafter, Victoria welcomed the Negro president aboard the royal yacht, which paid a courtesy call at Monrovia; Joseph Roberts thoughtfully pointed out that his government's premier good fortune was in men. This held for the fourteen members of its all-Negro legislature; for its distinguished three-member Supreme Court; its three-member cabinet; its commander of military forces and its collector of revenue—all enlightened men and men of color.

President Roberts was wholly confident that official recognition from the United States would be forthcoming within a very short time.

If one did not object to calling thirteen years, all grueling and critical ones, a very short time, one could grant that the young mulatto was absolutely right.

5

THE TODDLER

On July 26, 1847, the date of its Declaration of Independence, the Republic of Liberia included a land area of only 12,830 square miles—more or less clearly confirmed by treaties or other recorded negotiations with tribal chiefs or elders. Additional lands were being sought but those for which the American Colonization Society had already claimed "custodian's title" had never exceeded 10,000 square miles, the approximate area of the state of Vermont. The first and decidedly rough maps of the Republic of Liberia indicated a 285-mile strip of coastline, with inland depth averaging about forty miles. For the time, the immigrants' census was being guessed at approximately 4,500, including the recaptured slaves who had chosen to remain in or near the already established immigrant communities.

Young President Roberts pointed out cogently that although the new and only African republic was self-justifying as a symbol of the social and political liberation of a great and still cruelly enslaved race, its survival and growth demanded greatly expanded domains. Liberia would therefore seek more and bigger acquisitions of land and citizens by process of voluntary and wholly honorable "confraternity."

When the president toured European capitals he heard agreement from many sides, in notable part official. The British Foreign Office proffered a formal "trade and amity" agreement, which Liberia eagerly accepted. The official attitudes of France's Napoleon III, Belgium's Leopold I, and the Netherlands' Queen Emma were distinctly cordial.

Liberia's foremost disappointment was the continuing and in several respects ominous failure of the United States to grant formal or even post-factum recognition to the new Negro republic—with origins so convincingly American. Fortunately for Liberia and its proliferating needs, the American Colonization Society was taking a new lease on life. Its state auxiliaries in Massachusetts, New York, Pennsylvania, and New Jersey were beginning to rival the Maryland Society as revived givers and doers.

As Joseph Roberts recognized and discreetly stated, the specific attitudes of the still powerful proslavery lobbies and political blocs, particularly those in Washington, D.C., were perceptibly changing. By 1847 the unowned-Negro population of the United States was being conservatively estimated at 800,000 and its pressures and needs and burdens of inequities and of despair were growing much more than proportionately. Particularly in the South more and more slaveowners were in greater dread of slave revolt and were increasingly harried by the participation of unowned Negroes in after-dark enterprises to effect the liberation of slaves. The "underground railroads" that were gaining powerfully as collusive devices for smuggling slaves to Canada or other "freedom lands" were also persistent sources of worry for slaveowners. The pious-sounding export of unwanted Negroes to Liberia had attractive advantages.

From the jungle-crowded Negro republic, Joseph Roberts and his colleagues refrained from commenting on the stratagems of American slaveowning or the potential violence of unowned Negroes. They could not in good conscience evade the fact that the slave trade, without benefit of legality, was still booming in much of West Africa and remained a prime menace to Liberia.

During its first eight months of life the Negro republic was confronted by a particularly obnoxious example. Friendly tribespeople from directly downcoast brought word of a well-organized and heavily armed invasion of Spanish slave traders who were operating openly in treaty territory of Liberia. The slavers had already built stockades, or "capture stations," in the bejungled Cess Valley, where they were "snatching niggers" with the help of African mercenaries whom the slavers had hired and armed.

When Liberian government scouts confirmed the report, the president and his three-man cabinet summoned the militia commander and the aging Elisha Johnson and shaped plans for what they hoped would be a crusade to end slave grabbing within Liberian territory. The president decided to request help from British and United States naval patrol units stationed at Freetown. Within two weeks the U.S. Navy corvette *Yorktown* and a British man-of-war, the *Kingfisher*, put in at Cape Mesurado to join Liberia's schooner, the *Lark*, and take on about 200 volunteer militiamen.

Early in November (1848) the force made a landing at the mouth of the Cess River, located the slavers' headquarters, and, with veteran Johnson in command, made a flank attack. The slavers' garrison opened cannon fire, which the *Kingfisher* and the *Yorktown* returned with compound interest. The Liberians closed in, dislodged the slavers and set fire to their village. Then they surrounded the *barracones* and set the captives free. Eight militiamen lost their lives and twenty-two were seriously wounded, but the guerrilla tactics of the volunteers had been both successful and brilliant.

Once the naval craft took leave the Liberians were faced with the formidable task of feeding the captives and provisioning them for overland return to their tribes. However, about a hundred of the victims chose to remain with their rescuers within Liberian boundaries, making it necessary to provide accommodations for them. The valorous and too little noticed campaign of redemption marked the infant black republic as a champion extraordinary of slavery fighting and reiterated that the slave trade was still a premier menace of West Africa, Liberia included.

This provided moral ammunition for the president's second tour of European capitals in a continued quest for official recognition. Roberts repeated his conviction that the erasure of the slave trade could advance Equatorial Africa from the general status of Europe of the thirteenth century to the attainable equivalent of the seventeenth.

In Europe he was again warmly received. But the chilling silence from Washington continued. The obtaining American views on slavery grew increasingly contradictory and emotional. The new industrial centers, particularly those in New England, the Middle Atlantic, and the nearer Midwest, had largely abandoned the use of slave labor. One outcome was the intensification of state statutes to restrict or prohibit slave ownership within their respective boundaries. By feverish and emotional contrast the principal slavery states of the malarial South used their still powerful proslavery political blocs and lobbies to aggressively exploit recently attained slavery territories.

The Treaty of Guadalupe Hidalgo, signed on February 2, 1848, had turned out to be almost as brutal and corrupt as the Mexican War which it terminated. The treaty text named the Rio Grande as the southern boundary of Texas, predestined as a hell-roaring slavery state, and ceded to the United States all Mexican territories north of a line extending latitudinally from El Paso to the Pacific. Along with vivisecting the economy of Mexico, the appalling land grab made possible virtually doubling the slavery territory of the United States and provided a tremendous boost to the renewed importation and merchandising of slaves. Stated another way, while Liberia was striving so gallantly to rid its approximately 12,000 square miles of the curse, the United States was sustaining and perpetuating slavery throughout American areas approximately a hundred times as big.

Liberia meanwhile was a double recipient of American ambivalence regarding the Negro. The cotton-growing South was substantially living from human chattels. Slavers were still growing rich, in part from within the still dimly marked boundaries of Liberia. The American Colonization Society and its veritable horde of affiliates, with membership ranging from the most to the least conscientious of Americans, was again increasing the consignments of Negro settlers, thereby adding to the already heavy burdens and responsibilities of the republic that somewhat mushily was being termed the rising star of Africa. On the less unfavorable side the free-slave immigrants were beginning to include a more favorable percentage of tradesmen and better-skilled workers.

But at most, or best, the funds contributed to resettlement were not adequate for effecting comfortable transition intervals for the new arrivers. For the most part funds barely sufficed for paying ship's passage from an American embarkation port to a Liberian landing port. Indeed, in more and more instances, the settlers were paying their own way throughout, including purchase of their lands and buildings and equipping their new homes in Liberia.

Even so, the thin-pursed Liberian government continued to try to provide all needy settlers with farm plots and/or village lots. Government land buyers treatied and bartered with tribe chiefs for additional lands. By 1851 the proliferation of block purchases, ranging in cost (usually of barter goods) from $100 to $9,000 per transaction, had lengthened the new republic's coastal front by almost 400 miles and had doubled its area.

During 1852, a fairly typical settlement year, about 1,200 immigrants, or "pioneers," including roughly 200 from the West Indies and perhaps 175 recaptured from slave traders, received from the Liberian government free title to approximately 1,000 farm plots averaging about ten acres each, and about 250 one-acre town lots. These, in effect, were gratis homesteads, to be earned by specific improvements and two years of residence. The government supplemented with improved "fee lands" for the most part priced at about one dollar per acre.

There was crucial need for governmental continuity. As already noted, the Constitution limited presidential and legislative terms to two years, senators' to four. Joseph Roberts had found his first term to be a brief "poro," or initiation. During 1849 he had campaigned vigorously and won reelection despite spirited opposition from the True Whigs. The latter had avidly introduced "color" as a political issue, terming itself the True Black Man's Party dedicated to Africa for Africans and opposing a "collusive veneer" of brown men. Roberts and his fellow Republicans had discreetly refrained from using skin pigmentation as a campaign issue.

Having won reelection by direct vote, Roberts formally stated that he regarded his pigmentation as an act of fate, that he proposed to serve and speak for all Liberians and to continue shaping the armor of a righteous cause that all other civilized nations could reasonably and justly heed. In his second inaugural address he reported happily that the Kingdom of Prussia had recently recognized Liberia's sovereignty and mentioned somewhat wistfully his "ground for hope that the United States government will not much longer withhold this token of friendship." He also reported that the British government was encouraging its nationals to provide "cleaning machines" (gins) for advancing the introduction of cotton as a commercial crop for Liberia and providing a steamship, the *Flamer*, for carrying Liberian-grown cotton to British markets. He also submitted a proposal by one George Wright, a Liverpool importer, who sought a license for introducing a palm-oil press for use by Liberians and offered his services in devising a much-needed system of copper coins for use of the new republic—these were in the denominations of one, two, and three cents.

The latter was apropos in view of the fact that Liberia was, indeed, counting pennies in a brave effort to confirm its independent solvency. The government's total revenue intake for 1851 reached $32,039. Most of this sum had been spent for acquiring lands from the nearer hinterland tribes. The incidental expenses included building a lighthouse ($237.87), other public buildings ($1,708.90), payment of foreign claims ($11,272.43), military expenses ($532.62); total expended, $34,039.14. The fiscal deficit of $2,000.14, which deeply disturbed the president, was fortunately offset by the previous year's surplus of $4,657.

Directly after Roberts' third inauguration France formally recognized the first African republic and proffered a "treaty of amity and trade." Across the Atlantic, Brazil followed suit, thereby taking its place as the first American nation to recognize Liberian sovereignty formally. During 1853 and even more significantly, about 3,000 tribespeople applied for and received citizenship status in the new republic.

As a return compliment the diligent president instituted an annual nationwide tour to "fraternalize" with tribespeople and personally visit settlers and encourage them to expand their plantings and join neighbors in countryside improvements. He further appealed to the Colonization Societies to send more farming experts as colonizers and boldly projected a first governmental scholarship program whereby young Liberians would be sent to the United States to learn "agricultural skills and knowledge."

The Roberts administration was admittedly learning its way; more than nine-tenths of its members were holding public office for the first time. The True Whigs were clearly bent on making it the last time. When the president opened his campaign for a fourth two-year term, he again met spirited opposition and a vehement revival of the color issue. The True Whigs again presented themselves as True Blacks in and for a purely Negro state and charged the "light browns" with perpetuating themselves as a dominating mixed-blood minority. The Republicans again stood on their record and won.

Roberts' third reelection for the then two-year presidential term was marked by another event of particular consequence to the new Negro nation. Maryland in Liberia moved to join the Republic. The Maryland Colonization Society agreed in principle and gave its blessings for an on-the-scene constitutional convention. On the following May 29 (1854), a special election marked the long-delayed union; Maryland in Liberia took its place as a county of Liberia, retaining local autonomy. But the move was a telling overture to effective political integration. In the new county as in the Republic as a whole observers were entitled to note that never had so many men with so brief a background in government governed so well and so unselfishly. Poor and remote as Liberia remained, it was by then the world's only self-perpetuated Negro republic. Haiti had fallen by the wayside; there were no other contenders in view. But there was evidence, both direct and indirect, that the United States government was in fact veering away from Liberia.

Along with several of his colleagues, Roberts was particularly chagrined by the continuing sequence of U.S. court rulings on what was being termed the Dred Scott Case. The former slave and his wife and children had gained freedom when their owner, a Missouri physician, had moved into the then nonslave territory of Minnesota.

However, on return to Missouri, then a slave state, Dred Scott's status as a free man was revoked by a decision of a local court. Successive appeals had proved of no avail. As a final and devastating climax the U.S. Supreme Court would presently rule both by fiat and by opinion that the United States government in its existing form had no authority to accredit the citizenship of any Negro or the descendants of a Negro. This meant that no Negro had right of hearing in any court maintained by the United States and that the "Missouri Compromise," by which the admission to the Union of free states and slave states had been "paired off," was itself unconstitutional. Liberians could and did assume that a "motherland" which would not accredit black peoples' citizenship might never recognize the Negro republic in Africa.

As he labored through his eighth year as president, Roberts announced his intention of bowing out of the office in order to spend his remaining life as a "helper boy" for his country. He nodded approvingly toward his vice president.

Stephen Allen Benson, a longtime farmer, trader, and lay preacher, who succeeded to the presidency, was also a mulatto. But long before entering government, Benson had been a cordial friend and champion of the tribespeople. He chose the improvement of friendships between immigrants and tribespeople as his first official goal and pledged that he would center his efforts on proving Liberia a self-provident Negro nation of and for all Negroes—"a luminary of hope and promise to Africa's sons in this distant land of darkness."

The responses, both local and international, were favorable. From the hinterlands native kings and other senior chiefs in handsome regalia paid ceremonial visits to Monrovia; litter-borne and with entourages of medicine men, elders, drummers, and other musicians—including those using horns made of elephant tusks—they came and went grandly. In Paris the prince-president (Napoleon III) saluted the new African republic as a "child of peace and love." European capitals echoed the sentiments; the American Colonization Society publicly announced its intention of amplifying support of the "Foundling Republic" without unduly stressing the fact that the foundling republic was doing astonishingly well at supporting itself.

Stephen Allen Benson renewed his predecessor's practice of making extensive friendship tours of the hinterlands. Accompanied by an entourage of public servants, expert farmers, teachers, and preachers, Benson led the way to the tribal towns and outlying settlers' communities. The informal official visits featured feasting and palavers, and served as recognizable forerunners of what are now known as agricultural extension services; they were designed to benefit in combination farming, government, and good feelings.

Benson's presidency could not, however, avoid forces that made for bad feelings. The frontier confrontations of the new settlers and the long-established tribespeople resulted in more or less inevitable intervals of strife. The most serious of these was an open clash in the Sheppert Lake settlement, where Grebo warriors struck en masse and killed twenty-six settlers. The president, with Joseph Roberts at his side, led a militia unit to the scene, set up a "council of umpires," including neighboring chiefs, and proceeded to weigh the grievances of both sides in open forum. Presently all were persuaded to join in writing and signing or X-ing a "treaty of friendship." Again the venture in what Joseph Roberts termed "peacemaking with backbone" was brilliantly successful.

The same did not hold for the most prevalent worry of the settlers. The shapes and overtones of a terrible civil war between the slave states and the free states "back home" were growing more ominous. With cause, Liberian settlers, whether from the United States or elsewhere, felt strongly that, however it turned out, what most Liberian officials regarded as a basically racial war and one surely materializing would afflict them grievously. For Negroes, whether slave or so-called free, would inevitably be in direct line of fire, exposed to death and suffering.

The nomination and raucously controversial election of Abraham Lincoln as president of the United States was cordially approved by Liberians who followed the homeland news, but with good cause most saw it as a certain forerunner of war. In distant, palm-fringed Monrovia, which was obliged to rely for most of its foreign news on ship's mail or travelers' reports anywhere from six to twelve weeks delayed, the *Liberia Herald* continued to appraise the unfolding American tragedy. The *Herald* pointed out quite rationally that, regardless of its outcome, the American holocaust over slavery would cut off Liberia's principal source of immigrants, including churchmen, medical workers, artisans, educators, and other "indispensable mortals." Inevitably the up-and-down support of the American Colonization Society would be reduced or obliterated. If the slaveholding states won, which seemed probable, the slave trade would presumably be resumed unfettered and Liberia would be ever more imperiled.

Slavery remained the perennial nightmare of the free Negroes' nation. Africa, for which Liberia would serve as a Christian doorway, still festered with human bondage, and as the *Herald* pointed out, "that devastating instrument of Satan" was consistently gaining in the United States. Despite the emancipation statutes enacted by individual states (beginning with Vermont, Pennsylvania, Massachusetts, Rhode Island, Connecticut, New York, and New Jersey), successive national censuses had shown unremitting increases both in numbers and values of slaves. The 1800 census had revealed that the United States had 893,041 Negro slaves; the 1860 census reported that the sixteen remaining slaveholding states had 3,953,760. Thus in six decades the numbers and average value of Negro slaves in the United States had grown more than fourfold. For weal or woe most of the slaveholding states would fight for the multi-billion-dollar valuation of their black chattels.

Meanwhile the nightmare of American civil war was storming into reality. Before 1860 ended, South Carolina seceded from the Union and issued an official "ordinance" declaring that ". . . the union now existing between South Carolina and the other States under the name of the United States of America is hereby dissolved. . . ." Belatedly but competently the *Liberia Herald* reported that on January 9, 1861, one year after Stephen Benson's inauguration for a third two-year term as president of Liberia, the state of Mississippi seceded from the American Union, and later off Fort Sumter in Charleston Harbor rebel forces fired on the government supply ship, *Star of the West*. The secession of Mississippi was followed by that of Florida on January 10; Alabama, January 11; Georgia, January 19; Louisiana, January 26; and Texas, February 1.

Three days later and exactly a month before Abraham Lincoln's inauguration, a congress of the seceding states convened at Montgomery, Alabama, to adopt a provisional constitution and elect as first president of the Confederate States of America Colonel Jefferson Davis of Mississippi.

On the ensuing April 17, Virginia seceded, followed in May by Arkansas and North Carolina, and in June by Tennessee. The slavery-permitting states of Maryland, Missouri, Kentucky, Delaware, and what would shortly be West Virginia, declined to join the Confederacy officially, but before mid-April the Civil War was undeniably begun. On April 12 rebel forces in Charleston fired on Fort Sumter. On April 15 Abraham Lincoln issued his call for

75,000 volunteers, and four days later while a Confederate force seized the arsenal at Harper's Ferry, Virginia, proclaimed the blockade of Southern seaports—to be effective, one gathers, as soon as the globally dispersed U.S. Navy could be reassembled.

Liberia's lone newspaper continued to record how the fortunes of war swung strongly to the South's advantage, with the feeble and far-dispersed U.S. Army of 16,000 regulars and the undermanned and untried U.S. Navy lamentably inadequate; how Colonel Robert E. Lee after great thought and conflict declined Lincoln's offer of field command of the Union armies to head Confederate forces in his native Virginia, and that on July 4 a special session of the U.S. Congress voted a half-billion dollars and an army of 500,000 men for the "saving of the Union."

The war news filtered into Liberia belatedly and darkly. Successive Confederate victories added to the concern of official Monrovia. Predictions of a cessation of American immigration to the republic were being sustained in fact. Trade with the United States virtually disappeared; of necessity Liberian exporters and other traders turned to European markets and to the surprise of many the predictions were largely successful. By 1862 Liberian exports, principally of palm oils, coffee, and cotton, climbed to $2 million, enough to keep the young nation solvent. Informed students of African trade regarded this as astonishing, almost miraculous.

And toddler or not, the new Negro nation was standing tall in other ways. A particularly impressive demonstration took place in September, 1862, when a British Navy patrol force off Liberia's Gallinas lands sighted a Spanish-flagged ship previously identified as a slaver. When the ship refused to stand search, a British gunboat opened fire, overhauled the slaver, removed the surviving crew and several slaves, then sank the ship. Spain's admiralty charged Liberia with having "devised" the action and dispatched a man-of-war to Monrovia to demand restitution. When the Liberian president refused, the Spanish shore party threatened to bombard the outpost capital. President Benson ordered the harbor fort manned and delivered a four-word reply: "Bombard and be damned!" The threat maker backed down.

Almost coincidentally Liberia's prime and painfully delayed diplomatic goal was at long last attained. Deeply preoccupied and distressed as he was by a war he abhorred, Abraham Lincoln maneuvered successfully to gain recognition of Liberia as soon as he could feel confident of Senate approval. Lacking a diplomatic representative and aware that many in the Congress still looked on Liberia as a pious front for the safeguarding of slavery, Lincoln instructed the America legation in London to arrange a "treaty of commerce and navigation with the Republic of Liberia." That treaty, formally signed on October 22, 1862, was the essential opener of the long-needed and long-awaited diplomatic recognition.

For the time, Liberia's gain was mostly moral and prestigious. Economically and otherwise the lone African republic continued, as its president proudly affirmed, to go it alone.

When he had completed his third two-year term, Benson bowed out gracefully to a Republican colleague, Daniel Bashiel Warner, another mulatto. Baltimore born, Warner had emigrated with his free-slave parents to the colony during 1833. He had grown up in Liberia; in his teens he had cleared and tilled his own farm, set up a successful store, then in his early twenties entered government service.

As the third president, Warner regarded uninterrupted immigration as his country's prime need and moved to restore it by shifting "solicitation" to the West Indies. Simultaneously he effected more generous land grants for all forthcoming immigrants. By early 1865 he was happily welcoming a first contingent of 346 Barbados Negroes, who turned out to be outstandingly good citizens.

As Liberia entered what promised to be its happiest year, the Negro nation was deeply grieved by news of Abraham Lincoln's assassination. Sensing his peoples' emotional upset, the Liberian president proclaimed a month-long period of mourning. Somewhat ironically in the course of this month the rival political party, the True Whigs, gained an abrupt resurrection and in the oncoming election again came forward as "the true black sons of Africa resolved to displace an oligarchy of brown men."

Warner barely won reelection, but boldly resumed his role as advocate extraordinary of Liberian self-sufficiency, insisting that the republic could not endure merely as a "petty imitator" of the United States. In keeping with this thesis, the third president demonstrated effective ambivalence by simultaneously promoting trade with the British Isles and Western Europe and seeking stronger amalgamation with the hinterlands tribespeople. (". . . In the bosom of these mighty forests lie the elements of the great African nationality.")

Both efforts were commendably successful. More surprisingly, the American Colonization Society was able to celebrate the close of the Civil War by dispatching to Liberia an exceptionally well-chosen contingent of 621 Negro settlers. Early in 1866 the Society announced its recruitment of 633 additional "voluntary pioneers" and published a résumé of accomplishments to that date. As of March, 1866, a total of 13,136 American Negroes had emigrated to Liberia; 5,722 black people recaptured from slavers had become Liberian citizens; "miscellaneous sources" had provided about 5,000 additional settlers. However, the Society estimated that the aborigines continued to outnumber immigrants at least ten to one, and there was little or no reason to anticipate any immediate diminishment in the proportions, since Liberia had succeeded in effecting tribal treaties which had brought its claimed area to almost 150,000 square miles and included a comparable number of tribespeople.

President Warner thoughtfully pointed out that, while the United States immigrant "floods" had overwhelmed the Indian aborigines on that continent, the role of the Liberian pioneer would doubtless be that of a durable and benefitting minority, and the destiny of Liberia would be to "remain black."

In the national election of May, 1867, Warner found his ethnic philosophy being vociferously supported, but with results that were calamitous to his own political career. James Sprigg Payne was a fellow Republican but an emphatic dissident. He argued that his party would gain by total immersion in the "black tide of destiny" and by purging itself of the image of brown men leading blacks. Undeniably James Payne was a black man and he was much more than a vocal racist. He had already put in sixteen years as a diligent, usually effective and unsalaried public servant. Although a native of Richmond, Virginia, Payne had been raised and schooled in Liberia, where he had entered government service at twenty-two. Like Joseph Roberts, he achieved presidential election while still in his thirties—specifically, thirty-eight.

Having promised to champion the needs and welfare of both the pioneers and the tribespeople "fairly and proportionately," James Payne emphasized the needs for finding out far more definitively who and where the "tribal neighbors" really were.

At the time, hinterland Liberia had never been mapped and principal areas had not been knowledgeably explored. The fourth president therefore authorized completion of a detailed hinterlands survey already begun by a former cabinet member and civil engineer, Joseph Anderson.

The Anderson mission immediately encountered the dispiriting fact that slavery persisted in Liberian territory, with black men enslaving black men. In Boporo country beyond the Mano River north of Monrovia, the Anderson group encountered Mandingo chiefs and elders who owned and used hundreds of slaves. These included both local or estrayed tribespeople, particularly Buzzis and Kpelles.

Some contended that the "owned people" were being held in serfdom rather than literal slavery, but that was largely an issue of semantics. The fact stood that the Mandingos, preponderantly Mohammedans and thereby cushioned with a religion that accepts slavery as tolerable, were indeed using fellow Africans of many different tribes as slaves, and they did not necessarily obey the Mohammedan mandate for treating slaves with kindliness. The Anderson party saw child slaves bearing disfiguring brands and observed men and women being cruelly flogged by taskmasters or by first or elder wives.

Fortunately, not all of the Mandingos practiced slavery. When the explorers pushed northward through the Great Forests, they presently reached the beautiful Massardo Plateau and located the town of King Ibramhama Sissi, the great chief of the "good Mandingos." Sissi's kingdom had no slavery, and in many respects was a kind of Utopia. The land was fertile; the rice plantings grew shoulder high; herds of cattle and horses grazed far-spreading pastures shaded by fruitful palms. Without difficulty Anderson and his party succeeded in drawing up a treaty, written in Arabic, whereby King Sissi agreed officially to place his country within the limits of Liberia and to use his influence to oppose slavery.

The explorers met other superbly governed tribes—peace-abid-

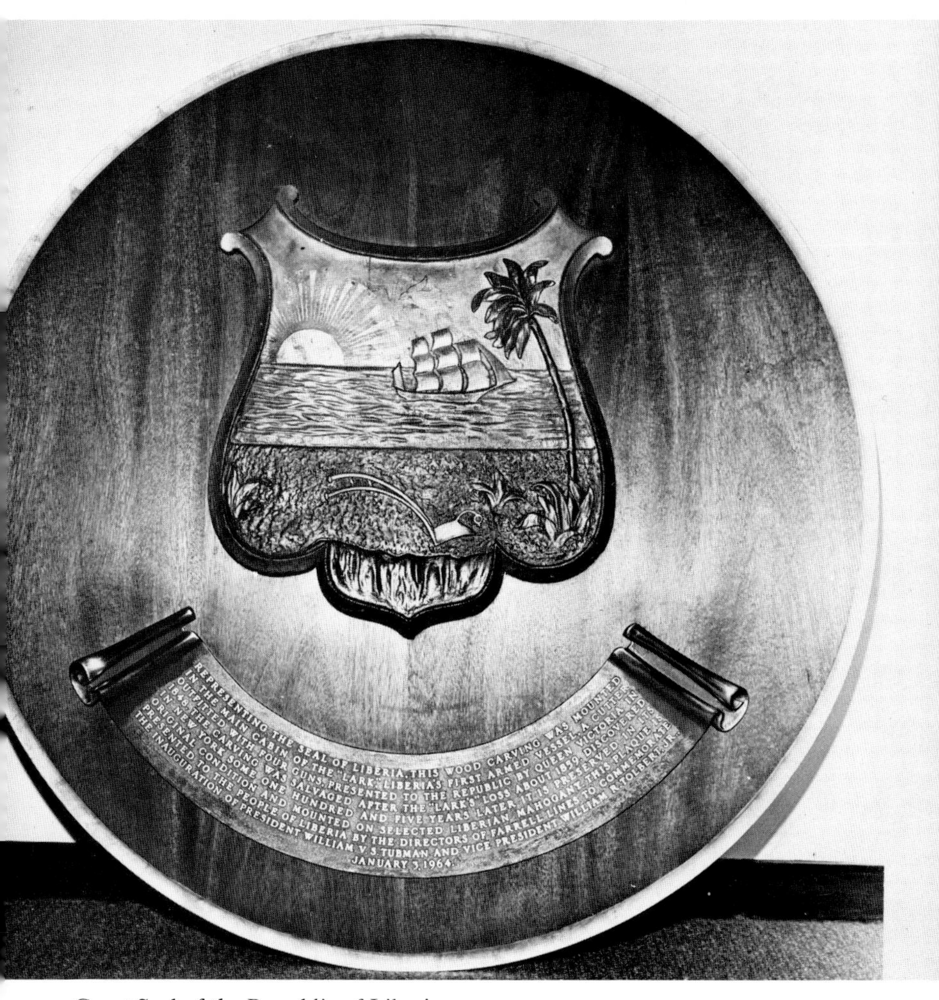

Great Seal of the Republic of Liberia

All photos by the author unless otherwise credited.

The Traditional Crafts. *Top:* Blacksmiths of the Bassa tribe. Note the traditional goatskin bellows and open fire. *Bottom:* Native weaving of "country cloth" being sold at a native market at Harbel.

Sports and Learning. *Top:* Soccer, a white man's game duly adapted. *Bottom:* Indigenous tribal Poro school for young boys.

The Performing Arts. *Top:* A native band at Kwangi—the horns are literally that. *Bottom:* Acrobatic dancers of the transient Mandingos are among traditional showmen.

V. Lewis

The Country Life. *Top:* Liberian women catch minnows in home-made basket seines. *Bottom:* Planting a cassava "garden" in Vai country.

Firestone

The Changing Workers. *Top:* A Liberian secretary. *Bottom:* A village tailor's shop.

Firestone

The Changing Government. *Top:* In his first State of the Nation Address, 1946, President Tubman (right center) inducts a fellow chief into the national legislature. *Bottom:* Three more native chiefs (wearing traditional robes) take official positions in House of Representatives.

New Builders of Liberia. *Top:* Drilling crews use modern pneumatic drills in building Monrovia Harbor. *Bottom:* A breakwater, 6,200 feet long, is a key factor in changing Monrovia to a world-influencing harbor.

Liberian Information Service

Liberia and Rubber. *Top:* First step in planting Hevea seed in a plantation nursery. *Right:* The rubber tapper at work.

Liberia and Rubber. *Top:* Early morning line of rubber tappers, Harbel area. *Bottom:* A convergence of rubber tappers for an entire plantation.

Liberia and Rubber. *Top:* Curded latex provides foam or solid rubber. *Bottom:* Most natural rubber is now processed and exported as liquid latex.

Distinguished Liberian Architecture. *Left:* The traditional hut begins with a center pole. *Below:* The wooden frame takes form without bothering with hammers, nails, saws or planes.

Distinguished Liberian Architecture. *Top:* Following completion of the frame, the mud walls and thatched roofs are placed. *Bottom:* A new tribal village is born.

V. Lewis

Liberian Crusade for Health. *Top:* The basic test for African sleeping sickness (trypanosomiasis), checking the cervical gland. *Bottom:* Modern surgery in a tribal clinic.

V. Lewis

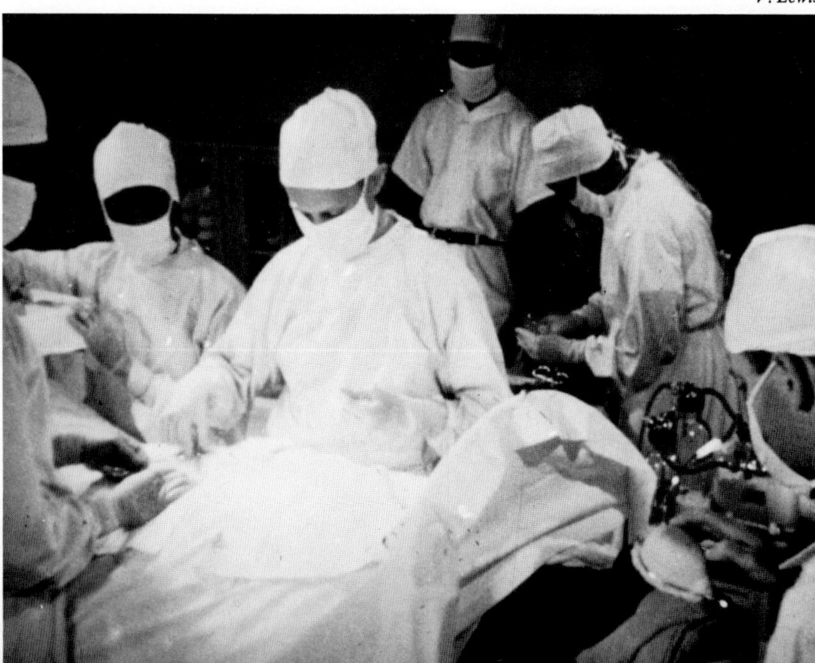

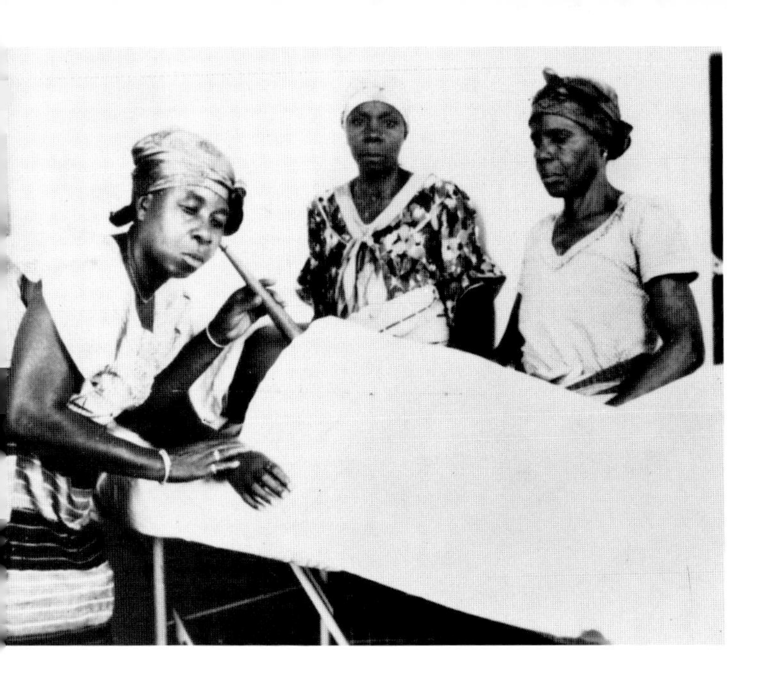

The Old and the New in Caring for the Sick. *Top:* Tribal midwives of Liberia. *Bottom:* Nurse and hospital technician at new Firestone Hospital.

Firestone

The Faces of Liberia. *Top:* Principals in a Kpelle tribal palaver, the indigenous town meeting of tribal Africa. *Bottom:* Liberian lumber mill workers.

ing, hospitable, and outstandingly honorable peoples who convinced Anderson that indigenous slavery could be rooted out by processes of moral persuasion and improved education.

President Payne agreed; he also saw the native slavery as one of the tragic fruits of extreme and persisting isolation. He therefore insisted that Liberia could gain growth and strength only by building roads and trails into the interior, which was generally lacking in navigable rivers. The outlook for effective roadbuilding by means of government income which totaled barely $50,000 per year overall was less than reassuring. Payne contended, however, that if more and better export crops could be developed and more Liberian-owned shipping instated, the roadbuilding could pay its own way.

But he found himself without time for proving the point. His political fortunes waned abruptly when the True Whig Party, with multiplying strength in outlying farming communities and its vehement proselytizing for true black men who could and would serve a true black Africa, gained ascendancy.

Edward James Roye came forth as the prophet-proponent of truly black leadership for a truly black nation. Roye was an exceptional black man. He was also a wealthy man, quite probably the richest citizen of Liberia. And he was not to be branded as a young upstart. Roye was fifty-five when he won the presidency and he clearly showed his years.

Edward Roye was born of a wealthy Negro family of Newark; he had received a college education at Oberlin in Ohio, and had multiplied his wealth as a successful manufacturer and realtor. Nobody could deny his acumen or intelligence. In his middle forties Roye had emigrated to Liberia, set up a shipping firm and a brokerage office, both successfully, and began "reading" law. At fifty he had won legislative election to the Supreme Court and after two years was advanced to chief justice. His superior record as leader of the judiciary was supported by an exceptionally successful business career, and his campaign for the presidency had stressed several commendable planks such as the development of an integrated national school system and a national banking structure.

Quite surprisingly Edward James Roye opened his presidential term with an appalling profusion of unwise moves that combined to antagonize the opposition party and direly alienate many of his supporters. One of his first painful mistakes was that of negotiating an outrageously usurious loan from London bankers. He countered with a "program" to improve trade and revenue collections which turned out very badly. He further weakened his position by indulging in recognizably dictatorial efforts to amend the Constitution by extending the presidential and legislative terms to four years and the senate term to six. The "extension act" gained passage by the True Whig-dominated legislature, but adversely cluttered the ensuing election into which the Roye amendment was dragged as a referendum entry. After a highly emotional campaign the True Whigs won by a very slight majority, but the referendum was challenged as having been dishonestly counted.

Roye angrily bypassed the challenge and contended that he was entitled to "extend" his reelection by four years. When the Republicans protested emphatically, Roye responded by again accusing the "light brown oligarchy" of conspiring to take over the government by collusion. Shortly thereafter the Republican opposition charged the strong-willed incumbent with unlawfully distributing firearms and employing armed mercenaries to perpetuate himself as a "dictator." The more extreme opposition climaxed the charge with what was labeled a "Manifesto by the Sovereign People of Liberia"; it would depose Edward Roye and his cabinet and set up a "provisional government" to be headed by an executive committee of three Republicans and one Whig.

The manifesto was clearly in violation of the Constitution of Liberia and was no less obviously an emotional and otherwise unfortunate move. Its issuance provided an opening for civil violence, the first and fortunately the last to afflict Liberia. Abruptly and without surely known instigation, armed mobs swept over Monrovia, seized the national arsenal and attacked and pillaged the president's residence. The mad mob action was followed by the unlawful arrest and jailing of leading members of the True Whig Party, including the president, vice president, the cabinet, and sixteen members of the Legislature.

Roye managed to escape and attempted to board an outbound ship. Insurgents fired at, overtook, and recaptured the fleeing president, pulled him ashore with needless violence, then with great brutality dragged him through the capital streets. A few hours later when the president died in a jail cell, a four-man junta that called itself an "executive committee" took over the government—leaving James Smith, the duly elected vice president, in the Monrovia jail. The tragic mayhem and illegality continued for sixty days, bringing Africa's first and then only republic to the brink of anarchy and ruin.

6

TROUBLED TRANSITION

WHILE THE MISNAMED Peoples' Executive Committee labored and fumbled, compounding the confusion and despair of both the illegally overthrown True Whigs and the legitimate and conscience-stricken principal leadership of the Republicans, Liberia was being whacked soundly by no fewer than a dozen major or lesser international powers.

With particular pomposity and venom the U.S. State Department conveyed and published notices of displeasure and mortification of the government of the United States (with the situation in Liberia). The official language was almost as vindictive as it was hypocritical. As all the world knew, the United States government had let itself be torn apart for more than four years by one of the most lethal and arbitrary of civil wars in known history. This marathon of malice and mayhem had by now weltered into its sixth year of dubiously named Reconstruction, which was leaving American escutcheons somewhat less clean than an unwashed cracklings kettle of a backwoods liquor still.

In the obtaining American language, the United States was in damned poor shape to castigate or deplore any other government anywhere on the whole earth. But the United States government nevertheless was a prime party in whacking and smearing the black toddler that had stumbled. And no clairvoyance was required to see that African colonies of Britain, France, Portugal, and perhaps others were observantly poised to close in and take over the mewling and troubled African republic.

There is no evidence that the United States or any other power had sought to investigate the unhappy turmoil that prevailed in and around Monrovia. But there was evidence of Liberian awareness of its very real perils. The seacoast and largely thatch-roofed capital had promptly reestablished a kind of spontaneous truce. The violence had shortly filtered away; comparative peacefulness had returned not only to Monrovia but to the outlying settlements and tribal hinterlands as well. The cogent *Liberia Herald* found itself unable to explain precisely what had brought on what the meditative paper chose to list as the deplorable and ridiculously emotional altercation.

Early in January, 1871, the Peoples' Executive Committee permitted and subsequently implored the national legislature to reconvene on schedule. With evident awareness that the republic's survival was in great peril, the legislators, including thirteen newly released from jail, joined in voting that the most distinguished elder statesman of Liberia be reinstated as president. The action was conspicuously unconstitutional, but the need was desperate.

Joseph Jenkins Roberts was well along in his sixties and preoccupied with his chosen public project—founding and serving as president of Liberia College, which was still aborning. The mulatto patriot agreed to accept the office on a temporary basis with the stipulation that he be permitted to stay on as president of the college-to-be. With that term accepted, Roberts took his presidential oath for the fifth time and again set out to guide his country on what he saw as a course of integrity. He moved quietly but promptly to issue pardons to all members of the rival party and others who had been unlawfully jailed. Next he announced his intentions of seeing the deplorably usurious London bank loan fully repaid. Then, with due awareness that his country was more than customarily a diplomatic outcast, the emeritus president sought to mend deteriorating relations with Britain, France, and the United States.

With the approval of his hastily salvaged legislature Roberts effected a resumption of constitutional elections, and even though he did not seek reelection, he found himself virtually lifted into a sixth term. By then the first president's health was rapidly failing, and "Old Faithful" found himself heavily dependent upon his colleagues. The situation imposed or involved deferment of school building, public health services, road and trail building and other greatly needed public works; first priority was given to keeping peace and seeking to build friendships among the tribes. The strife or altercations that bothered the hinterland were largely of rivalries among the backcountry tribes and were more of growing pains than of slaughterous violence. Most of the principal tribes were gaining in both total population and numbers of clans, and were understandably seeking more living space and more favorable markets for their homecrafts and harvests.

All this was contributing to intensifying competition between Liberian traders, in greater part American or West Indian immigrants, and the usually more affluent British, French, or Dutch traders. The tribespeople rationally associated expansion of land holdings with the quest of more and better farming lands. Some of the tribes of the nearer hinterlands were seeking additional lands and village sites, as were some of the immigrants.

The Grebos were a case in point. Their "united kingdom" was believed to number about 25,000 people; about half again as many as the prevailing total of Liberian immigrants and easily ten times the then current census of Maryland County. Early in 1875 there were disturbing reports of Grebo collusions with British traders and of raids by tribal warriors on outlying Liberian farming settlements. As usual the exact facts were not easy to sift; also as usual there was clear evidence that depredations were being committed by dissident petty chiefs, in some instances abetted by alien traders, rather than by the far more responsible "native kings," or paramount chiefs. In any case the development was neither simple nor happy, and it was placing Liberia in the position of an obligatory arbiter.

Since he was seriously ill at the time, Joseph Roberts assigned his vice president, Anthony Gardiner, the task of effecting arbitration between the Grebos and the outpost settlers, using as need be a show of strength. Gardiner used his president's earlier "routines of persuasion" as a blueprint for the Grebo-land maneuver. He would muster a volunteer militia force, proceed to the stronghold or town of the offending chief, demand that the erring chief and his henchmen make restitution of destroyed property. That accomplished, the government agent would assemble a convention or palaver of all available chiefs and tribe elders as well as Liberian settlers and lead the group in drawing up an open-forum treaty of peace and friendship.

But Vice President Gardiner, another attractive and intelligent mulatto, was handicapped by a lack of experience. His initial mistake, one gathers, was in mustering too large a militia force. He had recruited about 800 men—enough to establish the appearance of a combat army rather than an arbitration party. The error was compounded when an armed guard of 200 Maryland County volunteers joined the initial force as it landed at Cape Palmas. The combined army moved against Beneleu, a principal Grebo town, where the tribal defenders were forewarned.

Scouts had reported the apparent invasion and the chiefs had assembled every available fighting man in the entire tribe. The advantage in numbers was overwhelming and the Grebo warriors were expertly led, positioned, and ably armed with the usual long bows, battle axes, spears, and more than a few muskets. Without forewarning they stormed the militiamen from three sides, killed or wounded several and routed the rest. The government troops eventually regrouped but were obliged to build stockades and shelters and remain as a garrison force for safeguarding the nearby settlements from resumption of petty raids. The total lesson was self-evident: Liberia was no longer merely an immigrant black colony on the fringe of the black continent; its needs and responsibilities were surely African.

As Anthony Gardiner served out his trying and humiliating assignment, another election saw the mortally ill Joseph Roberts succeeded by the hard-used James Sprigg Payne, who had earlier been defeated by the tragically terminated Edward James Roye. The incorrigible independent (Payne) read in the Grebo story what Gardiner had painfully proved, that a varied and durable plurality of tribespeople demanded acceptance as an enduring reality. Liberia's immigrant minority, however valorous and determined, could not be assured of military victories against the larger tribes or predictable cooperation of the indigenes. The Roberts principle of show-of-force arbitration was meritorious, but it was not infallible.

Liberia would stand or fall with the native tribes, not against them.

James Payne was a realist and, as he had repeatedly stated, a Negro's Negro. He was also a courageous gambler. On that basis he resolved to appeal directly to the then new American president to serve as outside arbiter for the unsolved Grebo stalemate. Payne was well aware that in Liberia's quarter-century of sovereignty the American government had proved itself about as helpful as hip pockets on a pig, but to his great surprise and comfort he received a prompt answer in the affirmative from the president of the United States. General U. S. Grant promptly ordered the U.S.S. *Alaska* to proceed to Cape Palmas, and instructed her master, A. A. Semmes, to serve as "mediator" for Liberia and the Grebo Tribal Kingdom.

Captain Semmes, accompanied by President Payne, opened by calling a conclave of all Grebo chiefs. As a first move the chief negotiator established the common acceptance that Grebos were Liberians and willing to behave accordingly. After several days of palaver the group joined in drawing up a peace treaty, dated March 1, 1876. The document bore an engaging list of at least nine Grebo tribal chiefs' signatures representing the entire Grebo Kingdom. The terms provided for "perpetual peace, equal rights in land ownership, trade, and commerce, and complete amnesty for all political offenses either committed or alleged." The Liberian president forwarded his thanks to Washington, and asked no further favors.

Payne's determined stand to keep his country self-sufficient proved generally successful. Export trade climbed to $3 million a year; imports stayed close to $1 million. Government revenues reached a then impressive $80,000 a year, enough to attend the precommitted debts and still keep the tiny government solvent.

At the same time, Liberia's somewhat staggering responsibilities to provide land and emergency supplies for large inflows of immigrants were being substantially eased. The final "mass party" of Negro emigrants from the United States was a self-led group of about 300 black farmers from the Deep South, mostly Mississippi; they settled and promptly began clearing and planting a community of farms in the St. Paul Valley. The southerners were superb settlers, and models for other highly self-sufficient although smaller immigrations.

Anthony W. Gardiner, meanwhile, was duly vindicated and immensely encouraged by his subsequent election to the presidency. However much surprised he may have been by "adoption" and nomination by the strongly revived True Whig Party, Gardiner stood boldly as a "True Black Man Truly for Africa." As the sixth president he was entirely willing to grant that getting along with all accessible tribespeople was both a prerogative and the prime obligation of being president, or, as he put it, Chief of Chiefs, of Liberia.

The loser of the Grebo war set purposefully to improving what he termed "living relations" between the settlers and the tribespeople. To his very deep consternation Gardiner found that his most aggravating difficulties were being revived by the white man's lack of ethics in colonialism. The French Foreign Office resumed its pressures on Liberian frontiers. Even more disturbingly the British Foreign Office diligently revived claims on north Liberian territory on behalf of Britain's crown colony of Sierra Leone. The Freetown authorities were again charging that Liberia's land treaties with the interior tribes were implicitly invalid, insisting that the Negro republic was demonstrating "incompetence" by failing to provide necessary communications and other public services to its hinterlands.

The self-evident answer was that in the main the same could be said of Sierra Leone and most other colonies of West Africa. There were some few impressive exceptions. But on the whole the Liberian government was doing better than most colonial governments in winning friendships of the hinterland tribes. This was conspicuously true in the northwest region which the British colony was poised to seize. In several instances the stronger chiefdoms or tribes were voluntarily building trails and, in the Sennequellie area, were patrolling them (in some cases the better forest trails were still infested with highwaymen), while back of Cape Palmas the Grebos were opening about a hundred miles of particularly strategic pack trails into the wilderness.

Neither the Liberian president nor any other informed person could deny that, depending on the season, crossing Liberia still required as much as two months of foot travel. It was also true that as of 1876–77 the Liberian government was able to spend no more than $8,000 a year for roadbuilding and maintenance. The prime truth held that it was a trying time for the small republic with many obligations and little cash to spread over many areas of need.

For the time being Her Majesty's Foreign Office seemed willing at least temporarily to permit territorial claims to stand. The Liberian president temporarily could breathe more easily. But he was again deeply disturbed in late 1878 by another ominous infringement. This began when a German merchant ship ran aground off the lower Liberian coast and vandal tribesmen plundered the wreck and robbed some of the passengers. The German government waived the procedure of peaceful redress and dispatched a gunboat to bombard and destroy several Kru villages along the Liberian coast. Without avail the government at Monrovia protested the slaughter of innocent persons. Having paid the German injury claims from a hard-drained treasury, the president appealed to the United States to protest the German killing of Liberian tribespeople. He received no response and was similarly humiliated by the refusal of the French government to intervene.

The combined mistreatment and rebuffs apparently led the Negro republic to turn more intensely to internal affairs, for the British press soon accused it of practicing "torpid isolationism." But continued efforts to improve relations with the tribespeople, who were obviously intelligent and in some respects hardier than the settlers, were bearing fruit. During 1882 Lincoln University of Pennsylvania used competitive tests to choose eight young Liberians for fellowships. Only one of the eight was an Americo-Liberian; four were Bassas, two were Congolese (their parents had been recaptured slaves), and one was a Vey. The sought-for integration was proving beneficial on both sides. That tribal agriculture was benefiting the settlers may be deduced from the marked improvement of the prevailing diet. At Monrovia on July 26, in celebration of Liberia's Independence Day, a public dinner provided a menu ("a typical Liberian meal") of baked and fried fish; chicken, stewed, baked, and fried; venison; whole baked porcupine; rice; palm butter; cassava dumplings, and pound cake made of home-mortared cassava flour.

But while the obtaining agriculture showed improvement, the foreign relations again took turns for the worse. British claims on Liberia's north frontier were aggressively reinstated when, on March 20, 1883, four British Navy gunboats abruptly converged off Monrovia. Sir Arthur Havelock, the newly appointed governor of

Sierra Leone, accompanied by a landing party, served the astonished president of Liberia with an ultimatum demanding that he yield to British occupation the territory north and west of the Mano River and reimburse certain British traders for claims of losses suffered from "Liberian interference." Gardiner regarded the demands as wholly unjustified, and pointed out that the proposed territory grab would diminish the Liberian coastline by at least 150 miles and that pushing the boundary down to the Mano River would lift away at least 50 million acres of the republic's better farming lands.

While peering out at leveled Navy deck rifles, the president begrudgingly passed along the decision to his Senate, which firmly refused the demands. Its members reiterated that the proposed territorial infringements were outrageous and that most British traders claiming damages had in fact openly defied the sovereign rights of Liberia and in many instances had fomented discord among the natives. The British sea force withdrew briefly, then repeated the show of force. Weary and harassed, President Gardiner submitted his resignation to the national legislature. Vice President Alfred F. Russell served the remainder of his term, protesting futilely while the British Crown Colony of Sierra Leone began to occupy the territory between the Sherbro and Mano Rivers. The disputed lands were easily a fifth of Liberia's total area as then established.

Russell was succeeded by a True Whig but Republican-supported slate headed by Hiliary Richard Wright Johnson, a son of the soldier-founder, General Elisha Johnson. Johnson took office in January, 1884, as Liberia's first native-born president. His talents were most remarkable.

Johnson had served Liberia College multiply as head of the preparatory department and professor of *belles-lettres* and moral philosophy; he was a classics scholar and a gifted musician. He also was an engineer and surveyor, a successful farmer, and a long-time editor of the *Liberia Herald*. At twenty-five he had won election to the legislature as a "True Whig Black Man," and subsequently twice served as Secretary of the Interior.

At the time of his presidential inauguration Johnson was forty-five, competent in many things, experienced in government and certainly one of the best-informed students of the hinterland tribes, and a dedicated integrationist. He strongly advocated encouraging tribe participation in both county and national government; he submitted that founding mixed settlements of Americo-Liberians and tribespeople was the most feasible means for stabilizing the country's frontiers and hinterlands.

But the first native president also confronted the certainty that successfully governing the frontiers was his supreme challenge. Britain, France, and Germany were evidencing dire intentions of lifting away Liberian lands. Maintaining peace among the tribes was difficult and precarious. Foreign traders persisted in evading the payment of duties to the Negro republic and incited the tribes-people to do likewise. The republic could collapse for want of revenue. Johnson's plans for promoting frontier colonies in the Cape Palmas area were impeded by civil strife apparently incited by white traders.

France's official policy toward Liberia again changed for the worse. A *Bulletin des Lois* clearly indicated French determination to extend drastically the claims of additional territory. As Sierra Leone continued its invasion of the north and west, France turned avidly to the south frontier, specifically claiming the territory between the Cavalla River and the San Pedro Valley, plus dimly defined but large areas of Maryland County and adjacent Grand Bassa lands. Thus Liberia found itself on the chopping block, being dismembered by the two greatest powers of the West.

Both the British and the French rationalized their actions by claiming that Liberia was too poor to adequately serve the tribal peoples or control them. The Liberian president pointed out that poor and struggling as it was, the lone African republic by then was maintaining forty-three public schools and benefiting from fifty-four mission schools. This was nowhere near enough, but on a per capita basis it was at least twice as many as Sierra Leone, the French Ivory Coast, and French West Africa colonies were providing.

President Johnson continued to demonstrate his father's gift for evolving lucid defenses. He celebrated his reelection by instituting an engaging potpourri of "special missions." As a former teacher he visited all the schools then open and organized and supervised teaching clinics. He led school improvement rallies and solicited the help of tribal chiefs in setting up additional schools.

The diligent and versatile black president next directed an updated survey of churches and missions within the Negro republic. By 1888 the Methodist church led all denominations with a membership of about 2,200 and with mission schools which accommodated about 300 children. The Baptists had in all about 2,000 members; the Episcopalians with only a few hundred Liberian members nevertheless led with numbers of missionaries (thirty-four), and enrollments in mission schools (415). The president granted that the "Christianization" of tribespeople was not advanced impressively. He estimated that perhaps 1,500 had by then become converted to Christianity and a probable 15,000 to Mohammedanism, but the preponderance still followed the indigenous tribal religions.

The first native-born president continued to proselytize for more widespread participation by the tribespeople in the government. He persuaded the national legislature to support this mission with a more generous "full rights of citizenship" statute for all aborigines who were willing to take the citizenship oath. Following his second reelection Johnson succeeded in winning legislative approval for a series of what he termed "worthy causes acts." These included the granting of government scholarships for Liberia College, the establishment of national agricultural fairs, and the beginnings of another crop's-introduction program.

In recommending a successor the younger Johnson pointed out philosophically that an effective first officer of the first African republic, which was by then the only enduring Negro republic, must be a hard-working detailist, a bold spirit who enjoyed people-benefiting combat, and a man capable of bringing yesterdays and tomorrows together. Appropriately, the True Whig Party, which by then had diminished its accentuation on black skin color, chose as its next nominee a "true dirt farmer" who had taught himself to read and write and had prospered by the skill of his hoe.

Joseph James Cheeseman had done all these things and much more. He had also studied law, served as a common pleas judge, accepted ordination as a Baptist preacher and the presidency of the Liberian Baptist Convention. The unobtrusive black man from backwoods Grand Bassa applied all his talents and experiences on his assumption of the presidency. His beginning tenure showed outstanding promise.

Cheeseman instituted a peace-and-order crusade which he eagerly extended to the tribes. He won the friendship of several of the more recalcitrant chiefs and gained their effective help in such diverse areas as discouraging smuggling and improving farming practices. His services as an agricultural way-shower were truly brilliant; he personally demonstrated the respective agronomies of an impressive list of exportable harvests including medicinal plants, oil palms, and special-use fibers. Perhaps his most impressive success was his championing of piassava, a strong, durable fiber obtained from an exceptionally hardy palm (*Attalea funifera*). Following its initial import from Brazil, the palm had gone wild throughout great areas of Liberia. As Cheeseman demonstrated, threshing and drying the fiber requires no expensive machinery, and the market value of the harvest was sufficient to provide a basis for excise duties. During the succeeding administration the development of Liberian piassava provided revenue which helped finance Liberia's first college and several government-supported primary schools.

But Cheeseman's leadership, including enlightened agricultural planning, was very seriously impeded by the continued seizure of Liberian territory. Late in 1891 the French Foreign Office bluntly notified Liberia that the Cavalla River would thereafter comprise the French territorial boundary and the "lower limit" of Liberia. The takeover was the more punitive because it clipped away more than 200 additional miles of Liberian coast front. Protests directed to Great Britain brought evasionary treatment that strongly indicated that the British Foreign Office was in collusion or *sub rosa* agreement with its French counterpart. The distressing records showed that the French Foreign Office was supporting Sierra Leone incursions from the north and west while the French colonies were most literally moving up from the St. Andreas to the Cavalla River.

Since it was lacking any real facilities for defending itself militarily, Liberia again turned to Washington to plead for protection. The White House reportedly instructed the American legation in Paris to seek "an equitable agreement" between France and

Liberia. The Paris legation welcomed and recommended the offer of Baron de Stein, a Belgian citizen, to serve as counsel for Liberia. The French Foreign Office responded by repeating its stratagem of first claiming a huge area, then professedly compromising by scaling down the extent of the takeover. But the intentions were all too clear; French colonial troops were already directed to invade Liberia's Cape Palmas. Official Monrovia waited despairingly as the Paris negotiators came forward with a recommendation for what was termed a moderate compromise. By then French territorial troops were already occupying more than 1,000 square miles of long accredited Liberian hinterlands with a seventy-mile ocean front. The Negro republic continued to protest. James Cheeseman, shaken and saddened, was also mortally ill. His death followed in 1896.

At least briefly the nightmare of land seizures showed promise of abatement. William D. Coleman, Cheeseman's vice president and successor, was another intelligent and gifted black man with great dedication and a sincere if not exceptional knack for elementary diplomacy. The latter was rooted in a gentle but courageous talent for persuasion. The hour was too late for this gentle prowess to halt the territorial rapine already being effected by Britain and France, but not for the looming threat of an empire-building Germany.

In 1895 a German trader submitted a claim for restitution in the amount of $13,000 for alleged injuries suffered at the hands of Liberian citizen traders. Before the claim could be verified a German Navy gunboat put in off Monrovia and discharged a landing party which proceeded to the president's home to demand instant payment of the claim—in gold. Coleman declined but confirmed his country's intention of paying all just obligations in keeping with accredited procedures.

When an investigation was completed, the Liberian government made the required payment. Simultaneously, Coleman forwarded to the German Foreign Office a thoughtful reappraisal of trade possibilities between the two countries. The Kaiser's Foreign Office agreed that such possibilities existed and had not been adequately explored; it then assigned an experienced tropical trade expert to serve as German Consul General at Monrovia. As a result trial shipments were developed for Liberian piassava fiber, medicinal plants, vine rubber, ivory, and various other products. Within three years Liberian trade with Imperial Germany had quintupled and was accounting for almost a third of Liberian exports.

But that was Liberia's first winning play in a discouragingly long list of losing plays in foreign relations. Coleman was a man capable of recognizing a good omen when he had planted one. But as the nineteenth century swept toward its end, Liberia continued to experience a marked shortage of good omens. At very least the first African republic, after its first half-century of life, was much more than a theorist's dream, a lobbyist's front, or politician's pawn—or even a small black satellite of the United States. It was still a poor, small, loosely devised, jungle-edge body politic. It was still being pilfered, rebuffed, and consigned to diplomatic peonage, but Liberia had survived as a black republic. It was still struggling toward sovereignty and freedom at the jungle-littered gateway of a most magnificent continent which remained in greater part enslaved.

7

LIBERIA AND AFRICA

AS THE NINETEENTH CENTURY, which more and more commentators were beginning to designate the American century, neared its end, editorialists of the *Manchester Guardian* led in the prediction or augury that the twentieth century was taking shape as the African century. The *Liberia Herald* vigorously agreed and augmented with the prophesy that Liberia, a creation of the American century, would stand or fall as an African nation of the oncoming African century.

The *Herald* reiterated that as it reached its half-century mark (1897), Liberia's international position was somewhere between that of a lesser Balkan state of Eastern Europe (such as Montenegro) or a formative American Balkan state (such as Honduras).

The exceptionally lucid Monrovia newspaper did not hesitate to describe its capital town as a tropical seaside slum with a few high hats and a great many tomtoms. But the *Herald* was well aware that Monrovia was a truly memorable doorway to a truly memorable continent and that Liberia was already one of the most meaningful land surfaces on the face of the earth.

Furthermore, Liberia was rounding out its first half-century not only as a small but enterable doorway to a continent but as a living key to the most profound story of the nineteenth century—the liberation from slavery. The jungle-strewn lands between the two distinguishing capes, Mesurado and Palmas, still showed the markings of slaver trails that had helped perpetuate the international slave trade for more than three centuries.

Liberia had been a particular bailiwick of the seventeenth-century Portuguese "explorer" who had opened the slave trade to the Western Hemisphere. The Pepper Coast, of which Liberia is a part, had supplied black chattels who had made possible and profitable the sugar plantations of Brazil and the Caribbean, the world-supplying cotton plantations and tobacco plantations of the gifted realms of British North America that would presently be the United States. What is now Liberia had also given the world the individual black man who turned out to be a particular talisman for the liberation of black men by recourse to the law.

Legal students will recall the escaped slave, Youmans, and the London barrister, Granville Sharp, who befriended him. Back in 1770 the youthful barrister found a sick, emaciated Negro abandoned in a London alley. Sharp nursed and fed the maverick and in 1772 instituted a protracted law suit which ended with Lord Chief Justice Mansfield's pivotal judgment that a liberated slave who sets foot on the land of England is thereafter a free man.

The ruling was vehemently challenged, the more so because the former slave had been reclaimed and sold back into slavery by his former owner. Powerful West Indian planters, in alliance with wealthy and influential slave traders of London, Bristol, and Liverpool, aggressively challenged the Lord Chief Justice's sustaining decision. But the slave traders and slaveowners lost, and the anti-slavery movement was begun.

To its untarnishable glory Britain led the nineteenth-century world in opposing the slave trade. During 1807 Parliament enacted a statute declaring that beginning January 1, 1808, all manner of dealing and trading in slaves in Africa or in their transport to any other nation or area was "utterly abolished, prohibited and declared to be unlawful." Any British subject violating the act would be punished and any British ship used as a slaver would be forfeited to the Crown.

Liberia was even more notably a beneficiary of Britain's climaxing Abolition of Slavery Act of 1833, which authorized direct compensation of British citizen slaveowners for effecting emancipation of their slaves. It followed that during the same century Britain had intermittently served to light the way for and imperil the survival of the African republic.

The chronicle of France for and against Liberia had been even more paradoxical. French-African relations had begun dourly with slave trading openly countenanced and profited from by the courts of both Louis XV and Louis XVI. Then, shortly before the first valiant free slaves reached Liberia, French *émigrés* had begun moving into Africa. Beginning in the mainland Cape Verde area now known as Dakar, the *voyageurs* rented colony sites from compatible chiefs. The first wave of settlers was destroyed by the endemic "fevers." But while the first Liberian settlement was taking form, another party of Frenchmen led by Jean Boudin moved into the valley of the upper Senegal and there began clearing and tilling farms.

The French colonization was courageous, and eventually effective as it began to include indigenous tribespeople of the north. From Dakar colony the French farmers and traders infiltrated much farther, establishing land occupancy and trading treaties with hundreds of individual tribes. As the American Civil War ended, the French government completed a wharf and working harbor at Dakar, and in 1878 began building a first African railroad from Dakar to St. Louis, the interior capital of the Senegal Colony.

From there increasing influxes of French farmers and traders moved into the huge, soil-rich Sudan and followed the ancient trader trails into the valley of the upper Niger and the beautiful midlands of Chad. The French also moved south and west into the Ivory Coast and farther into what would shortly be French Equatorial Africa, the French Cameroons, the Gabon coast, and the Ubangi country north of the materializing Belgian Congo. In many respects it was brilliant colonizing and effective elemental diplomacy; as Liberia neared its fiftieth year, France, still with a combined nucleus of only about 60,000 troops, white settlers and traders, all told, held or claimed more than two million square miles of tropical Africa.

As the colony-building took shape and figurative bone structure from winning or inveigling the compliance of resident tribes and luring or driving them into confederations that were based on geographical proximity or ethnic backgrounds or hopes for improved livelihoods, the African tribe was being made the prime supplier of the slave trade.

The prime irony was that as the British opposition to the slave trade gained force and effectiveness, the evil feat of slave supplying shifted more markedly to Africans. As the overt slave raids diminished, corrupt traders and fallible chiefs joined in the "blood business" of supplying fellow Africans to the slavers. Liberia, as we have noted, had repeatedly and valiantly fought off or otherwise opposed both African and white participation in the slave trade.

Vastly greater forces were emerging to oppose slavery. The defeat of the Confederate forces in the American Civil War permanently erased the most lucrative of slave markets. Slave traders who sought to smuggle and sell Africans to developing plantations in the South Pacific met ever more aggressive naval patrols. In 1876 the Sultan of Zanzibar, which at the time was the world's largest slave-trading base, abruptly outlawed slave trading throughout his domain and decreed and began enforcing the death penalty for violation. This blow was particularly ruinous to the would-be revival of an international slave traffic.

But the tribulations of Liberia were being bestirred by an ominous changeabout in the rudiments of African colonization; the particular ogre was the white man's government-sponsored and profits-hungry colonization corporation. Germany had provided an especially aggressive demonstration. During 1884 the German Colonization Society, first operated in Pacific tropics, moved forcefully into both East and West Africa. The German, or so-called Karl Peters technique, usually made entry by means of "friendship and trade treaties" with specific tribes. The chosen chiefs were prevailed upon, usually by an admixture of flattery, bribery, and threats, either overt or implied, to make their X's on documents purporting to transfer certain "civil amities" to the German "society." Thereupon the Imperial German Government would "recognize" the transaction as comprising a concession and proclaim a protectorate over the area indicated and, quite frequently, neighboring territories. In repeated instances the so-called treaties were established with only local chiefs without the knowledge or consent of the paramount chiefs or sultans. The latter were pressured into acceding, and regions were grouped into "spheres of influence."

By the middle 1880s these spheres of influence were being recognized or affirmed by treaties or other official agreements among Berlin, London, and other European capitals. Other colonial powers began to emulate the German concept of the "officialized" Africa company. By 1888 the British East Africa Company was industriously paving the British way throughout that part of the world; by 1895 British protectorates extended along most of the rich east coast.

British involvements in the Sudan and the Upper Nile country had brought about still another structure of power politics to the black continent. Egypt was the prime proving ground. Until 1878 the Khedive Ismail had ruled Egypt under the nominal overlordship of the Sultan of Turkey. But the Khedive's stature was weak. During 1882 France moved in to take over the "chaotic finances of Egypt"; Britain promptly intervened to set up "dual control"—a revolt in the Egyptian army had led the Gladstone government to view with alarm a possible threat to the Suez Canal. By means of naval craft and Sir Garnet Wolseley's army the British overwhelmed the Arab rebels and captured Cairo. Egypt would wait until 1922 to regain even nominal status as a sovereign state.

During the latter 1880s Britain's programming known as "constructive imperialism" was strongly implemented in the resources-rich Kenya protectorate by the British-directed building of the Uganda Railway, which linked a most strategic coastland with the immensely fertile interior. The tides of British colonizing shortly resumed in West Africa. Long before—directly after the end of the American Revolution—Britain had established the Sierra Leone Colony, which in 1810 had been made the site of Africa's first Negro refuge colony. By the 1860s the British Colonial Office was conspicuously interested in expanding its pioneer African colony and adding to its holdings in West Africa. The bold German move into the coastal Cameroons further stimulated British interest in the comparatively neglected but obviously rich West Coast.

Relationships with major tribes emerged as a decisive issue during 1872 when the formidable Ashanti army with some 40,000 armed warriors crossed the Prah River, overwhelmed the Fantis (then under British protection) and took over the British-held port of Elmina. A British combat fleet arrived at the scene and Captain John Glover and Sir Garnet Wolseley landed a force of Royal

Marines to supplement the spears and bows of defending tribesmen with British firearms and seasoned combat troops.

The British led a combat force against the Ashantis, defeated their army, and in 1874 enforced a treaty of surrender. Subsequently they put down another Ashanti uprising and merged the Ashanti kingdoms into the newly founded Gold Coast Colony. The prime incentive was the development and proliferation of highly profitable trade. By 1879 British traders began forming themselves into an association that soon became the long-dominating United Africa Company. During 1886 another charter corporation, the Royal Niger Company, had been incubated with government encouragement, and fourteen years later this company was refurbished as the British "protectorate" of Northern and Southern Nigeria.

By this time the international scramble for West Africa had become accelerated, with Liberia a ready-placed grab bag. France acquired "treaty claims" to the upper Niger and the large areas subsequently called French West Africa and French Equatorial Africa. British takeovers included the promising but undeveloped coastal holdings along the Gambia River—Sierra Leone, the Gold Coast, Lagos, and Nigeria.

Liberia, as a jungle-edge onlooker, was finding itself more and more directly in line of the empire *putsch* while being tantalizingly bypassed by the growing trickles of trade. There were other visible and tempting fruits of colonization which the struggling Negro republic could see and question but could not wholly deny. Frederick Dealtry Lugard, speaking as Her Britannic Majesty's first Crown Governor of Nigeria, extolled what he termed the British system of indirect rule—leading Africans to lead themselves—"in such a way that the latter's resources are developed on the one hand for the benefit of the native inhabitants, and on the other for the benefit of the world at large."

The Liberian government could not and had not sought to evade or underestimate the many splendid attainments of missionaries, teachers, physicians, and other African benefactors. Dr. David Livingstone and his renowned missionary career were finding admirable counterparts in West Africa. Among those in hinterland Nigeria was Nurse ("Sister") Mary Slessor, who beginning in 1876 spent thirty years ministering to the sick, serving as judge and counsel on request for the native courts and as devoted benefactress of the tribespeople near and far.

Sir Ronald Ross, earlier of the British Army Medical Service in India, who discovered that the Anopheles mosquito was a vector of malaria, had begun to move into people-saving research and various other phases of preventive medicine in the Gambia basin and the frontiers of Sierra Leone. Malcolm Watson, his brilliant disciple, would carry his splendid enterprise further by developing the use of oil sprays and field-sanitation devices for combating African fevers and other lethal diseases.

During the 1890s two other eminent British medical pioneers, David Bruce and Charles Swynnerton, would come to West Africa to open their epochal studies of the tsetse fly and sleeping sickness (trypanosomiasis). Bruce later traveled and worked in Uganda, where the sleeping sickness had brought death to at least 20,000 tribesmen in a single year. When the eminent medical pathologist made his last great stand in Nigeria, he was succeeded by one of the most remarkable researchers of the era. Charles Swynnerton, born in England in 1877, came to Nigeria to work as a minor employee in a jungle-edge trading post. He became interested in the fascinating natural world about him and presently "bought" a three-month holiday to study the tsetse fly. From that beginning the self-taught naturalist and lay medical scholar built his own way as a premier defender against African sleeping sickness.

As Liberians knew so well, all these and many more attainments were rooted in a most demanding environment. Travel, whether for native or immigrant, was perilous, and accomplished for the most part by means of dugout canoes or by tramping narrow bush trails afoot, or being borne in hammocks on the heads of native carriers. In most of Liberia as in much of Africa drums served inadequately as the most effective means of communication. Tribes might live for generations no more than fifty miles apart and never see each other.

European colonization was providing the first really telling defense against the age-old afflictions of isolation. Between 1900 and 1910 British capital and talent, assisted by tribal laborers and imported labor would complete and place in operation approximately 15,000 miles of railroads in Equatorial Africa, including some of the most difficult construction in all the history of railroading. Britain did not build railroads in tiny Gambia, but in the nearby Dakar area and in the Ivory Coast and other parts of French West Africa, France built about 4,000 miles during the same decade.

But the enormously expensive railroad construction did not touch Liberia, nor did the Republic have the capital or facilities for the needed roadbuilding which French and British colonizers were able to effect. Worst of all, Liberia was not able to build even the direly needed harbors and riverside piers made crucially necessary for effective trade where natural harbors were virtually nonexistent.

Liberia's leadership was also aware that British, French, German, and intermittently other colonizers were contributing importantly to the agricultural development of West Africa. Some of the really outstanding pioneering works were being directed by British trading firms that, beginning in the lower Niger Valley, were making the largely wild-growing African oil palms the basis for a most profitable export trade and tribal barter, as well as a most valid native food crop.

Palm oil was and still is an indigenous "natural" of and for much of Equatorial Africa. Beginning in 1886 personnel of the British colonial Office established another basic trader's crop when they successfully propagated cacao seed from Venezuela and lower Central America in a government nursery in the Gold Coast Colony. Colonial Office agronomists had distributed the young trees to chiefs and other tribal landholders throughout the area. During 1891 the port of Accra was the scene of the first export of eighty pounds of cacao seeds or beans. Within forty years the first eighty pounds had grown to more than 250,000 tons annually of the source of cocoa and chocolate, easily half of the world's supply.

There were many other successful agricultural introductions that were effected or aptly encouraged by the colonizing powers. Early in the twentieth century Britain effectively established cotton growing in Nigeria, and other crops, many from the American tropics, were developed. There were also some highly effective innovations in political establishments which showed particular British skills. By prevailing standards Britain's African colonies were competently, in several instances brilliantly governed. Each was being headed by a governor-general appointed by the Crown and responsible to the secretary of state for the Colonies in London. The governor-general presided over a lawmaking and legislative council, essentially a legislature of resident Africans, in great part chiefs. The legislative council was supplemented by regional councils made up principally or entirely of local chiefs, elders, and other tribe members.

All this was by no means Utopian government, but at least temporarily it represented an effective compromise between indigenous tribal governments and the self-imposed white man's. In functional ways the British-style colony government had undeniable advantages over the Liberian government, which was and still is constitutionally similar to that of the United States. Nobody could deny that Liberians had worked devotedly and in great part ingeniously to adapt an American-conceived republic to life and usefulness in tropical Africa. Nobody could deny the presence and the growth of Liberian political talent. But judging in terms of readily discernible results, the imposed British formulations of African government were more effective than Liberia's valiant implantation of an American-conceived republican government.

In mighty Africa, where the criteria of good and bad, right or wrong, are so powerfully stamped by environmental demands, Liberia waited in a dark, dense mist of vagaries and problems. The waning of the infamous slave trade was its most special beacon of hope. But colonialism was ready materialized as a truly baffling Pandora's box which was already opening to show a most amazing assortment of death's heads and masks of good fortune.

II. Meeting the Twentieth Century

8

THE NEW CENTURY

FOR AFRICA AS A WHOLE the twentieth century began as a baffling intermixing of good auguries and bad. For Liberia, which lacked both the shield and the shackles of colony status, the new century dawned very darkly indeed. An item of supporting testimony materialized during December, 1900, when the handsome and philosophic William D. Coleman resigned his office as President of Liberia with the forthright explanation that, as he saw it, his country was being forced to withdraw dismembered "into the forests." The thirteenth president of what was already the oldest continuing Negro republic stated with quiet eloquence that he would no longer be an administrative party to the ravaging of his country.

There were those who believed that William Coleman was unduly discouraged. For four years he had served creditably and in great part valiantly as the chief executive officer of his country. His record as a patriot was beyond challenge or doubt and his knowledge of West Africa was unquestionably extensive.

At first glance the Coleman complaint of his country's under duress retreat into its forests seemed somewhat rhetorical. The truth was that most of the people of Liberia had not yet come forth from their forests. Most, at very minimum nine-tenths, of the then resident Liberians were long-established tribespeople, still dwelling in forest clearings or on forest fringes; left to their preferences few would choose to change abode. Most were of comparatively small tribes; partly because of this most were disposed toward being peaceful.

The resigned president, of course, was the last to deny the foregoing. The handsome American-descended Negro was well informed regarding the Liberian aborigines. He had repeatedly professed and demonstrated that he loved the tribespeople; as a capable arbiter and persuader, Coleman had worked manfully and successfully to maintain peace and neighborliness among the tribes. For good measure he had labored valiantly to persuade the Americo-Liberians to deal more justly with their tribal neighbors and better support "the greening promise of national unity."

William Coleman had also striven to revive and maintain at least an embryo of a public school system. He had more or less successfully pioneered the ingenious move to effect the reopening of Liberia College by developing a specific crop export (piassava fiber) as a basis for excise revenue with which to support the nation's first and then only college. However, his attempts to effect adequate government financing of schools were admittedly inadequate; as of 1900 they remained no better than feebly operative in Monrovia and six other Americo-Liberian towns, leaving the hinterlands to keep with their own folkish educational devices, and where available the frequently brave but usually feeble mission schools.

But the root of the Coleman despair was the apparent unattainability of Liberian sovereignty. The nation was being robbed of its territory, and its solvency was thereby being placed in double jeopardy.

William Coleman had been confident that nationwide public education and agricultural solvency could be attained in time if, and he had found the "if" discouragingly big, the all-important, all-sustaining lands could be held intact and available for Liberian use. But here, as Coleman saw and felt it, was the eraser of rational hope. Liberian lands were being remorselessly snatched from Liberian control. The pilfering had grown monstrous with the so-called Treaty of 1892, when the French Foreign Office, employing largely vapid and imagined claims based on alleged and previously unannounced tribal treaties, had at one ruinous swipe claimed and begun occupying for France's West African Colony about 40 percent of Liberia's original territory as defined or indicated by prior treaties with the tribe occupants. Many of the existent treaties between Liberia and the various hinterland tribes were vague and quasi-literate, but it was common agreement that most predated and were fully as valid as the French and comparable colonial claims. But with ruthless absoluteness the French Foreign Office had named the Cavalla River as the "official" north and east boundary of Liberia. This outrageous grab had taken away about 60,000 square miles and had included some of the best potential agricultural lands in West Africa, almost half again the present total area of Liberia.

That was only the biggest bite. Britain's colonial claims, repeatedly preluded by overt occupation, had lifted away another 30,000 square miles of the north and west frontiers. In all, Liberian-claimed territory stood at about one-quarter of the 167,000 square miles that as recently as 1866 had been generally conceded as Liberian domain. With the land grabs, of course, had gone the people grabs. Although there were no official West African censuses in 1900, there was reason to believe that Liberia had also lost somewhere near half of its legitimately claimed native population, hardly fewer than 600,000 people.

The losses of the lone Negro republic included valuable coastal frontages, river routes and fertile valleys, vast quantities of valuable timbers, fishing sites, wild-growing crops, particularly palm kernels, and poorly surveyed but recognizable mineral wealth.

Protests had been of little or no avail. The mere fact that scores of the Liberian government's annexation treaties were hardly more than perfunctory letter agreements signed with X's scrawled by chiefs or headmen, and acknowledging token payments of barter goods, granted no implicit superiority to conflicting colonial claims. Justice had not prevailed. William Coleman saw a violation of Liberian sovereignty as an assured prelude to economic insolvency.

Since his elected vice president, Samual A. Ross, had become another casualty of the "fevers," the discouraged president recommended his secretary of state, the intelligent, hardworking Garrett W. Gibson, as his successor. The national legislature responded agreeably by enacting a joint resolution directing that Gibson serve the remainder of Coleman's second two-year term of the presidency.

The Gibson administration encored with another valiant but

largely futile try at reestablishing a hold-the-line government, but the twin afflictions of poverty and isolation held on relentlessly, each perpetuating the other. President Gibson succeeded in temporarily and at least apparently improving relationships with the British and French colonial secretaries but failed to penetrate the continued evasiveness of official Washington. His efforts to expand and upgrade foreign trade were far from successful; revenue collections dragged at barely $80,000 per year. This meant, of course, that government workers either served without pay or for pittances. The hoped-for program of building schools again floundered and roadbuilding was largely reduced to efforts to persuade the more compatible tribe chiefs to open a few additional trails into their more accessible forests.

After toiling manfully through his remaining term and a then two-year elective term, Gibson chose to bow out of the presidency in favor of another likable mulatto, his secretary of the treasury, Arthur Barclay. Again the outgoing president spoke with a brave man's candor. Garrett Gibson warned openly that Liberia was at the verge of bankruptcy, a calamity that could very well bring an end to the nation's sovereignty. The collapse of the Liberian treasury would be tantamount to anarchy. Britain, France, or Germany, separately or collusively, could and most probably would impound all revenues collectible, seize the sources, and still worse, take over the fallen government on pretext of debt claims. If this menacing nightmare seemed unduly lurid, an American precedent, also related to a Negro nation, was even then taking form.

Among the well informed and deeply feeling onlookers was the incoming Liberian president. Arthur Barclay was West Indies born. His family had emigrated to Liberia from the West Indies during the Civil War years. This fact, added to his personal success as a businessman and as a civilian party treasurer, caused Barclay to feel confidence that he could revitalize his country's financial status. Furthermore, Barclay had traded successfully with several of the hinterlands tribes and built up numerous friendships among the chiefs and tribal elders. Accordingly, he pivoted his presidential campaign on improved financial management, and in his inaugural address he promised that he would "strike the rock of national finance with success and effect."

But try as he did, Barclay could not strike the financial rock hard enough with the staff at hand. His determination to keep Liberia solvent was unquestionably amplified by the most painful fate of a Caribbean country which he knew at first hand. This was the aspiring Dominican Republic, the unhappy island neighbor of the first and tragic Negro republic Haiti. The Dominican story had long been complex and rife with violence. But early in 1904 the treasury of that preponderantly black nation had run out of money and negotiable credit. Real and pretended creditors had used admiralty rulings and other subterfuges to term the Dominican Republic a "public bankrupt." Creditors had swept in to seize any kind of negotiable public property. The United States government had intervened and on presidential order assigned customs collectors as treasury receivers and ordered the U.S. Marines to "maintain order." The unhappy Dominican state had thereby forfeited its actual sovereignty, and the United States takeover was destined to linger for twelve years, when the Woodrow Wilson administration made its disastrous move to set up a "military republic" with an obviously phony national election "refereed" by James M. Sullivan, a Tammany Hall sachem with conspicuous Banco Nacional connections.

Arthur Barclay made no claim to being clairvoyant with regard to the future of the Dominican Republic. As a perceptive scholar he might well have anticipated that the United States takeover of the bankrupt and tragedy-ridden Caribbean nation was there preparing a viable rootbed for perhaps the most tyrannical dictatorship that has ever afflicted the Western Hemisphere.

The Liberian president was determined that his own country would not be crucified as a bankrupt. He moved boldly to institute a program of what was then termed pump-priming finance; a modest loan in gold with which to stimulate productive facilities, and thereby increase revenue collections (particularly customs, since tribal taxes were being paid in rice, palm oil, labor, and other barter goods that were not dependably negotiable).

President Barclay therefore proceeded to London to seek a commercial bank loan of £100,000 (then $500,000). The London bankers politely but firmly declined to make a direct loan to the Liberian government and joined in demanding a corporate underwriter or trustee.

That provided the entry cue for one of the most unctuous promoters of the era. He was Sir Harry Johnston, a Marx brothers concept of the African explorer, who was additionally talented as an avid promoter and a surprisingly fluent journalist.

Johnston swooped down on the troubled Liberian president with plans for forming a Johnston-controlled limited-liability corporation ("Liberia Development Company" alias H. Johnston) with which he agreed to underwrite and "trustee" the sought-for loan in return for an official lien on all Liberia's customs collections. Just to be doubly neighborly, Johnston agreed to attend to the disbursement of the bank loan after it had been procured.

The Liberian president acceded with hesitancy but with awareness that his country was desperately in need of the treasury nest egg. Just how desperately was clearly indicated by his acceptance as a last resort of one of the most outrageous documents ever foisted upon a chief of state. Specific entries read:

Ordinary and Extraordinary Interest Payments, $30,000 per annum
Operating Expenses, Liberian Developing Company, $35,000
Servicing Internal Debts, $125,000 [No mention of specific debts or how they were to be serviced.]
For Banks and Roads, $315,000 [At the time Liberia had no banks and virtually no roads.]

Arthur Barclay very soon rued the day that Sir Harry Johnston had befallen him. The distressed president had cause to criticize vociferously the Johnston disbursements and insisted that at least $200,000 of the bank loan had never left the "trustee's" hands. Johnston answered publicly that if the Liberian government had wished a "formal accounting" it should have "petitioned it at the proper time." The Barclay answer was that he had petitioned at the proper time and in vain.

But the bargain had been sealed. Johnston held remorselessly to his lien on customs; he collected in full and in blood, and his somewhat flatulent two-volume *Liberia* provided a bonus dividend for the grand old sport of nigger-cheating.

The Barclay administration, trusting mostly to God and the peacefully inclined tribes, managed to survive and repay the not too figurative pound of flesh. By 1911 a depressive dip in foreign trade again placed the Negro republic in a critical shortage of funds. Barclay turned unwillingly but compulsively to Washington, where the stodgy, foot-dragging Taft administration finally got around to heeding the appeal. William Howard Taft was not averse to being described as that jovial fat man from Ohio who lived at 1600 Pennsylvania Avenue, but the former varsity heavyweight wrestler from Yale did not treat the Liberia loan application jovially.

He opened by instructing a minor assistant to list "certain conditions." The American president would do no more than "indicate approval in principle" of a commercial loan; other "conditions" were that all but $400,000 of the principal amount of $1.7 million be applied to Liberia's already accrued foreign debts and claims, and once more specified that all Liberian customs revenues be impounded for amortizing the loan.

To add pain and insult to hardness, Taft and his cohorts revealed that at the request of the "cooperating" American bankers the president of the United States would appoint an official receiver on behalf of the American lenders and request that the respective British, French, and German governments each appoint its own "referee receiver," all at the expense of Liberia, and at salary plus expenses, which in each instance exceeded the income of the Liberian president. Insofar as neither Britain, France, nor Germany was advancing so much as a farthing, sou, or pfennig of the loan, the latter "condition" also smelled very bad. Even so, the so-called American loan of 1912 may very well have saved Liberia from outright bankruptcy and literal foreclosure.

By March 4, 1913, which marked the inauguration of Thomas Woodrow Wilson as twenty-eighth president of the United States, Daniel Edward Howard, who had served devotedly throughout the Barclay presidency as Liberia's Secretary of the Treasury, was well along in his second year as Liberia's sixteenth president. Still in his thirties, Dan Howard showed embarrassment when he was pointed out, however accurately, as the world's handsomest chief of state. The impressively black Liberian had more than good looks in his favor. During his very early twenties he had made himself a successful merchant, an effective teacher, and an exceptionally popular lay preacher. All of these vocations had provided him revealing acquaintance with hinterland Liberians and helped to make him an effective befriender and protagonist of the tribespeople. The Howard skill as a party organizer had also won him popularity among his fellow Americo-Liberians.

Daniel Howard was also a dedicated advocate of peace. He had moved effectively to win hinterlands acceptance as an arbiter of tribal disputes and proved himself superior as a friendmaker in tribal capitals and villages as well as the Americo-Liberian towns.

As a businessman in public service the young president was well aware that his government did not have sufficient income to maintain an army and navy and accommodate other more demanding services, and he therefore moved to disband the military completely. He was perceptively aware of the dangers involved, but he could and did point out that his country was already and quite unavoidably at war with bankruptcy, sickness, and extreme want. He knew too that a very serious European war seemed to be brewing; and that insofar as Liberia was little more than a crayon dot on the map of colonial Africa, it should make every effort to maintain a policy of "absolute neutrality." To that end the "Beautiful President" had selected as his secretary of state a gifted and engaging young attorney-about-Monrovia, Charles D. B. King. Howard correctly sensed in young King the makings of an outstandingly able diplomat.

Charles King was also a dedicated pacifist. But he believed and said that he regarded the portentous European war as unavoidable and foresaw his country being "swept inevitably into a torrent of strife like a dot of wood carried on the surface of a rampaging river."

During the summer of 1914, beginning in July when the Great War exploded into bloody reality, the pertinency of King's prophecy became evident. Liberia hastened to announce its position of absolute neutrality, inevitably moving at cross furrows with its colonial neighbors, which of course were precommitted to stand or fall with their respective "motherlands." By 1915 all of colonial Africa was technically belligerent.

As the solitary, undersized neutral, Liberia began to experience the particular pains and perils that dog the well-intentioned impecunious noncombatant. Commercial shipping, drastically reduced in most African sea lanes, began to bypass Liberia completely. While most of Africa was hampered by isolation, Liberia found itself almost strangled by it. African colonials or territorials sought and in many instances found profitable opportunities to produce and export various war materiel and other strategic goods to their "motherlands." The lists came to include palm oils, utility fibers and timbers, important ores and minerals, coffee, cacao, and other priority harvests. Liberia had available or potential supplies of many of these, but no merchant shipping and virtually no access to hired cargo space.

Directly before the war began, Liberia's leading exports had been leopard pelts and ivory. Neither was "war priority." Inevitably all customs revenues, including excises, plummeted. The treasury plight veered downward from impoverished to imperiling; the ugly threat of bankruptcy emerged again.

President Howard kept with his announced policy of neutrality, changing the adjective from "absolute" to "exquisite." But by 1916, with the national treasury on the verge of collapse, he yielded to the no-longer-postponable need for seeking a replenishment or survival loan. There was no place to look except Washington.

Robert Lansing, who had lately replaced the premier pleader for peace, William Jennings Bryan, as Woodrow Wilson's secretary of state, favored approval of Liberia's application for a $5 million intergovernment loan. Lansing's arguments included "moral responsibility toward a heretofore ill-used colored stepchild." Woodrow Wilson's implementation waited on enabling legislation by the Congress. The timing was disastrous. The supporting legislation became hopelessly lost in a flood of poorly coordinated "emergency" bills; it did not emerge from committee until early February, 1917, and promptly met defeat in the Senate, which obviously could not see Liberia as a responsible credit risk.

Meanwhile Britain had won the propaganda war, and the United States was accelerating her move toward joining the Allies as a combatant. The State Department under Lansing was applying strong pressure on a host of lingering neutrals, but especially on Liberia, which the secretary correctly termed the only remaining American gateway into vast Africa. Lansing employed modifying phrases, such as "Ally in waiting," apparently forgetful that the Negro republic had already suffered a long and leaning siege of waiting.

On April 4, 1917, when the United States Congress formally declared war against the Imperial German government, President Howard and his secretary of state were parrying for time but felt themselves and their country being stripped of any alternative course. The price for neutrality looked more and more like total collapse as a sovereign state. Liberia lacked the facilities of a combatant. On the other hand to join the United States as a noncombatant ally was also rife with danger. The United States was not able to offer immediate military aid. Germany, still strong in terms of its African empire and still possessing submarine strength in African shipping lanes, was in good position to attack and destroy the unprotected Liberian ports, when and if it saw fit.

Liberia formally declared war on January 12, 1918. On the morning of April 10 a German submarine surfaced directly off Monrovia and moved into position to attack. When the aging revenue cutter, the *Lark*, at the time Liberia's only armed vessel, interceded, the submarine surfaced a torpedo which shattered and sank the lone defending vessel.

Having positioned deck guns, the U-boat next landed a shore party of three officers and an armed escort, which proceeded to the capital to demand of President Howard that he acknowledge the "technical surrender" of Monrovia and deliver to the submarine commander certain aliens, presumably British citizens then present in the capital. The Liberian president refused the demand, but as procedural course consulted his government colleagues, including the vice president, cabinet members, and several leaders of the legislature. The consensus confirmed the president's refusal, agreed that Liberia would "yield no bodies" and "abide no tyranny."

The attackers posted 2:00 P.M. as the final deadline, and shortly before that hour opened an indiscriminate shelling of the tiny, highly flammable (then mostly thatch-roofed) capital. Three buildings were destroyed, two citizens were killed, and several destructive fires started. The U-boat gunners meanwhile purposefully blasted away the French-owned shortwave radio headquarters.

However, within the hour a British armed merchant ship hove in sight and opened fire on the submarine, which cleared decks and submerged. Monrovia was able to tend its wounds. Liberia once more endured. Following the Armistice the Negro republic became the first African nation to seek and receive membership in the League of Nations. With tremendous effort the Howard administration avoided national bankruptcy and as a protective measure against the postwar unrest that afflicted much of tropical Africa, managed to revive and equip a minimal frontier guard force. Daniel Howard's summation was lyrically direct: "Liberia has endured, but her young men in government have grown old overnight."

Early in 1919 the extremely diligent secretary of state won the True Whig nomination and the ensuing election as Liberia's seventeenth president. During the following January Charles C. B. King began a particularly encouraging tenure. He had already gained accreditation as one of the most effective of Liberian diplomats. He enjoyed exceptional popularity among the still politically dominant Americo-Liberians, but he had also gained stature and following among most of the chiefs and principal numbers of the tribespeople. One effective reason was his toleration and gracious recognition of the Mohammedans and the various indigenous religions. "A true Christian such as I strive to be can do no less," the new president explained convincingly.

The moves King made to improve relations with the hinterlands were discreet and generally effective. His crusading zeal for establishing public schools was valiant, but still limited by shortage of public monies. Despite these the diplomat-president succeeded in having built and staffed at Monrovia a first public hospital. With effective vigor the tall and cavalierlike Negro president launched a well-planned move to improve harbors and effect the building of a first line of lighthouses to aid the storm-harassed coastal shipping.

His most successful venture related to planning and correlating plans for establishing employment for Liberian labor. The most noticed move, as already mentioned, was granting a major concession for rubber growing. One recipient, the Firestone Plantations Company, leased a million acres of land directly below Monrovia for planting to Hevea rubber trees. The initial terms were modest, with annual rental of the total lands at six cents per acre and payment of one percent ad valorem excise duties on produced rubber. But the related terms included Firestone's agreement to organize the Finance Corporation of America for the specific purpose of favoring the Liberian treasury with a still crucially needed loan of $5 million—which the Negro republic devotedly repaid.

Meanwhile, Charles King expanded his efforts to make possible more extensive employment of tribal labor. This was a worthy cause that was doomed to a woeful outcome.

9

THE AMBIGUOUS NIGHTMARE

"SLAVERY" IS A RATHER UGLY WORD with somewhat fuzzy meanings and rootage. A typical dictionary definition: "1. Continued and wearisome labor; drudgery; 2. the condition of bondage; 3. the institution of slaveholding."

Self-evidently the first definition catches almost everybody; there are few employments or occupations that are completely free of continued or wearisome labor; drudgery is not easily avoided. Liberia of the 1920s could still find all three of the commonplace definitions of "slavery" more than comfortably pertinent—especially to the tribespeople.

The African tribe, whether in Liberia or elsewhere, and despite its many merits, is a way of life in which thighs and elbows unendingly rub against restrictions and taboos. For the tribe member remains part of an ethnic commune in which the individual's personal and property rights are rather severely limited. A participative tribe member is not a freeholder in the usual reach of that term; he or she is committed to the accepted authority of his chief to share his earnings with his tribe. On chief's orders the member is obligated to contribute to the fulfillment of tribal needs. By command of his chief or chiefs the member may also be required to perform work away from his home or homeland or village; he may be assigned to work in alien places with his earnings assigned partly or wholly to his chief. The tribeswoman is similarly committed to serve as a homemaker, childbearer, as a farmer or miscellaneous provider.

Until the 1930s, when the Liberian government made the practice illegal, "pawning" children was still another accredited practice at least on the periphery of slavery. In return for money or other provision, a baby or child, even an adult, could be given over to serve and be kept by individuals or families not its own. Despite its self-evident faults, pawning has no doubt contributed to the integration of Americo-Liberians and tribal Liberians.

There was and occasionally still is the tradition-rooted practice of enslavement by way of personal indebtedness—not too different from dealing with the Ideal Loan Company of Anywhere, U.S.A. When a tribe member owes another and does not pay, by recourse of palaver or open trial or on order of the chief, the debtor may be obliged to accept servitude to his creditor until his debt is "worked out."

These and related mores, abetted by the ever crucial need for wages, had sustained the long-accredited practice of exporting tribesmen as contract workers.

One of the first and most notable beyond-boundary labor markets was provided by British shipping companies, which had eagerly employed Liberian Krus, the most outstanding seafaring tribesmen, as port, small-craft, and shipboard laborers. The recruiting was presently extended to other tribes to include contract or term labor for plantations or logging operations. By tradition or long-time precedence, workers were employed by permission of their chiefs, who received a prescribed share of the earnings in money or barter goods.

Beginning about 1910 the rapid expansion of cacao, or "chocolate tree," plantings in the British Gold Coast Colony and other areas of West Africa strongly stimulated the export of tribe-contract labor from Liberia. By 1912 Spain's island colony of Fernando Po, off the Bight (Bend) of Biafra, about a thousand miles down-coast east from Liberia, began gaining strongly as a cacao-growing center and importer of contract labor from the mainland. The Liberian tribesmen were long recognized as outstandingly competent and peace-abiding workers. The mountainous island is a small (800 square miles) area, and its resident population of about 25,000, mostly Spaniards and Spanish-Negroes, had neither the numbers nor the disposition to work the chocolate crop, which more or less requires a hot and humid climate. Its workers customarily received very low wages. Bad as they were, they were actually no worse than the wage scales then obtaining in most other colonies.

The Fernando Po planters, most of whom lived in the comparative comfort of Santa Isabel, the island capital, joined dispatching ships and agents to recruit and take aboard "gangs" of tribesmen on two-year contracts. At first the arrangements were made wholly with native chiefs. Then, during 1914, following repeated reports of brutality and other bad-faith practices on Fernando Po, the Liberian government arranged with the Spanish Colonial Office to standardize the work agreements and provide for accredited Liberian consuls to serve as "referees" to serve the needs and interests of Liberian contract workers. There is general agreement that most of the referees served competently, but the Liberian government erred in permitting a "citizen committee" to supervise the labor recruitment and to collect fees or bonuses which were paid by the island employers.

Anyone who has had firsthand and varied experience with tropical labor grows aware of the implicit faults and evils of agency or syndicate recruiting procedures. As in ticket scalping, not even the best is good enough. A study of the records suggests that labor recruiting in Liberia was not implicitly corrupt, but presently became infested with hangers-on and pretty commissioners who might better have remained asleep in their hammocks.

Meanwhile the prevailing health and living conditions on Fernando Po, although better than disastrous, were distinctly less than acceptable. Imported laborers suffered excessive disease casualties, particularly from endemic malaria, which in all, according to the fairly respectable Spanish Colonial Office records, by 1915 were producing death rates among cacao workers as high as 7 percent yearly. That, of course, was deplorable; it implied about 65 deaths among the 928 Liberian laborers who were "on export" in Fernando Po during the year of maximum death tolls.

With due cause the British Colonial Office publicly deplored the situation. The Spanish Foreign Office concurred in principle, but insisted that the Fernando Po recruiting was competitive with the

British contractors who were operating virtually without supervision. The Spanish government officially stated its willingness to use its "good offices" to improve the situation. From Monrovia the Liberian government restated its concern for its "exportees."

The British Colonial Office also appealed to Washington to intervene in this and other Liberian affairs. Various observers began to suggest that the actual British position was that the independent success of Liberia as an African republic would motivate British and other "territorials" to demand substantially greater autonomy. That affirmation or reflection would recur again and again.

But the Fernando Po chronicle continued to fester. In 1920, Charles Dunbar Burgess King, on his inauguration as the fourteenth president of Liberia, turned again to the export-labor quandary with which he had earlier wrestled as a cabinet member. King was aware, of course, of Liberia's needs for wage earnings and the fact that many tribe chiefs fervently insisted that labor contracting to Fernando Po be continued. The new president proceeded to reorganize the supervisory board, of which he made his vice president, a member of the Supreme Court, and a senior cabinet member ex officio members. He further sought the legislature's permission to employ an accredited personnel expert from the United States to serve as administrative director.

The Liberian Senate accepted; the House of Representatives held for the continuation of what it termed a private employment syndicate to be officially directed by the vice president. President King, understandably disappointed, accepted what was given, and succeeded in persuading the Spanish government to appoint an accredited committee of supervisors. The Liberian government meanwhile authorized the employment of three additional consul-grade "labor referees" to serve on Fernando Po.

There was evidence of improvements. During 1927 an official party of plant explorers, including Dr. P. G. Saunders, a respected specialist in cacao, made a detailed study of the cacao industry of Fernando Po and rated it as somewhat above prevailing averages of both Latin America and British West Africa. The Fernando Po cacao wages averaged about 93 cents a day, reputedly the highest agricultural wages obtaining in or near Africa at the time. The Saunders report was confirmed by the International Cacao Institute, then headquartered in Amsterdam.

But there were continuing charges of lethal exploitation, and at least a few roving reporters insisted that the lone Negro republic which had so vehemently deplored slavery was permitting what amounted to the profit-seeking impressment of its own people. The journalistic uproar grew more and more stentorian.

During 1924 a former British colonial secretary of Gambia, Henry Fenwick Reeve, published from London a no-holds-barred book entitled *The Black Republic of Liberia,* which heatedly criticized the King government. The Reeve explosion was echoed in kind, although better informed critics pointed out that by his own admission Reeve had never visited Monrovia, or any other principal area of Liberia. This did not, however, repress the Reeve conviction that the African republic should be taken over by a "civilized power or powers"—white, naturally, and one somehow suspects Britain would have been his first choice, with possibly the United States as second.

Reeve's sweeping pronouncements were strongly supported by an itinerant American, Raymond Leslie Buell, who wrote and published a volume entitled *The Native Problem in Africa.* Buell had at least glimpsed Monrovia; he explained that he had been aboard a ship which paid Monrovia a brief and necessarily offshore call. However, his appraisals of Liberia were openly contradicted by reports of the *Harvard Expedition to Liberia,* as published in 1929.

The really devastating blast and the most luridly purple prose materialized in 1929 with the publication of a book entitled *Slavery.* The author was Lady Kathleen Simon, the emphatically outspoken spouse of Sir John A. Simon, a Member of Parliament who was Britain's oncoming Secretary of State for Foreign Affairs.

Sir John provided the foreword and served as publisher for what appears to have been one of the most profoundly undiplomatic tomes ever put out. The entire presentment was lurid and tabloidish, but its chapter on Liberia (which Lady Kathleen admitted she had never seen or gone near) was relentless and libelous. Her ladyship openly branded Liberia a "self-perpetuating conspiracy" of Americo-Liberians—all engaged in the flagrant and profit-motivated practice of "slavery." The vehement Lady Simon also admitted that she had never seen or gone near Fernando Po; obviously she had not permitted herself to be prejudiced by the study of any accredited records. She charged the colonial government of

Fernando Po with open participation in "slave running." But Her Ladyship's knockout blows were directed at the Negro republic with the absolute recommendation that Liberia be taken over by "the civilized intercession, specifically by a government of strong-willed white men."

A study of Kathleen Simon's sources suggest that a strong-willed black man had provided most of the muckraking ingredients, some of which had appeared, also with impediment of quotation marks, in the books of Reeve and Buell. He was the American-born Thomas J. Faulkner, then a perennial candidate for the presidency of Liberia, and a two-time loser to Charles King. The Faulkner assets included the so-called People's Party of Liberia, which he had personally organized and dominated, and the vivid collection of unconfirmed but not unsensational allegations regarding the "blotch" of slavery.

The point of real consequence was that Kathleen Simon's book promptly took over as an international bestseller with undeniable striking power. On the latter basis the work proved most hurtful to Liberia; it condemned totally the Negro republic, emphatically denied the black man's right of self-government and his ability to govern his fellow blacks, and bluntly denied Liberia's acceptability in the "family of nations."

The vehement book won quotations and still more imitators. For all of a year there were no effective refutations. That year was marked by the inauguration of Herbert C. Hoover as president of the United States. He chose Henry L. Stimson as his secretary of state.

There had been many expressions of doubt regarding Stimson's potentialities as secretary of state. But there were no grounds for disputing his status as a ready believer and an emphatic exclaimer or that he had read the Simon book. On his sixty-third day in office Stimson found time to direct a long and vitriolic note to Liberia's then secretary of state, Edwin Barclay. The principal content was a potpourri of unverified charges of official and illicit Liberian complicity in labor traffic with Fernando Po. It included several almost verbatim lifts from the Simon book about slavery, e.g., "A system which seems hardly distinguishable from organized slave trade," which was being enforced "by the services of the Liberian Frontier

Forces and the services and influences of certain high government officials . . . being constantly and systematically used."

The fact that the black republic was being humiliated and condemned without trial or routine procedures of verification was made the more hurtful by the handling of the brutal note which was released to newsmen and news services in Washington on June 7, 1919, a full day before its delivery to official Monrovia.

Deeply shaken, President King firmly denied the charges and termed them partisan and abusive. He pointed out that his government had made and was continuing sincere and constitutional efforts to correct any and all errors and evils relating to the exportation of contracted Liberian labor to Fernando Po. King next requested the League of Nations, of which Liberia was a member, to consider participation in a factual investigation of the Fernando Po situation, specifically a League-approved investigatory commission with one member to be appointed by the League of Nations, one by the United States government, and one by the Liberian government.

It was an entirely rational proposal, but its calamitous aftermaths were almost instant. League headquarters approved, in principle, then indulged in an interval of hemming and hawing. During this interval Liberia was being pilloried by press, pulpit, politician blowhards, and notice-seekers throughout much of the English-speaking world and beyond. The requested commission was chosen with appalling ineptness. Its American member, Dr. Charles S. Johnson of Fisk University, then one of the better-known Negro colleges, accepted with forthright protests, explaining that he had no firsthand acquaintance with Africa, knew extremely little about Liberia, and nothing about the Fernando Po controversy. Dr. Johnson also stated that he had no appropriate experience in investigatory procedures, and was accepting only from a sense of devotion to a cause and with the hope that God and competent colleagues would help him through.

The committee's Liberian member, a former president, Arthur Barclay, was highly respected but was aging and seriously impeded by failing health. This made it impossible for the elder statesman to travel when or where required. The aging uncle of the incumbent Liberian secretary of state explained that he would do his best, although reminiscence rather than active investigation would necessarily be his metier. The burden of work, therefore, fell on the League's representative, who was well intentioned but ludicrously unqualified. Dr. Cuthbert Christie was a practicing dentist from London's Soho. His firsthand acquaintance with Africa was limited to one brief tourist's visit to Nigeria. He knew little of proper investigatory proceedings and of international law. Dr. Christie was, however, very strongly opinionated, possessed of a dominating personality and an undeniable flair for drumming up publicity.

Because of numerous bureaucratic delays the group did not begin work until April, 1930, and for causes left unexplained the commission omitted any attempt at firsthand study of existent conditions in Fernando Po. The opening session of what the talkative dentist agreed to name the Christie Commission took place in Monrovia. Because the former Liberian president was seriously ill and the two non-Liberians lacked legal training, the majority decision was to dispense with conventional questioning and cross-examination; also with the presence of news reporters.

The "imprimis findings" confirmed that Liberian law does not permit the practice of slavery, per se; that by obtaining constitutional provision any citizen or resident of the republic was (and is) free to seek court's redress for infringement of his civil liberties. Further, any person found guilty of holding any adult against his will was and is subject to prosecution and/or lawful damage procedures and that the process of *habeas corpus* on court order was and is fully accredited.

However Dr. Christie and Dr. Johnson joined in recording their deduction that a "large proportion" of the Liberian contract labor exported to Fernando Po had been recruited with "degrees of duress." The two-member majority refrained from naming specific violations that were confirmable by available witnesses. They did, however, quote published material from non-Liberian sources which used such phrases as "slave raiding" and "willful impressment" more or less interchangeably.

The primary charges and issue, viz., the placement of unlawful work tenures on Liberian contract workers in Fernando Po, were almost completely avoided. There was no effort to investigate the prevailing living or labor conditions on the cacao-growing island.

The various investigatory reports that had been compiled and published by the colonial government of Fernando Po and by the supervisory agencies in Madrid and the meticulously neutral reports of the International Cacao Institute were also conspicuously missing. And there were no authenticated charges or testimony that Liberian or other tribal laborers had been or were being enslaved.

In all the Christie Commission spent four months in its studies but avoided any actual on-the-scene investigation of tribal labor recruitment. Christie personally noted that in the Commission's attempt to acquire information about hinterland labor practices by way of "trusted messengers":

> . . . A somewhat unique factor has been the extraordinary force of rumors. The Commission feels that it should, at the outset, indicate its awareness of frequent mischievous currents of discussion . . . [and] difficulty in disentangling evidence of fundamental economic and social conditions from an extravagant emphasis upon politics in the Republic. . . .

The published report reiterated that slavery in the "classic sense" did not exist in Liberia. That established, the dentist member, still without bothering with specific instances, dates, or supporting evidence, rendered a minority opinion intermittently supported by his American Negro colleague that there were indications of "criminal participation" in the shipment of "forced labor." The loquacious dentist charged several of Liberia's district commissioners, county superintendents, and some residents of Monrovia (although only Vice President Yancy was mentioned by name) of having acted in violation of good faith and in the willful quest of profit or personal benefit.

Portions of the Christie appraisals were released directly to the British news services prior to the completion of the report and its submission to Geneva. The vice president offered his resignation; President King stated that he would wait the completion of the report before making any "public response."

Early in September, 1930, the report was completed. It was by no means a consensus, but rather a volume of dissenting opinion in which only the dentist from London declared for extensive wrongdoings. Even so, the repercussions were immediate and, for Liberia, most hurtful. Literate Monrovia was deeply upset and chagrinned. In England, Lady Simon barged forth on another lecture tour which concentrated on lambasting Liberia. Included with her declamations was the unqualified assertion that "Descendants of American Negro slaves are now busy in slave owning and slave raiding in Liberia." From Monrovia the Liberian president avoided all acrimony and reaffirmed his willingness to devise and sponsor legislation "designed to correct all or any correctable errors." Unfortunately President King found himself in confrontation with a legislature which in the main was angered and humiliated by the "Christie Report" and openly outraged by the platform and publicity antics of the British Foreign Secretary's wife.

The situation grew still worse when the League of Nations Secretariat dispatched the "finalized" report of the Christie Commission to Washington—apparently with the assumption that although not a member of the League of Nations, the United States was in most effective position to chastise and castigate the African republic which it had done so appallingly little to help.

Secretary of State Stimson, at the time faring badly in the naval disarmament talks with Britain and even worse with the shouting insurgency of Adolf Hitler's incubating Third Reich, was evidently in the mood to whack the figurative daylights out of Liberia. One is entitled to wonder if the American secretary of state had actually read or instructed a more literate colleague to read the Christie Report. His responses did not prove or convincingly suggest that he had. Following his unexplained delay of five weeks in acknowledging the receipt of the report, the U.S. Secretary of State opened by denouncing the tardiness of its submission. That accomplished, Stimson on November 7 fired on Monrovia a bombshell of angry castigation generating ruinous heat wholly without light. Ten days later the first officer of the American president's cabinet resumed with a truly brutal condemnation that virtually assured the downfall of the King administration.

In his opening blow, Stimson clearly indicated that he actually knew little or nothing of the report of the Christie Commission, but he again demonstrated beyond doubt that he had read Lady Simon's book. Again and again he all but lifted verbatim its purple-splashed pyrotechnics. The opening salvo was distinctively of Stimson's own prose style:

The Government of the United States is profoundly shocked at this revelation of the existence in the Republic established in the name of human freedom of conditions not only in tragic contrast to the ideals of its founders but in denial of the engagements entered into by the Republic of Liberia through its adherence to the International Slavery Convention of 1926. . . .

In his onrushing of ensuing drivel the American secretary of state wholly evaded a literal barrelful of relevant historic truths. These include such absolutes as the fact that with enormous gallantry and at appalling risks the very earliest Liberian colonists, though impoverished, isolated, and ill-equipped, had fought against the slave trade while American citizens remained its principal exploiters; that the Negro republic's first Constitution, accepted and instated while the United States was indulging in the largest, most relentless and perhaps most conscienceless grab of slavery territory in recorded history, clearly prohibited slavery. Moreover, through the years of United States aggrandizement from the slave trade and slavery, Liberia had fought on and on and on to oppose it. As of 1930 tribal and immigrant Liberians alike had been participating in public elections for almost a century; at longest, American Negroes had been technically recognized as citizens for barely two-thirds of a century; at the time of the Stimson explosion Negro ballots were still not being cast or counted in most of the U.S. South; estimates were that fewer than 10 percent of our nation's Negro citizens were exercising their franchise. Aborigines of Liberia had been officially acknowledged as citizens for almost a century; American Indians had been accredited citizens for less than six years.

With a shocking disregard of documents and supportable truth, the U.S. secretary of state officially asserted that the Liberian "conspiracy to practice slavery" was being "permitted, if not actively indulged in, by nearly all the high officials of Liberia."

Defending the U.S. secretary of state from a direct charge of willful, malicious lying was thereby made most difficult. It would shortly be made wholly unattainable. But his closing delivery of a dire and to Liberia most terrifying threat was even less forgivable:

. . . Ten weeks have now elapsed since the formal submission of the report to the Liberian Government. The American Government understands that not only has no action been taken against the officials whose guilt was established therein, but apparently all of these officials continue to hold public office. . . . International opinion will no longer tolerate these twin scourges of slavery and forced labor. Unless these are abolished, and unless there is instituted by the Liberian Government a comprehensive system of reform, loyally and sincerely put into effect, it will result in the final alienation of the friendly feelings which the American Government and people have entertained for Liberia since its establishment nearly a century ago.

The Report of the Christie Commission had not "established the guilt" of any official of the Liberian government and had not so claimed. The American secretary of state was, however, irrevocably establishing that he himself was a liar and that his administration was indeed a lying accomplice. At least two months before the Stimson explosion the president of Liberia had delivered his assurance of taking proper and thorough remedial action if necessary; one official of the Liberian government was already the principal of constitutional impeachment procedures by the national legislature. Stimson's evocations of the "final alienation of friendly feelings of the American government and people" were too hypocritical, too degenerately crass for ready comment; in the American language of the time, they were stinking politician's baloney. Perhaps the feat of terming eighty-three years "almost a century" represented a new pinnacle of accuracy for the U.S. State Department. But to enunciate that the friendly feelings of the American government toward Liberia had been "entertained" for nearly a century was, speaking as an American, the near ultimate in absolute untruth. The American government had waited almost fifteen years before officially recognizing Liberia; during the intervening sixty-eight years the American government's friendly feelings were mostly those of a grouchy elephant for a country mouse.

One remembers also that the controversial report was assigned and accredited as a League of Nations document, and that the United States was not even a member of the League. The big Stimson stink was destined to endure. But the obtaining Liberian government was not. On December 2, 1930, Liberian Vice President Yancy fulfilled his promise to resign from office without awaiting the outcome of the legislative impeachment. On the following day President King followed suit, having graciously explained that insofar as American "acceptance" was indispensable to his country's survival, his prerogative as a patriot required that he voluntarily relinquish his office.

Except for Liberians, Cuthbert Christie was among the first to express regrets publicly for the almost instant aftermaths. In an address to the Royal Geographic Society, Christie closed a distinctly charitable summation of his "Liberian studies" by noting with his own flair for the obvious: "The resignation of Mr. King was probably not the best thing that could have happened in the interest of the Republic."

Many students of Liberia continue to agree. As herein indicated, this writer is numbered among those who would very warmly agree. It was my cherished pleasure and honor to have known and worked with President King both in Monrovia and Washington. Never in a now long lifetime enriched by a great many friends have I known a finer idealist, a kinder man, or a more perfect gentleman and dedicated public servant. For good measure, Charles Dunbar Burgess King loved his people, never excepting the tribespeople. He abhorred slavery, he adored freedom, and he loved the truth in government or anywhere else. The most absolute testimony of this was written in his face.

10

LIBERIA AND RUBBER

THE AUTOMOTIVE AGE reached Liberia by way of a shipping error. Early in 1916 the Ford Motor Company shipped a crated Model T to the governor of Lagos. By purser's error the "boxo" was landed by lighter at Monrovia. Acting on impulse and quite unofficially, Colonel Harry M. McBride, the American interim consul to Monrovia, volunteered to pay the amount of the C.O.D. and thereby acquired the distinction of becoming the first auto owner in Liberia.

The rub was in being the first auto user. Monrovia had no filling stations, no garages, indeed, no streets; it was then a foot-trail capital. McBride opened the crate, set up the little engine, placed the wheels, and succeeded in wheedling a can of "petrol" from a British motor craft then in or near the landing area. After a great deal of diligent cranking, what may well have been the first landside combustion engine ever to fire in Liberia popped and spluttered into action. At about that time the acting consul became aware that his powered vehicle waited on flat tires. By sheerest luck a local trader owned an air pump. It did not work well, but it was borrowable and Colonel McBride was energetic. Before exhaustion set in, the interim consul was duly reminded that the spark of the internal combustion engine is irrevocably committed to rubber, and that the automotive age is inevitably mounted on rubber tires.

Having inflated the tires Colonel McBride next realized that the "streets" of Monrovia would have to be widened, and he employed axmen to clear a wide trail from his house to the president's.

Meanwhile, when he returned the hand pump to the trader's storeroom (in that era pumps were not standard tool-kit equipment), Colonel McBride listened attentively while the trader proposed that in return for the use of the pump the diplomatic representative use his influence to encourage the gathering and export of natural rubber from Liberia. The trader, an observant Swiss, reminded him that the epoch of the automobile was surely arrived; already it was shrinking the earth; it would presently reach every nation, including Liberia. Everywhere autos would set up a need for roads, engine fuels—and rubber tires. The trader was aware that most rubber then came from a tropical tree called Hevea (*Hevea brasiliensis*), originally from the Amazon Basin of South America. West Africa was known to have its own rubber-bearing plants, but none was the peer of the Hevea tree. Situated as it is on the border of Africa's great rain forest, Liberia was well placed for any tropics-growing tree, including the stately rubber-bearer native to the Amazon. Furthermore, by natural decree, this West Africa was most favorable to tree crops.

Colonel McBride did not debate the issue. Actually he had already written and posted a departmental memorandum on the subject of natural rubber—as usual without avail. The gist of his memorandum was that rubber was then a staple commodity in multiplying world demand and that rubber production was changing from a jungle grab bag to a potentially profitable tropics grove crop. Commercial groves of Hevea were being established in the great areas of the Pacific tropics and in Equatorial West Africa, notably in the British Gold Coast Colony, Sierra Leone, Nigeria, and French West Africa. Beginning in 1910 a British company had planted a trial Hevea rubber grove at Mount Barclay, a few miles inland from Monrovia. The seedling trees had grown readily but apparently the choice of varieties had been unsuitable. Or perhaps the harvesting was inept. In any case, the yields had been so poor that British Africa Ltd. had decided to abandon the test planting.

But for the world at large the Hevea tree had taken over as the predominant world source of rubber. By 1916 exports were about 100,000 tons a year; by 1920 they would be 500,000, with double that quantity firmly predictable. Even in 1916 United States manufacturers were using about three-fourths of the total crude rubber in international trade. Meanwhile, commercial grove owners in British Malaya, the Netherlands Indies, and Ceylon were supplying about three-fourths of the production at prices which vacillated wildly from ten cents to more than two dollars a pound. American companies, led by Goodyear in Sumatra, had set out to establish their own groves in suitable tropics. In 1923 when Britain's Stevenson Rubber Restriction Act, the most audacious and successful commodity cartel of its era, succeeded in raising the world price of rubber from 14 cents to $1.23 a pound, several additional American manufacturers set about establishing their own sources, and thereby assuring their own basic supplies.

The most determined of these manufacturers was Harvey S. Firestone, the founder-president of Firestone Tire and Rubber Company of Akron. The astute little Ohioan, who had personally founded the Firestone Rubber Tire Company back in 1906, had watched the fade-out of wild-rubber snatching from the farflung wilds of the Amazon Basin and its replacement with grove plantings of South American Hevea in the cheap-labor hotlands of Southeast Asia and major islands of the South Pacific, particularly Sumatra. He also saw Equatorial Africa as the most likely escape from the British, Dutch, and French domination of rubber sources and the rubber buyer's special nightmare, the Stevenson cartel. Firestone was aware that the rubber-bearing plants that are native to Africa (the Lobelia vine is the best known) are inferior to the Hevea tree as an effective source of natural rubber. However, the farm-raised Ohioan also observed that the Amazon Basin Hevea is less harassed by disease in Equatorial Africa than in the dark misty wilds of the Amazon country.

Liberia, therefore, seemed a particularly promising choice of a rubber-growing base, the more so because its government was actively and at that time unsuccessfully seeking an international industry and revenue source. The employment of tribespeople was another prime incentive. As already noted, Liberia's affable and cogent president, Charles D. B. King, had actively championed the development of employment sources for tribal workers and, with the strong encouragement of tribe chiefs, including "paramounts" and "kings," had sought to stabilize the recruiting and export of contract labor by the appointment and training of "referees" who could be made responsible to the Liberian government. As also noted, the desire of the chiefs and their tribespeople to earn was strongly augmented by the national economic need for the increase of revenue sources. Government income had remained painfully short of minimal needs; annual revenue receipts were still being siphoned off directly into the distinctly usurious hands of international bankers. Liberia was deep in financial quicksand; a rubber industry might provide the crucially needed pull-out. The harvest would provide employment within home boundaries and a responsible and expandible source of excise revenues.

There were, of course, no legal means of selling the required lands to Firestone or anybody else; the Liberian Constitution restricts the literal or title ownership of all real property to citizens of African descent. The evident alternative was a long-term (up to ninety-nine years) leasing of available lands by means of concessions duly approved by the national legislature.

During November, 1926, the Liberian legislature on recommendation of President King and Edwin Barclay, then his secretary of state, enacted a special bill to lease to the Firestone Plantations Company a million acres of nationally owned lands for ninety-nine years at an annual rental of six cents per acre, plus one percent of the prevailing market price of all rubber produced, the latter to be collected as an excise. If the development were successful, the Liberian government would be assured of approximately two dollars per acre of producing groves each year along with the regular employment of tribesmen as tappers and miscellaneous rubber workers.

The Firestone concession was promptly put to use as a credit base for refinancing the Liberian government. This involved setting up a "complying" company, the Finance Corporation of America, as a subsidiary of Firestone, with immediate commitments to purchase a $2.5 million Liberian bond issue at no less than 90 percent of face value and to make available a like amount in approved loans to the Liberian government. The National City Bank of New York would serve as fiscal agent for the most forthright acknowledgment of Liberia's validity as a borrower thus far attained. The procedures were not without strings, but they provided immediate means for retiring the still strangling 1912 indebtedness; also a new basis for "internal borrowing" by the government, and a modest kitty of about $168,000 for use in building frontier clinics, sanitation facilities, and other urgently needed public services.

From the beginning, however, the good or bad of the Firestone concession was centered in supply and use of labor. Firestone's initial letter of intent stipulated,

> . . . The Company may employ any workers whom the Company may recruit or who may present themselves . . . . Such labor . . . shall be free to bargain for its terms of and conditions of employment and shall be free to sever its employment with the Company at its own will and convenience. We desire to point out to the Government that the success of our development in Liberia is largely dependent upon the organization of a permanent and contented labor force. This can be done only through free and unrestricted employment and upon terms and conditions which are agreeable to the workers themselves. . . .

The employment procedures were correlated to tribal traditions. Firestone agents traveled into the interior, usually afoot, to meet and negotiate directly with the chiefs, whether clan or village, paramount or "king." From the beginning the Firestone emissaries kept the "recruiting" distributed among all tribes who chose to participate. They were authorized to open negotiations by paying the respective chiefs a dash or gift for permitting his followers to accept employment and to accept the prevailing procedure whereby each worker returned a portion of his earnings to the tribe, this to be decided by the respective chief or tribe council. It was also agreed that the workers could receive part of their wages in food, primarily rice, the staple grain, at wholesale costs as a supplement to money wages, and that all would be provided housing and medical care without cost to themselves. There was to be no labor contracting as such. All workers were to be free to leave when and as they saw fit. The chief might stipulate that his tribe members return to their homes to help with farming during the dry season, i.e., "cut-farm"—this is an insurance against famines in the home countrysides—or otherwise serve his tribe during times of need.

Harvey Firestone and his son, Harvey, Jr., who headed the Liberian rubber-growing enterprise, explained in writing:

> . . . When an agent has assembled a group of natives—let us say about 200 —they start for the plantations accompanied by a "messenger" who represents their chief by supervising the welfare of his people. This trip along

a forest long trail, in some instances several hundred miles long, is a great adventure. Many of the men never traveled that far from home before.

Instead of living in "coolie lines" they build their own houses in their own way, setting up a new village in place of those left behind. They presently bring along their families to live with them. . . .

Here is a typical recruiting report ("CC" being Clan Chief, and "PC" Paramount Chief):

Chief	*District*	*Section*	*Tribe*	*No. Men Sent*	*Arrived*
CC Kpama Yomo	Kakata	Kpama	Kpelle	15	15
CC Kpabah Gbeles	Kakata	Gbelee To	Kpelle	10	7
CC Gbalokai	Kakata	Konoyea	Kpelle	11	11
CC K. Daniel	Kakata	Queline	Kpelle	14	10
CC K. Lupu	Kakata	Menkellie	Kpelle	14	14
CC D. Living-stone	Kakata	Sanoyea	Kpelle	10	8
CC Kpenbah	Kakata	Gbama	Kpelle	11	11
PC B. Zinnah	Bopolu-Suehn	Bopolu	Kpelle	24	24
PC Menyongai	Kakata	Gibi	Bassa	42	38
PC Vana Woo	Bopolu-Suehn	Kongba	Gola	13	13
PC Varfee Sirleaf	Bopolu-Suehn	Mecca	Mandingo	9	9
PC Mongru	Saniquel-lie	Gborplay	Geh	32	32
PC Mongru	Saniquel-lie	Stolay	Geh	21	21
PC Wydordea	Tappita	Messonah	Mano	27	21
PC G. Toweh	Tappita	Boe-Queela	Gio	18	8
PC Wydordea	Tappita	Yarwin	Mano	17	12
PC Weipah Paye	Tappita	Doe	Gio	16	11
CC Segbeh Dahn	Tappita	Gbai-Gblor	Gio	14	6
PC Nyonton Paye	Tappita	Kpiaplay	Krahn	16	16
			TOTAL	334	287

As rubber plantations were cleared and planted and the combined work force reached 30,000 (the foreseen minimum for a profitable operation), virtually every tribe in Liberia was represented on the work rosters:

Bassa	2,685
Belle	435
Buzzie	4,004
Chien	31
Dey	73
Gbandi	1,594
Gio	3,975
Gizzie	1,969
Gola	766
Grebo	2,585
Kpelle	5,486
Krahn	571
Kru	563
Mandingo	247
Mano	3,666
Mendi	1,197
Vai	259
	30,016

By 1928 the rubber plantations were materializing, but entailing some more or less inevitable errors. In terms of the commercial forestry of rubber, the most costly error was the initial use of scrub, or "run-of-the-jungle," Hevea seed. A typical grove acre of about 300 "native-type" trees could be expected to yield ("tap out") about 300 pounds of processed crude rubber in a year's time. That simply was not enough. By 1928 Dutch growers in the East Indies were taking the lead in demonstrating that bud-grafting young trees with higher-yielding strains of clones from "mother trees," and the efficacious use of cross-pollination or hybridization could even then establish grove yields averaging as much as 1,200 pounds of rubber per acre yearly. Subsequent advances in plant genetics and nursery and forestry practice clearly foretold even higher yields. That, of course, was and still is befitting the ever-growing world demands for rubber products. In great part as a necessary course, the rubber plantings in Equatorial Africa, including Firestone's in Liberia, were begun on a first-step-forward basis; the first steps included a systematic procedure for clearing the heavily forested sites, planting the Hevea seed in nurseries and adapting the seedling trees to prevailing topographies and climates. Hevea is an adaptable crop, but its successful development requires time, experimentation, and selection. The minimal growth time is about six years, depending on clone or variety; the maximum production wait may be several times as long.

Liberia's most impressive asset was the excellence of available workers. An effective rubber tapper must have superb eyesight, a surgeon's skill with a sharp knife, and the patience of an unrufflable Job. For aside from being the tireless harvester, the tapper must also be the astute nurse and physician to the rubber trees and the most manually skillful of all major harvest workers. Liberian tribesmen are especially blessed with all these skills.

Natural rubber begins as a white, milklike latex that oozes out of layers of cells located between the outer bark and the cambium layer of the tree's trunk. In terms of yields the bark is precious stuff, but the cambium is inviolable; it cannot be cut into carelessly or clumsily without irreparable damage to the tree. However, if the tapper's knife does not cut cleanly into the thin layer of "milk" cells, the latex cannot bleed adequately. It follows that the successful tapping cut must keep to within the thickness of a thin sheet of paper, never more than a millimeter.

The most exceptional skill of rubber tapping is based on several related items of natural history. When a Hevea tree reaches a waist-high diameter of about five inches it becomes tappable and accordingly may be numbered and assigned to a "task," usually of 250 to 300 trees; a task, in turn, is the daily work assignment of a tapper. The initial step is to mark the "panel," usually on the north side of a tree (to minimize latex coagulation by the sunlight) with cut angles of about 35 degrees and covering no more than half of the circumference of the tree. Ideally when the individual tree is tapped every second day, its bark is consumed at the rate of about one inch a month. Since a healthy tree is able to replenish its "spent" bark at about the same rate, expert tapping makes the potential yielding life of the rubber tree several decades long.

Tapping is early-morning work. Beginning at daybreak the tapper makes his cutting rounds, leaving the latex to flow into a small metal or porcelain spout that feeds into a cup made preferably of glass. The tapper carries a professional-looking work kit that contains a scalpel-bladed knife, a file and whetstone for sharpening the knife, a bottle filled with fungicide for disinfecting the tree wound, a panel pattern, and a sharp probe for verifying bark thickness. As a rule the latex bleeds anywhere from three to five hours, or until the increasing heat of late morning causes it to coagulate and thereby seal the cut or wound.

Collecting finishes the tapper's day. He places two large stainless steel buckets on a light shoulder yoke or "picul stick," and carries a canvas bag for collecting scrap rubber and coagulum. So equipped he again tramps his task, collecting the latex in his buckets and coagulum and scrap in his bag. The "pickups" have limited value, but the methodical collection is necessary for keeping a clean task. The entire gathering must be carried to the collection station. There the liquid latex is strained into receiving tanks from which it is delivered by tank trucks to the plantation or local processing center or "factory."

The total operation requires a host of diverse skills—from biochemists to master mechanics, but the decisive workers are the tappers who comprise about two-thirds of the entire work personnel. For the most part the tappers are young. A tapper's requisite manual skill may endure for ten years or more, but chances are that sooner or later he must move along to other works.

In any case, the Liberian tribesman's unique excellence as a harvester of rubber is a most memorable testimony of superior manual competence. That, plus a most special and wonderful feeling for trees. These and related endowments continue to accentuate the most exceptional skills of the indigenous tribespeople and their commendable ability to work together as all-Negro groups.

In keeping with native employee tradition the Firestone men set up "work forces" of from twenty to thirty men apiece. Each force elects its own leader, or head man, who doubles as interpreter. The leader so chosen may be voted out of office and replaced by majority choice. Any worker who is dissatisfied with his head man is free to join another force. If he feels misused, or is abused or unjustly accused or reprimanded, he has recourse to a palaver or tribe-style hearing. The supervisors, most of whom are also tribesmen, are confirmed by the head men; in keeping with tribal protocol the supervisors give orders or lodge criticism with the head men rather than the individual worker.

Tribe loyalties and distinguishing talents endure. Belles, for example, excel as builders; Krus as boatmen and fishermen; Mendes as policemen, Buzzis as technicians, Bassas and Gios as farmers, Mandingos as traders. Rubber growing requires all these skills and many more; it abounds in symbolism and not infrequently with errors.

In the Liberian epoch of rubber, errors of timing and delays have taken their tolls. The punitive delays began with the onset of the almost global depression of the 1930s, which saw crude rubber prices skid to less than three cents a pound. That made profitable operation of any property virtually unattainable, and Firestone's pioneering Liberian project was permitted to drag its feet for seven years. As a result, even with a second rubber plantation center in the downcoast Cape Palmas area, and with a sustained resumption of plantings in the latter 1930s, the Firestone enterprise was not sufficiently well timed in terms of the onrushing developments of World War II. Even before Hitler's conquest of Poland, rubber was clearly marked as the most imperiling deficit in so-called defense material. Synthetics were still unproved and land and air warfare were crucially dependent on rubber supplies. Japan's blitzkrieg conquest of the lower Pacific and Southeast Asia would shortly cut off from the Allies at least 85 percent of the prevailing sources. Civilian demands already in excess of 800,000 tons a year were being doubled by war demands. By 1940 the fate of many nations depended on rubber supplies.

By the date of Pearl Harbor Liberia's production of rubber already totaled 27 million pounds of "factory prime" per year—more than twice the combined yields of Brazil and all other sources in the American tropics. Largely as a result of intensive harvest, or "double panel" tapping, the Liberian production promptly reached 45 million pounds per year, and kept on rising. By 1942 Liberian rubber yields were 703 pounds (dry rubber equivalent) per acre of grove, more than double the then world average; during 1943–44 they increased to 999 pounds and by 1945 were about 1200 pounds.

The aptitudes of the climates and soils and the exceptional competence of Liberian workers were handsomely proved. The same held for the "basic economy." During World War II the "emergency" harvests of wild rubber in Latin America had cost the United States Treasury an average of $2.60 per pound; the United States was able to purchase the entire Liberian crop for an average of 26 cents by means of price ceilings established by the United States. This saving alone totaled approximately ten times the all-time total of U.S. money grants to the black republic.

Even more significantly, beginning in 1939 each successive year has witnessed a substantial increase in rubber harvests produced by citizen farmers and planters in Liberia. During 1939 Firestone nursery stock, in all 32,500 seedlings, was distributed without charge to interested Liberians. By 1942 the number of gift trees totaled 323,875. By 1947 more than 10,000 acres of bearing groves were owned and operated by Liberian citizens, including tribespeople. At present more than 10,000 Liberian citizens are operating about 135,000 acres of bearing rubber groves. Four major rubber companies based in the United States and three European concessionaires are currently operating Hevea groves in Liberia. But the totals are trending rapidly toward majority production by citizens.

Meanwhile, growing and processing natural rubber holds its place as one of the most exacting and complex of agricultural industries. It is a pragmatic joining of town and country, of machineries, chemistry, transportation, ranging from shoulder pack to tanker ship, and, most decisively of exceptional manual skill and alertness. As already noted the tapper is the indispensable factor.

Beyond reasonable doubt the establishment of commercial rubber growing in Liberia is one of the most impressive attainments in contemporary forestry, or, using a broader-based term, tropical agriculture, at least from the latter 1930s to the present time. Even so the absolute values of the Liberian rubber story cannot be measured adequately in acreages of bearing groves, or tons of product exported, or of wages paid (which are still much too low) or of progress in plant sciences (which as yet is not adequately appreciated).

From its beginnings, the most valuable contribution of Liberian rubber has been and remains the improvement of acquaintance with and appreciation of the *sine qua non*, the Liberian tribespeople. Liberian rubber has opened the way for the people—the most distinguished and valuable of Liberian resources—and provided motivation for their emergence from tall-bush isolation. That first step in integration has made possible successive steps for Liberia's most significant majority, a great and divergent and profoundly African people who continue to touch hands with both yesterday and tomorrow.

11

THE ENDURING TRIBES

YOU WALK down a country trail in late afternoon. You pass a black woman dressed in a gay red robe. On her head she carries a kerosene lantern in preparation for the night that will presently leap down from the giant forests. You notice a tribal postman with his mail pouch balanced competently on his bare head, securely weighted by his water jug. You may presently walk over a bouncy and extremely narrow foot bridge made of barkless poles bound with fibrous creepers and worn slippery by the passing generations of strong bare feet.

You may meet a tribal hunter clad in underwear shorts (quite probably imported from Red China via Hong Kong) persuasively peddling the meat of antelope or forest buffalo, and just possibly whetting customer interest by exhibiting a recently captured leopard cub which he carries in a homemade reed basket.

You come to a tribal town where women work and children play in the neat yardways of the thatch-roofed huts. You observe that these single-room, windowless, and usually wigwam-shaped dwellings are also homemade. The walls are likely to be built of hard-packed mud; the size and shapes vary from town to town, but maintain a democratic uniformity for the particular town you are visiting or viewing.

If it isn't too late in the afternoon, and if weather permits, you will see families, most probably including relatives and other visitors, gathered about a hutside kettle for the once-a-day meal. This, too, delineates both the living economy and long-time tradition of tribal life. Perhaps the townspeople have only food enough for one "full" meal each twenty-four hours. Or perhaps the diners prefer to limit themselves to a single meal, or "feast," each day and supplement it with intermittent snacks. In any case the eating routine is generally steadfast and the basic cooking and serving are traditionally from the same utensil—most frequently a heavy iron kettle from which the principal entree is ladled into bowls homemade of wood or burned clay. The total serving is commonly known as "country chop," and frequently includes toppings of peanuts, pineapple, or other locally gathered fruits or berries, and quite often, richly flavored palm oil. Below the topping one usually finds the great staple, boiled rice. The richly flavored "red" or dryland rice is preferred. Pod peppers or capsicums are among the most-used flavor factors for the "great kettle."

It is exceptionally colorful dining in exceptionally colorful surroundings. For in principal part tribal or hinterland Liberia is almost fabulously colorful; a flowery land, literally radiant with hibiscus, antigonon, giant violets, and blooming trees, vines, and miscellaneous shrubs. Back of these are the multitudes of palms and giant grasses and the very tall forest that appears to reach the sky.

Tribal Liberia revels in the natural and the tumultuously colorful. For it is a most special world built partly of clay and stones and most recently of iron; and partly of daydreams, and bright colors and, ever importantly, of lively sounds. The sounds include bird songs and calls, the ever-varied noises of forest and jungle animals, and the talk and chanting and laughter of people. Also the singing and the talking of drums.

During my first walking foray in Bassa country I received a lesson in drumming appreciation. My first tutor was a slender easy-smiling youth who had lingered at the trail side to prepare what he described as a "small-small beef." (In hinterland Liberia any meat is "small beef"; in this instance the provider was a woods mouse which the youth had captured and was barbecuing, with the long tail bound into the top of a "fire wigwam" built of dead twigs.)

When I inquired about the audible but very distant throbbing of drums, the engaging young man admitted that he himself was a "singer" (i.e., a drummer). Having finished his small feast he vanished hastily into the bush and presently returned with a leather-headed drum about the size and shape of a three-gallon water bucket. He squeezed it with his left elbow and began drumming with the fingers and "heel" of his right hand. "Drum talk sad," he began. "Drum tell somebody die. . . . Now drum talk happier . . . . Now a li'l baby comes. Now hunter takes meat. . . . Here come woman palaver. . . . Now drum say, 'Come eat rice!' . . . Now, 'Go 'way and hide, stranger people sneak in!' . . ."

The instructor's fingers began to leap playfully. "Dance time come. . . . War dance . . . tribe dance . . . line dance." His smile faded and the cadence slowed. "Drum get mad . . . Drum talk mean. . . ." The frown faded and the ensuing smile became almost angelic. "Now drum talk sweet . . . friend palaver with people upriver. . . . Drum your friend, tell all nice things. . . ."

More than any other medium, drums have spoken Liberian history. The largest of size and voice are, or used to be, the war drums. They are now comparatively rare; the only one I ever laid hands on was made of a sector of hollow log about three feet in diameter and covered with a tightly stretched piece of forest buffalo hide. It is listable as a war drum, but its most common use is for nonmilitary services, such as sounding fire alarms or other principal gatherings calls of tribespeoples.

Far more numerous and more frequently used are the "dancing drums." Traditionally these are made of home-cured parchments stretched over hollowed wooden blocks. There are also more extemporaneous and modern drums, made from oil or gasoline containers, or from abandoned military junk, including portions of fuselage of wrecked aircraft, or abandoned ammunition cases or other metal containers; or, funds permitting, commercial instruments supplied by traders or other merchants.

There are also homemade double-headed drums, generally similar to snaredrums and beaten with the fingers and heels of the hands. The smaller "talking drums" are sometimes shaped like hourglasses; they are carried under the singer's left arm and beaten with a stick, as accompaniment to bigger drums, or as inspiration for the women working in the fields or preparing a meal, or of axmen felling giant trees to make way for a new field. Chances are that a single block of hardwood is used for the big kettledrums; a balance brace, or "foot," protrudes at the bottom, and the head is ringed with bands of iron or brass to vary the pitch and give the instrument a "tinkle," or a kind of rhythmic counterpoint.

My gifted young informant and presently his uncle, a clan or half-town chief (I could not ascertain which), assured me that in some tribe communities every man has his own drum name or "call," and that drum telegraphy is so well coded that other tribes-people—even those who speak a different language—can send and receive messages.

Unquestionably the symbolism of drums reaches back into the green-misted dawn of tribal creation. There is a degree of confirmation in the fact that tribal drummers still serve as folk historians. The following, which is fairly typical, was recounted by a Gio drummer and leader of ceremonial dances:

> The first father of all people is Ye. There was a woman too, also named Ye. They were twins. They had a son named Abi. He in turn had one son named Za. Za had much power to bring good or evil upon people. . . . If one wants anything very much he makes this petition to Za, "Za, bo kende [help me]."
>
> Abi caught one of each animal of the town. If he had caught animals of the forest they would have run away again. The town animals he caught were goat, dog, cow, sheep, cat, and chicken. He said, "I don't want my son to be without a wife." He took his medicine and blew some of it on each of the animals. This turned them into six maidens. . . . Abi said, "You, cat-woman, you are my son's first wife because you stay around the house all day."
>
> The cat-woman was a peacemaker. She is the mother of peacemakers because she remains quiet and peaceful around the house. . . . The cat that was turned to a woman bore Za two sons, Sera and Zuakpwa, twins. To these Za gave all the other animal women. The cat-woman was his own. Her last son was Ma. To him Za turned over all his household because Ma was a wise man. He was the father of Ma-Me [Mano] and the Ge-Ne [Gio]. That is why these great tribes are wiser than Za's other descendants.

Whether told with drums or recounted by word of mouth or written language, each tribe has its own recitation of genesis, which usually abounds in such motivators as magic robes, singing waters, and petrified ancestors.

Again to cite a fairly typical instance: the great Mano tribe is a confederation of fourteen clans: Bei, Ga, Yemei, Kei, Gbana, Beua, Duro, Gbwai, Gbwen, Kpibe, Lau, Yalur, Yeka, and Za. The folk history is briefly this:

> In the beginning a man took a wife [where obtainable, several wives], moved into a favored part of the jungle and began a family. As he begat and as the jungle yielded more abundantly, the family head bought, captured, or otherwise acquired additional wives from other families or clans. In time and with due process of propagation the proliferated family grew into a clan. In time the members built their own village, added fields, and chose a patriarch or a strong man as village chief. When one or more additional villages were obtained, the strongest or best-liked of the village chiefs was elevated to clan chiefdom. Eventually clans and villages came together as tribes or rudimentary nations, each one led by a supreme or paramount chief.

Students of the tribes and related ethnic groups are inclined to agree that the earlier peoples of what is now Liberia were members of farming or hunting clans with homes in or adjoining the great forests. The need of mutual protection against the many forces of destruction was a first motivation for banding together in what eventually gained establishment as tribes. Paradoxcs or contradictions of goals developed as some of the larger and more aggressive tribal groups chose to take over weaker communities, in some instances capturing their villages, enslaving their men and taking over their women as additional "heifers," or owned wives. For at least a century one of the most distinctive tribes of Liberia, the Bande, was held in slavery by another still prominent tribe, the Kissi.

But this was the only known instance of its kind. The Liberian tribes were relatively small, with membership numbering in thousands, or at most tens of thousands, instead of millions (which prevails with the Fulani, Ashanti, Etobe, and various other more populous tribes). At least in some part because all of the Liberian tribes were comparatively small, they were mostly peaceful, certainly by comparison with the United States and other habituated warmaking powers.

For good cause the confederations called tribes continued for many centuries. In a great many instances when calamities such as floods, fires, and devastating epidemics struck them down the smaller communities were obliged to find some kind of union with a stronger clan or tribal group. A Loma tribesman gave the following typical account of how the clan from which he was descended was obliged to accept adoption by a more strongly developed neighboring tribe:

> Our fathers lived in hamlets of three or four huts each. Too many wars drove our ancestors farther and farther back into the high bush (forest). Some were taken captive, some were slain by marauders. So those who lived came together and drank medicine in which they had sworn they would live together in big towns and be brothers there and cease fighting among themselves and protect each other. That is why my tribe keeps with large towns. . . .

("Tribe town" is usually synonymous with hamlet or very small village. In hinterland Liberia most tribe towns have anywhere from a dozen to a hundred huts, or "roofs." Smaller or adjacent settlements with two or three or twelve huts are commonly known as "half-towns." Tribal towns with more than a hundred huts or dwellings are described as "big.")

There are great numbers of ghost towns, made so by lethal epidemics or floods or failing soils. One also finds numerous remnants or ruins of towns—the totals may well be in the hundreds—that were destroyed or caused to be abandoned by the slave trade. Most of these vanquished settlements were located on or near the earlier trails, by now returned to forest or jungle. The vestiges of time-worn remnants tell of generations and multitudes of agrarian Africans who were marched or dragged away under the whip and in shackles to seacoast stockades and slave ships. There is evidence that hundreds of other tribal towns and half-towns were purposefully abandoned as their people moved en masse or by individual families into taller forests and more distant bush in attempts to escape the slavers, black as well as white.

It follows that, although most tribes are older than the present majority of sovereign nations, most of the prevailing tribe towns are comparatively new. Few are more than a century old; a majority is no more than two or three generations old, i.e., fifty to seventy-five years. Even the roadside shrines—commonly known as "medicine huts"—built beside the trails as good medicine makers for safeguarding travelers from illness or robbers or leopards, snakes, or biting insects are frequently overgrown and reduced to dank oblivion within a single lifetime. The various sacred trees, including the native teak, most frequently used to mark the graves of departed chiefs, soon become lost in the aggressively crowding forests. All in all, it is advisable to look closely at today's towns when one has the chance—they may be somewhere else tomorrow.

The efforts to appraise tribe histories have been handicapped by various and chronic lapses. A troublesome factor here is the continuing lack (at least through 1970) of an authenticated census of the Liberian tribespeople. It is comparatively certain that by totals they comprise somewhere near 90 percent of all contemporary Liberians, but here again, the confirmable total is not surely available. During 1969 the incumbent Tubman administration estimated the overall population of Liberia as about 1.5 million. By inference this would suggest that somewhere near 1.3 million are tribespeople or, as the saying goes, "tribally related." This projection is supported by the fact that as many as 568,000 tribespeople are known to have voted in recent national elections.

However, United Nations estimates continue to place the Liberian census as around 1.21 million, of whom a probable 950,000 or thereabouts are tribespeople. There is no real question that the predominant tribes of Liberia now number sixteen pivotal entries. One who travels the Western Province can be assured of meeting three of the tribes, viz., the Vai, Gola, and Kissi, each with somewhere near 50,000 resident members.

In the Central Province and the upper third of the Western Province one will meet eight major tribes—the Dey, Bandi, Mande, Belle, Loma, Kpelle, Mah, and Gio. All have languages that are recognizably similar but each has fairly distinctive characteristics. The long-enslaved Bandes, for example, tend to be the least aggressive and perhaps the most gifted in music, dancing, and other performing arts. The Belles are an especially handsome people; some observers insist that their numbers include the most beautiful women in all Africa. This writer would never deny that the Belle women are beautiful, but to ponder as one homely and transient male, I am convinced that Africa has more beautiful women than any other continent, and vies with Latin America for world leadership in attractively feminine women. (Reportedly Africa also has about 2,800 tribes, most of which I have never seen.)

In the north part of the Western Province of Liberia and along the Guinea frontier one meets the stronghold of the Buzi (sometimes spelled Buzzi), or Loma, an exceptionally industrious people, socially conscious, strongly literate (they have their own written language), and deeply interested in the sciences and arts of government. The Bassas are comparably interested in government; thus far they have contributed more officials to the national government at Monrovia than any other tribe of Liberia.

The Mendes are an especially noteworthy border people. Most of them now live in the Republic of Sierra Leone, but Liberia's share are typically imaginative, artistic, and otherwise admirable. The Mah peoples, who include the Mano and Gio, are near neighbors, most of whom live in the northernmost corner of the Central Province. In the main they are "Africa Africans," strongly Negroid, well bodied, diligent as farmers, generous and warmhearted.

The Krus, who keep their eminence as mariners, are extraordinarily friendly—they verily glow with friendliness—and comprise the most populous of the coastal tribes. They are another most likable population sector. The Mandingos, still the most active traders, are hardly to be listed as Liberians; they reside and trade in no fewer than twenty of the African states.

At about this point it might be well to insert that the procedure of listing even the pivotal tribes as characterized by specific skills or emotional qualities or particular social customs is conducive to some degree of error. None can be termed wholly and permanently steadfast in characteristics. One is obliged to grant that the tribe is certainly not impervious to change. But the rate is much slower and the already assured changes are far fewer than one might surmise.

The truth is that despite all the destroyers of isolation, such as all-weather and cement roads, telephones, radios, and relentlessly invading television—all now present and proliferating in Liberia—the fundamentals of the tribes are almost unbelievably resistant to change. One very evident reason is the ever remarkable phenomenon of natural balance. As new roads materialize, and these are nowhere near as numerous or lengthy as the hurry-by correspondents indicate, earlier roads become quickly obliterated by the sheer might and wrath of tropical erosion. Historic trails are quickly erased by the enormously greedy and lusty jungles and forests. When telephone lines disintegrate, as they predictably do, signal drums once more "sing" their messages.

In many instances the tribe towns and their most distinctive and vital ways go on, with little change or none at all. There are some specific exceptions. More and more of the larger tribal towns now have commissioner's, or "Monrovia," houses built and maintained by the national government. But the most significant of the tribe town buildings is still the traditional palaver house. This is usually a kind of town hall where the resident chief and the elders hold sway; also where all tribespeople are entitled to gather for palaver, a deeply African materialization of the open forum or people's court.

Even though the palaver house may be a minuscule mud or log hut with a thatched roof, it is a hallmark and symbol and literal bastion for proving the implicit strength of the tribe. The palaver house may or may not be a thing of beauty per se but it is the symbolic marker for the tribe town which literally and figuratively is a thing of beauty, bringing together as it does the farm lands and the village in living and benefiting community. The rice paddies, cassava fields and other cultivations are outside of but usually within walking distance of the tribe town. Thus, throughout at least half of the year the tribe town is the farm center extraordinary. It is also the pivotal home for those who hunt, fish, or earn, or forage in the bush and those who go forth to work in mines or rubber groves or logging camps or other outside enterprises and thereby contribute to the tribe.

It follows appropriately that the tribe town is in one a wilderness outpost, a child's world, a man's world, and most particularly, a woman's world. Whatever or wherever the tribeswomen are, they keep their places as the prime contributors and stay-at-home heroines of tribal establishment.

The tribeswomen are the principal farmers as well as the indispensable homemakers. They prepare, cook, and serve the food which they have also planted, tilled, and harvested. Almost without exception they grow, reap, flail, and winnow the rice, harvest the palm nuts, and press out the edible oils. They care for the livestock, plant, hoe, and harvest the field and garden crops, carry the water, do the almost incessant creek or riverside washings; also the marketing, which includes selling or bartering the various produce they raise at home or dig, pick or otherwise collect from the wilds. The older children, of course, help with many of the home chores.

Tribeswomen also spin, dye, and sew the clothes. For the most part the men clear the land, build the huts, bring home the game, and constitute most of the wage earners. Men are usually the artisans: potters, wood-carvers, blacksmiths, etc., and, sometimes, the weavers.

Despite this, or perhaps better say because of it, the tribe must serve all the people. The tribe town must function as a refuge and haven for the young and old, the sick and infirm, as well as the work-capable and productive. The tribe town is also for the children who play in its clean, narrow streets, beat drums or pound buckets, patter rhythms with their bare feet, and play singing games and line dances or improvise new ones.

The tribe, its people, its town, half-towns, and nearby wilds, are also a most remarkable bulwark for most remarkable creativity. This includes an especially imaginative reservoir for the raiment and ornamentation and appealing fashions for men and women alike. The chiefs' and elders' dress features the toga and brilliantly designed headwear ranging from fezzes to "pate pads" strikingly ornamented with shells or beads in some cases. The chiefs' robes are with little doubt the most distinguished and graceful apparel yet worn by the human male.

By way of counterbalance tribeswomen, including those in Liberia, may well be the most interestingly dressed of all the daughters of Eve. For their clothes are an unending adventure in creation, not of fashion but rather of basic and progressive style. They begin with the winding and draping of apparels, in great part home woven and colored with native dyes, but in some part trader cloths vividly designed, eye-capturing batiks and pastels. For engagingly good measure, the home-styled creations of costume jewelry cause many of the tribeswomen to glitter and tinkle or radiate with rings, necklaces, earrings, hair ornaments, tiaras, anklets, and leg bands—of silver, gold, bronze, iron or wood beads and carvings, shells, corals, and so on.

Adornment is not a superficial veneer; it is undeniably tribe-related. And a brilliantly original and convincing reminder that the tribe is both a phenomenon and a composite of total living—tradition, worship, medicine, language, economy, arts, and artcrafts of community and an already long-lived culture.

The tribe is of and for all of these. For good and lasting measure it is also government, and the common defense of its members; it aids the sick and infirm and the aged; it seeks justice. The tribe is also for dying, for breeding, for play and laughter and dancing; for the pursuit of happiness and light and resurrection. Inevitably, therefore, the tribe stays the first sustainer of Liberia.

12

LIBERIA AND MEDICINE

As long as white people have known Equatorial Africa, they have reiterated the primary facts that (1) it is tribe country, (2) it is or has been a sick man's society, and (3) the tribes are enduring whereas the status of a sick man's society, although not necessarily permanent, is not easily changed.

This brief exercise in simplification is validly applied to Liberia, where, according to the United Nations studies completed as recently as 1969 at least 90 percent of all residents remain tribespeople or at very least maintain definite tribal affiliations. The observant and persistent counters and appraisers for the United Nations no longer rate Liberia as an *a priori* sick man's society. They clearly indicate that it is now a country with upward-bound health levels, but discreetly admit that serious public health problems persist, and also that the prevailing rise in health levels is not yet conducive to population gains.

The UN's highly respected World Health Organization has been less comforting in its intermittent but continuing reports and estimates of public health in Liberia. WHO is not necessarily renowned as a source of discreet and comforting summations. As regards Liberia it has repeatedly admitted that the vital statistics now available are incomplete—"abounding in gaps." In some part this stems from the fact that Liberia had no public health service prior to 1928, when the Charles D. B. King administration established the first

Bureau of Public Health. During 1930 King's successor, Edwin Barclay, led in expanding the agency, renaming it the Bureau of Health and Sanitation and persuading all the resident doctors then in Liberia—a total of three for the entire nation—to serve as bureau directors or professional counselors. Subsequently the Liberian government has had a public health department of one kind or another.

The menaces have included, and for that matter still include, a worrisome catalog of dread diseases ranging from grim and ancient tropical renegades such as yaws and leprosy to the ancient and endemic destroyers such as malaria and kindred fevers, some of which are still known only dimly. Tuberculosis persists very strongly; African sleeping sickness (trypanosomiasis) is now receding but remains among the most dreaded.

For public health works and for health scientists, Liberia is a particularly revealing laboratory and work field. For good and no less revealing measure, Liberia is also a most impressive stronghold of the practice of folk medicine. This distinctive and enduring heritage continues to hold very real and special values as therapeutic and other medical background materiel.

The subject and resource is not yet sufficiently explored and is only beginning to gain the considerate appreciation of students and researchers from without. One evident reason is that the so-called tribal medicine is linked to philosophy and religion as well as tradition and interpretive science. It is a medical lore of the spirit and body together, but primarily of the spirit. Its prime essence is of the soul, or more literally, the souls.

As the hinterland tribal Liberian believed, and apparent majorities continue to believe, every mortal being has several souls—a veritable congregation of souls. The most visible is the shadow one casts. The most continuously felt is the breath soul. The most exciting is the dream soul. But the most durable is the body soul, which lingers for a time after life leaves the body, presently departs from the corpse and proceeds to God's Town, which is far away.

Health, then, is necessarily of the soul realm and quite basic to its welfare. Good health is man's natural state and heritage. Disease is implicitly unnatural, an intrusion of outside and hurtful forces, magical or superhuman, but nevertheless understandable to perceptive people. All else is comparably understandable since all things are lives—including the grass beneath one's feet, the trees over one's head, the rivers, the mountains, the moon and sun, all "sky things" from the nearer planets to the farthest star. Every object, including those that less understanding people may regard as inanimate, has a spirit or soul or souls within it. Therefore, a knowing person may talk to a tree or a rock, river or cliff, or mountain with the assurance that its spirit or life essence hears. Any object or being controlled by spirit, as all are, is "medicine."

In the more or less pivotal Mano language the word for medicine is *nye*. Any means for channeling its power is *nye ke*—making medicine. The person who produces the medicine is the *nye ke mi*, or doctor. A true *nye* erases the implicitly unnatural phenomenon of disease. The more precious medicines also have the power of sight and speech; a few can, indeed, assume human form. In that event each becomes a fetish, a living thing in its own right, and for the doctor or health seeker an object for prayer or special sacrifice, or both.

A typical fetish is a *zang*, an oval, cone-shaped object hand molded of fiber and clay and sometimes smeared with eggs or fragments of eggshells. On occasion the *zang* requires a particular meal each month (such as a hen's egg served just as the new moon appears). As it elects, a fetish may travel about in human form saying and doing helpful things, but in time, even as you and I, a *zang* tires and requires refreshment.

The folk medicine of Liberian and many other African tribes is also vitally interrelated with prayers; prayers to Mother Earth at the time of crop planting to make abundant the people-sustaining harvests; prayers to waterfalls, which are the homes of the rainbow serpents that cause lands to be fertile; prayers to the sacred hills where the great rains live; prayers to fire and iron that restore and perpetuate mortal strength. For the tribal Liberian medicine and religion, if not wholly identical, are inseparable. The doctor, whatever his tribe, is priest, physician, and for good measure symbolizer. The Kpelle reveres his wayside shrine. The Mano marks his sacred trees and plants at his father's grave the kola palm, a venerated spirit tree. The doctor-priest proceeds on the principle that life is everlasting and that death is essentially an accident which people are duty-bound to prevent or, at very least, delay.

Zo, another term that is recurrent in several tribal languages of Liberia, combines the functions of priesthood, midwifery, medicine, and divinity or philosophy. Significantly, *zos* can be either men or women, but regardless of sex, must abide a degree of practitioner's secrecy. Accordingly, the *zo* avoids explaining his medicine to his patient because he (or she) believes or at least suspects that the sickness may be a spirit that is capable of hearing and thus of counteracting the curative force.

The duty of the native doctor ("witch doctor" is an inept white man's coinage), like that of any dedicated physician, is to attend the sick and seek to make them well in body and mind. To that end the tribal medicine man (or woman) uses many devices that are as ancient as any *materia medica* one can name. He gives enemas with long-necked gourds, uses selected reeds for catheters, and selects indigenous herbs for making poultices, herb baths, or douches. The *nye ke mi* or *zo* should be and usually is a deft anatomist; he is frequently obliged to improvise splints and set fractures without facilities other than his own skilled hands and alert mind. The late Dr. George W. Harley, the career medical director of the Ganta Mission (in Liberia) recalled:

> At Ganta . . . a Bassa boy was thrown violently by a Kisi wrestler, landing on one foot and suffering a Pott's fracture. The white doctor applied a plaster-of-paris splint in the approved fashion. The reputation of the local Mano specialist in fractures was greater than that of the white doctor. The boy had the plaster removed. The native "specialist" applied a light co-adaptation splint made of split raffia midrib. He removed the latter daily and massaged the foot with an astringent paste which dried on like a coat of stiff glue. The splints were reapplied each day. After a week the patient was urged to use the foot lightly. The aim was for a useful member rather than a perfect alignment. The final result was as good as could be expected. There was no deformity. The boy walked without limping.*

The expert use of native pharmacology is another time-proven hallmark of what Dr. Harley reverently termed tribal medicine. Traditionally the medicine man devises potions of native herbs for

*G. W. Harley, *Native African Medicine*, Harvard University Press, Cambridge, Mass., 1944.

treating such nuisance diseases as bacillary dysentery or the more common flesh ulcers. He treats severe wounds by poulticing them with selections of native leaves which have analyzable pharmaceutical values. Many *zos* make and use tourniquets for stanching severed arteries or "force draining" abscesses. Perceptive knowledge of medicinal herbs, roots, barks, etc., provide fairly effective disinfectants, salves, and counterirritants.

Extremely few tribal medicine men or women attempt internal surgery, and here is centered the most regrettable shortcoming of the native medicine. Among the many factors of counterbalance is an astute if rudimentary awareness of the basic pragmatics of "preventive medicine." It seems that in some parts of Africa (but not in Liberia, apparently) attempts at smallpox vaccination have been practiced by the indigenes for a long time. The working principles of quarantine have long been known, and here related is a seemingly almost timeless awareness that many common diseases are contagious. The "trader-missionary" Jehudi Ashmun, writing from Liberia around 1831, recorded that when a tribe member was stricken with smallpox, for example, he was, as he still is, removed to a "sick bush," or pest house, usually an improvised shack or hut at least a quarter-mile from the village or several hundred yards from the nearest home.

There the sick person remains in comparative isolation until he is recovered or able to fend for himself. If the illness is severe and prolonged, one attendant, usually a wife or other family member, necessarily shares the isolation and serves as the doctor's helper. In briefer illnesses relatives or friends bring food or drink, which they leave at a convenient distance. Even if ambulatory, the patient is resolutely confined to quarters. If he breaks away prematurely or otherwise violates the "taboo," he cannot expect to recover from the disease. There are tragic instances of isolated patients who have died of neglect, but such are the vagaries of the intriguing folk medicine.

In the not too distant past and more than occasionally in the present, the reckoning of time has been a troubling medical handicap. In the tribe country watches and clocks are still quite scarce and conventional calendars are virtually unknown. A typical testimony is evidenced by the folkish expedients which one may still see in use. When a smallpox sufferer is quarantined, a young rooster (preferably a red one) is placed near the patient, who is told that when the rooster is big enough to crow, he may leave the sick bush.

Various theories and practices for feeding the sick are also noteworthy. Frequently the sick man's diet consists of sugar cane, a sweet palm oil (for restoring strength), and one of several brews of herb soups as tonic. Where money is scarce or nonexistent, doctor's fees are usually paid in barter plus a "dash" for good measure; sometimes as a final bounty—as in smallpox cases—the medicine man is permitted to take the time-measuring rooster home for his own cooking pot.

Like their colleagues throughout most of the world the tribal medicine men of West Africa were flabbergasted by the pandemic of influenza that swept over Africa and most of the rest of the world during 1918–19. Dr. Harley told me about an especially studious Mano medicine man who dreamed of the "right" medicine to combat the virulent flu germ. The potion consisted of a handful of genezola thorns *(Combretum aculeatum)* burned to charcoal, then ground to powder, mixed with red palm oil, and rubbed on the ankles, knees, and elbows of the sufferer. One gathers that the dream remedy proved about as effective as any other influenza medication.

Quite commonly indigenous Liberian medicine treats fevers with teas brewed of lemon grass, lime juice, or "feverleaf," which the Manos call *geazu* and the botanists call *Ocimum confusa*. The inner bark of a small tree known as *mo a yidi* is also used as a fever medicine; also a tea or broth made of the leaves of a bushy vine called *yini za (Morinda confusa)*, to which is added a small quantity of "country salt," actually a crystalline potash lye made by leaching wood ashes.

Measles, which is still commonplace throughout hinterland Liberia and most of Africa, is sometimes treated with the leaves of the cotton tree beaten to a pulp and mixed with white clay or kaolin, which in turn is diluted with water to form a paste. The measles sufferer (or his attendant) smears the paste over his body and the patient sleeps alone in the open. Each morning he bathes himself with water strained from the leaf pulp, then reapplies the clay paste. As the rash begins to disappear the patient returns to the standby African treatment of a daily hot bath, after which palm oil flavored with various aromatic herbs may be rubbed into the skin.

Appropriately, whatever the ailment may be, if the patient willfully violates the medicine man's instructions, the latter cannot be held responsible for the patient's failure to recover. If an obedient patient dies, the bush doctor is obliged to replenish and appease his fetish; if his professional score continues to be excessively bad, he eventually is forced out of his trade, either by order of the chief or the elders, or by a determined boycott by the tribal clientele.

Rheumatism, prevalent in most tropical countries, is usually treated with liniments, such as those made by mixing together soft clays and water, particularly the gray clays recovered from ant hills—possibly with a content of formic acid—and lime leaves or other kinds of leaves that are beaten to a pulp. After the liniment is removed, the patient, lying prostrate on a bed of heated leaves, is treated with an application of a soothing powder. Counterirritation is also a common strategy for treating rheumatic ailments.

There are "therapeutic fringes," such as the teeth-reddening eating of kola nuts, which contain caffeine and act as a mild stimulant to overcome fatigue. More standard regimens include a much used diuretic made from the dried bark of the *bo* tree *(Mitragyna stipulosa)*; usually the bark is beaten to a powder and diluted with palm wine.

In common with the world at large, respiratory diseases, particularly the common cold, bronchitis, and pneumonia, are formidable enemies. Tribal medicine takes special heed of the respiratory ailments. One of the traditional cold remedies, perhaps with efficacy at par with U.S. averages in the field, is made from the root of a common perennial plant called *suo longo (Ethulia conyzoides)*. The recipe is: Cut the root into small pieces, add capsicum (red) peppers and wood ashes, boil well, and let cool overnight. The usual dosage is a half-pint; the appalling taste and mouthburn causes one to forget his cold for at least an hour.

The boiled root of the *goa* bush is a commonly used remedy for biliousness and colic. For intestinal worms, still a menace in tribal Africa, small green figs serve as an effective vermifuge. Another standby worm remedy is made of the inner bark of corkwood (*wolo* to the Mano and *Musanga smithii* to botanists), beaten or ground with the seed of *dua di (Afrimonium baumanii)*, and diluted with cold water. A purgative dose from a quarter pint to half a pint is usually effective for ridding the child patient of ascarids. An adult sufferer often eats especially prepared dishes such as the buds of the *woma* tree *(Trema guniesis)*, mixed with a meat dish or cooked plantains, and washed down with a vermifuge made by boiling finely beaten *ti mana (Millettia sanagana)* root in water.

As one studies the medicine man's use of pharmacology he grows aware of legitimate and enduring value. There is undeniable merit in such entries as the still most used sore-throat remedy made of dried portulaca leaves *(Portulaca oleracea)* mixed with dried ginger root and made into a tasty broth.

The list of curative agents is enormously long and in greatest part still unpublished. The witch doctor's utilization of medicinal plants establishes an exciting scholarship. In a less tangible though certainly no less tantalizing way the same holds for what some would designate as medicinal magic. For the medicine of hinterland Liberia is a synthesis of a spirits world, one of magical conceptions and projected causations; one in which the pleasure or anger of spirits relates to and intermittently supersedes all natural sciences, including the health sciences. Yet there is impressive folk logic in much of the diagnostics and there is much of ingenious psychotherapy.

At least in some instances the witch doctor regards congenital deformities as an outcome of evil magic; appropriately, they require magical treatment. The condition of hunchback is one example. There is a common jungle tree called *kue* (*Pentaclethra macrophylla* Bent), which invariably grows with a hump or twist of its trunk. The medicine man converses with the spirit of the tree, after which he takes a rock and breaks off some of the tree's bark. Then he pounds the bark into a portion of clay, seasons it with pepper seed, and rubs the paste over the hump of the hunchback.

"Punitive medicine" is still another phase of the jungle-edge psychotherapy. Dr. Harley has reported a technique for correcting (punishing) a woman who has a "big mouth"—i.e., who is loud and insolent. The medicine man begins by taking a young shoot of *fai*

(Manniophyton africanum) and picking off the leaves, speaking a magic word for each leaf removed. Then, using his left hand, he strips the leaves from a branch of *pu (Deinbellia piniate)*, in the same way. He beats up the double handful of leaves and rolls the mass over the ground where the woman has urinated. Direct dosage of this appalling mess is said to produce bladder irritation—quite probably an understatement. In time the woman pleads with the man of magic to make her well. When he agrees, the loudmouth is supposedly cured both of her polyuria and her loudness and insolence.

In common with medical sciences and arts at large, the tribal physicianry can be, sometimes is, put to even more illicit uses. For example there is, or quite recently was, the Mano Cult of Thieves, whose members reputedly used potent herb brews to protect themselves from arrest or capture while stealing. In the main such strategic "medicines" have not been strong enough to impress the government's courts.

With the passing years some procedures of tribal folk medicine inevitably fade away. Others endure for the very good reason that they are functionally sound and worthy of accreditation by and in any capable medical practice. Among the latter is the traditional practice and appreciation of cleanliness. In body as in mind tribal Liberians as a whole are among the cleanest people to be found anywhere. Daily or twice daily bathing is traditional and, for most, mandatory. As a rule a tribal village is impressively well kept and clean. Although usually lacking sewage or piped water (these facilities are gradually materializing in some of the tribe towns), "night soils," garbage, and other wastes are consistently removed from the huts and meticulously buried or burned.

This is listable as traditional disease prevention. There are many other traditional pivots for preventive medicine but the total validity and worth of the folk medicine must be measured in continuing, live-or-die needs. Liberia, like most of tribe-rooted Africa, stays profoundly dependent on the *zo* or *nye ke mi*, the tribal midwife, and the many other bona fide savants of health and survival in the still preponderant hinterlands.

What is hopefully termed modern medicine is gaining in tribal

Liberia and tribal Africa as a vast whole, with a distinguishable share of its gains directly attributable to or correlated with folk medicine.

But dependence on the latter remains momentous to many newcomers or first-time visitors, almost terrifyingly so. The indigenous tribal practitioner is still very much needed both as doer and wayshower.

The writer, who doesn't always comprehend quickly, grasped the scope of dependence on folk, or *zo*, medicine during his very first day of Liberian hinterland exploration. I set out to gain some small degree of acquaintance with the Mano "nation," which includes several thousand square miles of north central Liberia and extends boundaries into the valleys of the St. John and Ya rivers. In all, the Manos number somewhere near 200,000 people. At the time (1945), two physicians with M.D.'s were available to serve the entire population. As this is written the total is reportedly four, but only three are in active practice.

South and east of the Ya Valley are the rolling or hilly forest lands of the Gios, and beyond, the Kpelle country. As of 1945, all these tribespeople were totally dependent on native doctors with only peripheral help of two medical missionaries and one mission nurse. The native tribal practitioners were serving or striving to serve their own and neighboring people as general practitioners, obstetricians, pharmacists, epidemiologists, and bone setters.

Here again the vista is changing, but by no means decisively. Without the help of folkish practitioners the present sprinkling of professionally schooled doctors and nurses would be situated very much like one small weary pygmy committed to herding two huge herds of wild elephants predisposed to travel in opposite directions.

In many ways—through the years and at present—the folk medicine and its practitioners have proved helpful to the more formally qualified physicians and other health scientists. In a few instances the tribal lores have impeded, but as usual and in the main, the exceptions have joined in confirming the rule.

During my first stay in Liberia I became reverently acquainted with Nurse Portia Jensen, a Norwegian-born, American-schooled registered nurse who took on a career mission as a Lutheran missionary to Liberia. Some twenty years before my time Nurse Jensen had "chopped her way" into the extremely remote Santoya country, then about seventy miles inland from any faint facsimile of a road. Throughout the ensuing thirty-five years she remained the only white woman and the only formally qualified nurse in what was expertly listed as the most completely isolated hundred square miles of all Equatorial Africa.

Nurse Jensen, still remembered by the more elderly tribespeople as the white god-woman, centered her almost fabulously busy career on founding and directing a children's clinic.

That prime devotion, of course, required complementary service as obstetrician, dietician, supervisor and "trainer" of native midwives, public vaccinator (when required materials were available), open-bush practitioner, and emergency surgeon. In career line of duty Nurse Jensen also qualified as a most dependable and charitably objective appraiser and colleague of tribal medicine men and women. She insisted that through the years she had learned more from them than she had taught them, granted that she had taught the *zos* a great deal, and for the most part had found them rewarding students.

The beloved Portia learned at first hand of the limitations and lapses of tribal medicine along with its many practical advantages. In line of self-assumed duties she recognized its severely limited facilities for combating such pathogenic enemies as venereal diseases, pneumonias, malarias, and many afflictions of both superficial and internal parasites.

Tribal medicine cannot fend against the ravages of leprosy, the filariases, sleeping sickness, the snail fluke disease, yaws, and a great many more. But Nurse Jensen astutely recognized the very real psychotherapeutic values of *zo* medicine and did her unassuming best to utilize and perpetuate them. Before her death in 1956 she had been able to assist medical researchers and medical scholars in exploiting the knowledge, perceptiveness, the profound human understanding of tribal folk medicine.

An old Buzzi proverb says in effect, health and harvest fail or thrive together. Angie Brooks, Liberia's tribe-born assistant secretary of state and first woman president of the United Nations Security Council, points out with exceptional pertinence that improved health, harvests, and government are as interdependent as the three legs of a mammy sitting stool, and that the three require the "marriage" of the folkish and time-proved old ways with the cogent and practiceable new. Like enduring wild-growing plant life, Liberia's great heritage of tribal medicine endures and challenges and waits to benefit.

III. Yesterday and Tomorrow

13

"TO LIVE TOGETHER OR PERISH ALONE"

THROUGHOUT the 1920s Charles C. B. King had grown to be an affable and meaningful hallmark for Africa's lone republic. This was no happenstance. The King presidency had completely filled the decade and it had contributed ably to bringing tribal Liberians into the national community. In his first inaugural address King had stated that his country's absolute choice was whether to live together or perish alone.

Anyone could see that perishing alone would be easy to attain, whereas living together—tribe with tribe and sovereign nation with neighboring colonies, remained much easier to say than to do. Accordingly, and as an inveterate scholar, King had sought, as he put it, to learn his way along. As secretary of state he had vigorously studied the obtaining practices in international relations and read what he termed the darkly distorting mirrors of African colonialism. As president he had shifted his focus of study to the needs and complexities of Liberia's component tribes. Before the 1920s ended he was undeniably one of the best-informed students of tribe life, traditions, economics, and miscellaneous assets and needs. The foregoing was astutely proved in 1928 when King and his administration managed to establish Liberia's first health department, which was predicated on a well-weighed comprehension of the merits and shortcomings of tribal medicine.

King was well aware and freely admitted that when he resigned from the presidency he had led Liberia in what he termed a great dark vale of adversities. The Fernando Po affair had left very deep scars. The prestige of Liberia was severely pummeled and bemired and the aftermaths were being negatively scored in areas other than diplomatic and prestigious. Included was an excessive and almost instant slump of the already anemic foreign trade.

In recognizable and substantial part, the alarming trade losses were in correlation with a relentlessly growing and increasingly worldwide depression. As early as 1928 African trade with Europe, particularly the United Kingdom, France, Germany, and Spain, had been showing disturbing lapses which traders termed "tightenings."

The total story was not easy to analyze or recite convincingly, but well before 1930 the proposition was entirely evident that Africa was in line for being a first major overseas casualty of the "tightenings." Understandably France and Britain, then with the largest colonial holdings in Africa, were making somewhat better than nominal efforts to hold trade doors open to their own colonies; the same held for some of the smaller colonial powers, particularly Belgium and Italy.

But the broader quandary was that throughout most of the previous three decades African trade had been rather consistently even if very unreasonably subordinated to that of the Pacific tropics, particularly lower Southeast Asia, including Malaya, and the then Netherlands East Indies. The United States remained a strong contributor to the less than wholly rational favoritism. By 1930, the United States led all nations in volume and values of tropical imports—due principally to rapidly multiplying American demands for rubber, palm oils, and special fibers. But almost 95 percent of American imports were from the Pacific tropics. Roughly four percent, in greatest part coffee, was from the American tropics, and, at most, one percent from Africa.

Liberia's export manifests, in which leopard pelts and palm kernels continued to vie for first place, clearly indicated the commercial cross that the undersize African republic, which still lacked a dependable commercial sponsor, was doomed to bear.

The persistently darkening depression aggravated the disadvantages.

By 1930 Liberian revenue collections were again on the skids and heading toward the near-collapse levels of the 1870s. The fulfillment of routine government obligations, such as public education, health and sanitation, and minimal road maintenance, dawdled at the brink of collapse. Africa was poor but Liberia was even poorer than most of its colonial neighbors. And Liberia's unjustly imposed diplomatic peonage certainly wasn't helping.

King's successor, Edwin Barclay, was the philosophical, enormously sensitive, frequently brooding nephew of the "Magnificent Mulatto" and former president, Arthur Barclay. Like his revered uncle, Edwin was a devoted worker, an aristocrat and, as he said, a habituated wonderer. He was also an exceptionally able prophet. Even before 1930, when he assumed the presidency of Liberia, the younger Barclay clearly foresaw the outbreak of the Second World War. I personally became acquainted with Barclay after he had served his fourteen-year "tour" as president, but his amazingly capable memory permitted him to recall virtually any day or circumstance during the years that he termed the Great Wait.

The Barclay clairvoyance termed Hitler's loud, bold "scrapping" of the Versailles Treaty, beginning in 1933, as the actual beginning of World War II. Edwin Barclay promptly foresaw the oncoming efforts of the Third Reich to effect a takeover in North Africa, using propaganda as an entry wedge. He insisted that Germany's forfeiture of its African colonies, by the hard and contriving terms of the Versailles Treaty, had permanently obliterated possibilities for legitimate or constructive German participation in African affairs. But he had never believed that the structures of nineteenth-century colonialism could survive in Africa without profound revision. He regarded the British mewlings about African isolationism as absolute hypocrisy, and he listened to pitying remarks about Liberian "depressive economy" with a somewhat mocking smile. "What other kind of an economy have we ever really known?" he inquired.

But Barclay was determined that even if his country could not prosper, it could and would maintain neutrality with regard to the surely developing super war. "Liberia is and will remain a bona fide, self-sustaining, honorable pacifistic nation," he insisted, adding that in attaining this Liberia had no choice other than to play a waiting game.

"Waiting game" was the essence of Liberian foreign policy throughout the 1930s. The president neither promised nor anticipated any marked alleviation of its poverty or its increasing isolation. "We must let our people, particularly our tribespeople, and the world at large come to us in peace and as friends," he reiterated. Barclay waited graciously and approvingly while more and more tribespeople came to Monrovia to seek and give help, and as Bassas, Vais, Golas, and many other tribal "talents" continued to form attachments with the national government.

Meanwhile Barclay continued to work stubbornly and in great part deftly to improve relations with the United States. These labors were severely impeded by a number of persisting lacks. One of these was the penalty of poverty which forced Liberia to make do with an extremely small diplomatic corps. For several years the black republic did not even have an embassy in Washington; its "American representation" was limited to one consul-general, located in New York. Barclay sought to serve as ex officio and in absentia ambassador to Washington. His efforts met with considerable success; at least by 1936 the Franklin D. Roosevelt administration was showing recognizable friendliness toward Liberia.

In keeping with Barclay's predictions, American relations continued to improve. There were pragmatic motivations which the Liberian president had vividly anticipated.

The years 1940 and 1941 merged into a vast, bloody holocaust. The war, which FDR was terming the Global War, was roaring along with Nazi Germany conspicuously ahead. Hitler's Germany had substantially taken over Western Europe, penetrated Scandinavia, opened its great, mad eastern front. France had "fallen." Britain was holed up for its absolute fight for survival. The USSR was bleeding into place as the military savior of the West. Meanwhile, like Napoleon, Hitler had moodily recognized Africa as the "continent of decision" and North Africa as the "crossroads of destiny" for the white man's world. The United States, with an already assumed place as the "arsenal for democracy," was being more and more specifically committed to fight in Africa. Inevitably Liberia was the most efficacious entranceway.

This recognizable fact of life and strategy was very intelligently reiterated by the Harriman mission to Moscow in 1941. The Harriman party had traveled by air and chosen to return by way of Africa. Its leader had cogently noted that the second largest continent of earth was still virtually lacking landing fields, without which the Allies could not rationally hope to win, or even gain the offensive.

The few extemporized military air strips then available were small and almost wholly lacking in essential weather-forecasting and radio facilities. The United States war supplies services were already meeting extreme difficulties in "ferrying" aircraft to prospective Allies by the northern routes; Japan's Far East conquests were virtually blockading the Pacific air routes. Attempts to utilize the southern lanes via South America and Africa were largely invalidated by the appalling absence of airport facilities in Africa.

During 1940 the Airport Development Program, for which the Pan American Airways System was serving as "agent" or aircraft deliverer for the Allied Forces in Africa, had already confronted the impediment which the Harriman report summarized. Pan American engineers had already recognized the strategic advantages of placing a long-range air base in Liberia; the recommended site was the Farmington valley, about fifty miles below and inland from Monrovia.

Without a formal contract but with the consent of the Liberian government, the Firestone Plantations Company began clearing land and building a first "long-flight" airport, at the time the largest in Africa. The site was named Roberts Field, honoring Liberia's first president.

Early in 1942 the U.S. Army Air Force took over the enterprise and with a regiment of Negro troops at hand, completed the primary base for the South Atlantic aircraft ferry. By then the so-called Atlantic Narrows were the prime route to lower Asia and the South Pacific; Japan was in control of the Hawaii-Midway-Wake-New Guinea routes. Roberts Field, meanwhile, held the additional advantage of being within bomber range of the temporary "Rommel Reich" in North Africa and of what Churchill termed the underbelly of Nazi-held Europe. Almost overnight Liberia's Roberts Field became one of the really crucial air bases of the Allies.

Yet the fact persisted that Liberia was still neutral. The act of granting lands and permission for the great, pivotal air base was perilous and potentially ruinous as well as unprecedentedly bold. A Rommel victory to the north, which "experts" were predicting, and the ensuing Nazi sweep over Africa would almost certainly see the black republic crushed like a dropped egg.

Yet here a direly imperiled Negro nation, still technically at peace, was delivering to the United States one of the most courageous and endangering entrustments ever made by one sovereign power to another. By "executive agreement," without support of formal treaty, Liberia yielded additionally to the United States the right to build, control, operate, and defend any and all "desirable" military and commercial airports in its territory, including a seaplane base at Fisherman's Lake, and permission to preempt lands for building roads, fortifications, storage for war materiel, including "housing and communications." Liberia further granted the privileges of police power. The one restriction, recognizably astute, was that the United States withdraw from Liberia within six months after the "official ending" of the war.

By 1943 the multiple operation of Roberts Field was fully effected. Hundreds and presently thousands of U.S. aircraft used the great airport, either for combat base or for a ferrying stop en route to India, the Middle East, Russia, China, or the South Pacific.

All this was a prelude for critically important peacetime uses. By 1946 Pan American Airways would be using Roberts Field as a "work base" on its Congo and South African flights; other international airlines would follow suit. Meanwhile the U.S. Army Air Corps proceeded to build and open a dozen landing strips in the Liberian interior, and a major hydroplane base on Fisherman's Lake.

Liberia, of course, was able to leaven its risks with self-evident rewards. During the early 1940s the black republic was still appallingly lacking in surface communications. All Liberia then had barely a hundred miles of public roads. There was no pavement and the longest travelable stretch was the forty miles between Monrovia and Harbel.

During 1943 the U.S. Army Air Force, using a company of Army engineers as construction workers, undertook to extend the "jungle ribbon" to the French Guinea boundary, thereby providing a first land route from the farthest inland point to the sea. The Army roadbuilders were withdrawn before they could complete their task, but a Firestone Plantations work force, financed by a holdover of U.S. Army funds, presently established the mirey beginnings of a first trans-Liberia road. Various tribes joined in opening access roads, in completing the throughway from Monrovia to Tappita, and, in the Eastern Province, opening new pack trails. The persisting difficulties were in completing the would-be travel ways.

In the steep hills and higher plateaus of the farther interior there was a need for machinery, expert engineering, and complex bridge installations that the tribespeople were unable to provide. By almost miraculous stages the first dim shapes of a nationwide highway system began reaching into such fabulously remote places as Zorzor in the Western Province, previously accessible only by foot trails, and finally into the lost wilderness of Kolahun, one of the least known of "wonderlands" of Equatorial Africa.

By the latter 1940s substantially more than half of Liberia had been made somewhat better than theoretically accessible to automobiles. No less amazingly, autos splashed and puttered in to accommodate. The earlier echelons were mostly erstwhile Army Jeeps, some time-battered sedans owned by traders, and the ubiquitous pickup trucks. Almost instantly the tribespeople were zestful for the automotive life. As the internal-combustion engine proliferated, nobody could convincingly explain who taught whom to drive or how gasoline found its way into so many tanks. There were no more than a dozen or so filling stations in the Republic; none at all in the hinterlands. But the tribespeople joined in the great mutation. Within a very few months chiefs and commoners and their wives and offspring were all plunging and sloshing awheel and, no doubt, enjoying every moment of it.

The more remarkable development was in the sequence—the air age had reached Liberia ahead of the auto age, and both were ahead of ocean shipping from a deepwater harbor. Liberia's ocean front had never been blessed with so much as one natural harbor site suited to deep-draft shipping. Through the years Monrovia, the most used port of entry, had remained a so-called lighter port, afflicted by most incompatible tides, shoals, sand or mud bars, and otherwise unable to admit any sizable ships to pier services.

The shallow estuary of the whimsical Mesurado River could

provide only minimal docking facilities for surf boats and portage craft for ships that were obliged to wait at anchor well out to sea. Bushrod Island, which the Mesurado River separates from Monrovia, marked the most feasible site for building a harbor. The mouth of Liberia's most used traffic stream, the St. Paul (or St. Paul's) River, is about five miles north of Bushrod Island, but like the Mesurado's its headwaters had remained formidably littered with sand bars.

Building a harbor would be difficult and costly. Even the preparatory work involved the formidable task of erecting at least two mile-long jetties for restraining the very vigorous tides. These projections would, of course, have to be built of rock, and the only adequate source of this was a hillock outcrop of granite, which is notoriously difficult to quarry. The eventual cost of an efficient port terminal would unquestionably add up to many millions of dollars; twenty million was a minimal estimate.

Franklin Delano Roosevelt, homeward bound from the historic Casablanca Conference, chose to have a firsthand look at what he described as the harbor that wasn't a harbor. FDR had been advised correctly that operation of Roberts Field, the crucial air base, was being seriously handicapped by the lack of a competent shipping port. Petroleum tankers, for example, were obliged to discharge plane fuels into buoyed pipelines reaching a mile or more seaward. The awkwardness, and, in view of the war needs, the dangers of the situation were evident. Roosevelt was in an arranging mood. He tersely addressed the Liberian president: "I understand you want a harbor built at Monrovia. I think it can be arranged."

By means of the Lend-Lease Act and with the remarkable competence of Liberian workers it was accomplished. Preliminary details were completed in June, 1944, at the White House, where the Liberian president (Barclay) and his newly elected (May, 1943) successor, William V. S. Tubman, were guests. It was the first such hospitality ever shown the Negro republic. The first forthright move included surveys that sagaciously recommended that the work be done by a private American construction company.

Again without the formality of a treaty the Liberian government agreed to provide the site and approve the building not only of a harbor but a free port, i.e., "a free foreign trade zone to be operated for the mutual benefit of the United States of America and the Republic of Liberia, and all nations with which the United States of America and Liberia maintain friendly relations, under such conditions and by such means as may be hereafter provided. . . ."

"Such conditions" provided for the establishment and supervision of a port authority; also the repayment of the United States' monetary advance by recipient Liberia from revenues derived in operating the port and its incidental facilities and from other Liberian sources. The African republic also granted to the United States "the right to establish, use, maintain, improve, supplement, guard and control such naval, air, and military facilities and installations at the site of the port and the general vicinity thereof as may be desired by the Government of the United States of America for protection of [its] strategic interests in the South Atlantic. . . ."

Obviously it was no easy bargain or blooming philanthropy; clearly the initial allocation of $15 million in Lend-Lease funds was conspicuously inadequate. The astute choice of Bushrod Island as a base for the "free trade zone" also required building a major bridge and railroad connection—at the time Liberia had a railroad but the harbor building was not possible without railroad facilities.

There were red tape and government-lawyer delays immediately forthcoming from official Washington, and the usual gushings of gobbledygook. But the undertaking presently moved into action. Its most effective resource was the ready availability of Liberian labor, headed by an initial employment of about 2,000 tribesmen. Washington planners had originally envisaged the importation of construction labor; Brazil was being suggested as a source. The drawback there was that Brazil did not have anywhere near enough construction workers to fill its own home needs. As Firestone had done two decades before, Raymond Concrete, as contractor, turned to the native workers and found them not only good, but superior. The Raymond management set up both a training school and an apprentice system for helping tribesmen qualify for the more complex assignments. About 1,800 of the first 2,000 employed eagerly volunteered for the technical training.

Within weeks young tribesmen who had never seen dump trucks, bulldozers, draglines or caterpillar tractors before were successfully operating all these and many other kinds of construction machinery. Others who had never seen a rock quarry qualified within a very few days as expert quarriers and drill men. Many more, who had never seen a railroad, joined in building and presently operating a shortline, "Tom Thumb" railroad. Native canoeists changed quickly to steam barge or towboat handlers. Throughout its three years of building time the free port had proved the truly amazing adaptability and competence of the tribal workers.

Monrovia Harbor began to materialize as one of the most impressive of manmade ocean ports. As soon as the jetties were completed hundreds of acres of seafront were dredged out sufficiently to provide anchorage for sea-going vessels. Railroad trackage, storage facilities, bridges, tank farms, a power plant, connecting and access roads, modern houses, and many other facilities materialized; all were alien yet all provided tangible proof of the impressive adaptability of the tribespeople.

By 1949 the Monrovia Port Management Company, a Delaware corporation, took over the temporary or interim management of the free port. Nine American companies which were or planned to be operating in Liberia took over as temporary principals of the management company. They were committed by the company's charter to serve the Liberian government as a "proper agent" for "managing, operating, and administering the port and harbor of Monrovia and the appurtenances thereof in the public interest and in a nondiscriminatory manner." The charter also confirmed the Liberian government's authority to grant concessions that are "customary or desirable in free port districts." The temporary company received a fee of 10 percent of the gross income of the free port and delivered the remainder of "net income" to the Liberian government but with all income committed for transmission to the United States government until the construction costs were repaid.

Within less than a year after its completion date the free port's trade volume rose from about 5,000 tons to 16,000 tons a month and continued to grow. The almost instant benefit of trade affected virtually all of Liberia and fully half of Equatorial West Africa, where a superior seaport is a most special gift from heaven. Having provided the site and the indispensable workers, the first African republic set about paying the tab.

Among the almost instant beneficiaries was Liberia's first industry and then principal export, natural rubber. World War II was

Armageddon on rubber tires, and as the biggest of all the international brawls neared its climax, Liberia took its place as the most effective supplier of natural rubber, with transportation a primary advantage. As soon as Roberts Field was in operation, the Firestone Plantations Company began pressing raw rubber into midget bales for airplane shipment to the United States. For the first time the crucial urgency of war caused a bulk raw material, in this instance about 50,000 tons of it, to gain what amounted to airmail status. War needs justified this, but understandably, legitimate peacetime needs and markets could not perpetuate it. The most provident source of wartime rubber supplies could not endure without improved processing and shipping; the new free port of Monrovia made both possible.

Most of the time since 1930 Liberian rubber had gone to sea from a most unsuitable surf port at the coastal village of Marshall. The longtime practice was to move baled rubber to shipside by barge or lighter. By the middle 1940s the rapidly advancing rubber industry had proved that carefully refined liquid latex is much preferable to baled, pelleted, or any other form of cured or hard rubber. The changeover to liquid latex called for a complete revision of transportation. When the new free port was completed, Firestone was able to use tank ships, set up pier tank forms, and otherwise pioneer in the changeover. Other growers, including citizen owners of rubber groves, were able to follow suit. The new port at Monrovia had most to do with making the industry-saving advances possible.

An even more significant development was in the immediate offing. That, as time would shortly prove, was the exploitation of the superior Liberian iron ore. Observant people who had traveled or explored Liberia knew that a great deal, somewhere near half, of the country was a potential iron mine. My own awareness of this dated back to my misadventures in Liberia in 1945, when, in tramping the hinterlands, I discovered that a compass is simply not dependable there. Surface lodes establish that fact of elementary science. As I presently learned, too, even aboard coastwise ships compasses behave peculiarly, frequently misleadingly; but when one ventures into the hinterlands, reliance on a compass may assure getting lost.

There was plenty of less mortifying evidence of the presence of iron lodes. In the Zorzor country where I stopped at a tribe village to ask directions, I found myself in a community of native blacksmiths who smelted out their own supplies from ores obtained from their yardways. They "burned down" the iron-rich subsoil in simple clay ovens and used the recovered iron for making hoes, rakes, and other hand tools, also the small twisted iron sticks that many hinterland Liberians still use for money; at the time twelve of the "twistos" represented the value of an American quarter or a British shilling.

During the same backwoods ramblings I gained my first acquaintance with the Bomi Hills, located about forty miles north of Monrovia. In this area I discovered that a compass almost instantly goes completely berserk. More expert eyes had made like observations many years earlier.

I learned in any case that about ten years previously a geological survey team employed by a Dutch mining firm, the Noord Europeesche Ertz en Pyriet Maatschappy, had made a painstaking survey of the Bomi iron lands which indicated the presence of tens of millions of tons of recoverable hematite and magnetite with iron contents of 60 percent, or thereabouts, of bulk. The estimated recovery proportion was higher than that of Sweden's Kiruna mines, a prime source of Swedish steel, and substantially higher than that of the already fading Mesabi Range in the Michigan–Great Lakes region of the United States.

But for reasons other than geological the huge granite-lined basins which hold the Bomi lodes intact had waited without takers. The entire countryside then grew in tall, dark green forests that admitted no roads and extremely few trails. The first survey had not been taken seriously; rumors were that its sponsoring company had Nazi associations and the Liberian government would not deal with it.

In 1938 an exploration party sponsored by the United States Steel Company resumed the survey, but abandoned it because the searchers recognized that no deep-water shipping facilities were available for economical export of the ore and that a difficult and expensive ore-carrying railroad would have to be built. More recently—during 1943, in response to a request by the Liberian president (Edwin Barclay)—the U.S. Department of the Interior had dispatched a surveying team to appraise the overall iron resources of Liberia. (This writer has never been able to locate the results of the Interior Department's survey.)

During the following year a venturesome Long Islander named Landell Christie came into the Bomi Hills, originally in the quest of strategic sites for air strips. Christie was the derring-do type. At seventeen he had gone on a one-boy gold hunt in the frontier Klondike. Surviving that, he had next gained admission to the U.S. Military Academy; he endured two years at West Point. The "washed-out" cadet next braved the political jungles of the New York waterfront and took over the direction of a successful barge company.

Directly after Pearl Harbor, Christie received an Army commission and was assigned to Africa as a transportation officer. His ensuing service tour was impressive. Captain, Major, and presently Lieutenant Colonel Christie located and directed the building and opening of a "string" of military landing strips and temporary air bases from Cape Town to Cairo. While "chasing down" possible landing strips in Liberia, the Colonel gained acquaintance with the Bomi Hills.

Following discharge Christie visited in Monrovia, met the president and other principals, organized the Liberia Mining Company, employed one of the original Dutch surveyors of the Bomi Hills as a senior consultant, and obtained a first exploitation concession for iron and all other minerals—excepting gold and platinum—within a 3-million-acre "slice" of the Bomi Hills lands. It was a very poor concession from Liberia's standpoint. Initially the Christie company agreed to pay to the Liberian government a royalty of five cents a ton on iron ore "withdrawn" plus a microscopic honorarium ranging from two cents to as much as twenty cents per ton on Bessemer-grade pig iron recovered from the Liberian ore. The obviously avaricious agreement did not avoid venality, but it did provide a specific working entry into an impressive new realm of iron. The concessionaire agreed to build motor roads and presently a railroad to connect the mining site with the oceanside capital. The enabling factor was the excellent new harbor of Monrovia.

In 1949 the Christie company began building its iron-ore railroad. This proved to be an exceptionally difficult and colorful venture, the more so because the route led through some of the densest forests remaining on earth and some of the more incompatible swamp lands in all of Equatorial Africa. By then, Republic Steel had got into the act by providing supplemental credit, experienced counsel, and advance orders for the superbly rich ore. The Export-Import Bank also came through with a $4 million "assistance loan" that covered most of the cost of the railroad building. Finally on April 16, 1951, Liberia's first trainload of ore, on its first cross-country railroad, moved from mine site to the nation's first deep-water harbor.

The reach and consequence of Liberian iron resources would multiply. But for better and for worse the beginning was made. The enchanting and once wildly remote Bomi Hills are beginning to be gouged and scraped by uproarious excavating machinery. Work camps and new villages have been nicked into the great forests; new farms, stores, and native markets came to life. The Christie enterprise was deftly publicized, at least in the United States. *Fortune* lauded the Christie acumen; *Time* labeled him astute businesswise; the *Wall Street Journal* was more cautious but nonetheless favorably impressed; the financial pages of the gently moldering New York *Herald-Tribune* cheered his plays with reverent headlines and a prose ode that carried over among advertisements on page 41.

Apparently the American commercial press overlooked the fact that the Christie concession was a memento, one can hope a final one, of nineteenth-century colonialism. Its original text, now voluntarily revised, was a restatement of the Karl Peters "philosophy" of public good by way of private advantage. On that basis Colonel Christie and his colleagues had proved themselves persuasive and effective promoters. More importantly, the Liberian government, with the strong new Tubman administration then in charge, had taken a fling at implementing an open-door policy purposefully aimed at attracting investment capital for opening a great and at the time undeveloped resource of an underdeveloped country. The darker side was that the Christie concession was cynical and privileged. Fortunately it was not indelible; it could and presently would be "liberalized."

Liberia, meanwhile, was gaining another tally in its struggle to beat down the long-hurtful forces of isolation.

14

THE ENGAGING CHEERLEADER

THE LATE Edward R. Stettinius, Jr., was a preeminent American success story of the 1920s and '30s. He was handsome, wealthy, socially delightful, and almost fabulously successful as a corporation stairs climber. Still in his twenties he was a high ranking vice president of the nation's largest industrial corporation; in his mid-thirties he was chairman of the board of the world's largest steel company.

Then in his very early forties he abruptly emerged as an internationalist and an ardent champion of what were then being termed racial appreciation and social justice. His fervent championship of Liberia was a noteworthy demonstration of this transition or, as many interested onlookers believed, this resurrection.

In any event, "E.R.S." began his most unusual career as an engaging hallmark of the aspirations of almost any believing member of the Junior Chamber of Commerce and climaxed it by substantially enlarging that hallmark.

Edward Stettinius, Jr., was also a favored child of the era of great American affluence, a Prince Charming of the most secure royalty now remaining on earth, the very wealthy American. Chicago-born in 1900, he was timed with the advent of the American century of vast wealth already accumulated by the privileged few, who included his own family.

In keeping with his background Stettinius attended Connecticut's Pomfret School, and from there entered the University of Virginia, where as the saying went, he smiled his way through the four-year course in five years. His more notable collegiate achievements included winning the nickname of Abstemious Stettinius and serving as head cheerleader for a varsity football team that almost invariably lost.

The last-mentioned shortcoming did not hold for Edward's subsequent business career. Following his college graduation in 1924 he was figuratively blasted into the General Motors orbit by being made employment manager for G.M.'s Hyatt Roller Bearings Works in New Jersey. From there he moved to Detroit as a General Motors executive assistant, and following a two-year stint as assistant to Alfred P. Sloan, the great freewheeling and most revered General Motors president, he emerged at twenty-eight as Vice President for Industrial and Public Relations. From General Motors Stettinius moved upward to U.S. Steel. There at thirty-six he was made chairman of the board of directors, the youngest chairman of the nation's first multibillion-dollar corporation. By then he held directorships in more than a dozen major corporations and was beginning to receive a continuing trickle of honorary college degrees and other special citations that collectively almost buckled the type frames of *Who's Who in America.*

At thirty-eight, using Franklin D. Roosevelt's personal presentation of a symbolic penny box of matches for burning his bridges behind him, Stettinius resigned from U.S. Steel and joined what was being labeled the Second New Deal. By then Roosevelt was proving himself the most prolific political kingmaker in the long history of American appointive politics, and there was materializing evidence that Edward R. Stettinius, Jr., home address, The Horseshoe, Rapidan, Culpeper County, Virginia, would shortly emerge as one of the New Deal's most prodigious princes.

From tryout posts in the Council of National Defense and the chairmanship of the enormously powerful priority board of the Office of Production Management, the photogenic and prematurely gray young man, early in 1941, was Roosevelt-lifted to the then extremely important post of Lend-Lease Administrator. From that elevation Stettinius heard of Liberia and the incubations of the Monrovia Free Port Project. He heard more during his ensuing tenure as special assistant to the president of the United States and during his subsequent brief and turbulent tenure as secretary of state.

As first officer of the cabinet and successor to the magnificent Cordell Hull, Stettinius had what he later termed "one heck of a tough time." He held the secretaryship only from November, 1944, to June, 1945, but during those eight harassed months he had opportunity to give a great deal of thought to ways and means of helping developing nations help themselves, and also to gain on-the-scene acquaintance with Monrovia.

Stettinius later confided to this writer that his "feeling interest" in Liberia and Africa as a vast whole took root directly following his attendance at the Yalta Conference as official advisor to FDR.

"I'd never really seen Africa before that trip," he reminisced, "and in a very short time I saw a mighty lot—in great part hard to believe and impossible to accept as unavoidable or necessary. I saw poverty more abject and humiliating than I had ever before even glimpsed. . . . People who had never worn shoes, never seen a dentist or a medical doctor, or known how it feels to be decently fed or dressed even for one day. For the first time, too, I sensed the really splendid potentials of the native Negro tribe as a basis for improved government and economic development in Africa. I saw that the wonderful people and other resources of Africa are for real, but they weren't and aren't getting a Chinaman's chance. I glimpsed about-to-be mothers in horrible pain because they had no anesthetic—not so much as a can of ether in a thousand miles—they lay dying while giving birth. . . . I saw chiefs' wives who are still whip-driven slaves . . . and half-starved men, women, and children clawing out wild-growing roots from soils as fertile as any in the world. And I said to myself, 'Ed, we've got to do something about this—something real, and now!' "

Stettinius had very few comforting memories of his tenure and attainments as secretary of state, and he did not remember his service as Lend-Lease administrator with his customary warming smile. He described the building of the harbor and free port of Monrovia as "setting in a door for a house that hadn't been built."

He could and did correlate Lend-Lease participation with "the new internationalism," but contended that "living, doing friendship among nations is the very least we can aim for, and that is America's first order of business." His greatest pride and satisfaction were based on his labors as a "peace builder." Successively and in great part competently, Stettinius had served as chairman of the Dumbarton Oaks "conversations" on international security, as delegation head for the Mexico City Conference on Problems of War and Peace, as an aide at the Yalta Conference, as chairman of the American delegation to the United Nations Conference on International Organization, and as first U.S. delegate to the United Nations Security Council. He looked on while Liberia was admitted to the United Nations and plugged for its subsequent election to the Security Council as a first African member of that group.

From the vastly publicized galaxy of peace plannings and sweet theorizings about internationalism, Edward Stettinius gained substantiation of his belief that "enlightened corporate business, a special hallmark of American organizational talent," provided the best way-builder to enlightened internationalism. He saw Liberia as a particularly appropriate testing area.

Accordingly, beginning in 1947, after the Truman administration had less than subtly heaved him overboard, he set about organizing what he purposefully named the Stettinius Associates–Liberia, Inc. That accomplished, as its board chairman he next approached the person and administration of William V. S. Tubman, who was valiantly launched on his first term as president of Liberia, with a "statement of understanding for the development of human and natural resources of the Republic of Liberia."

This statement, which the Liberian president approved after extensive revisions as "a distinctly loose and philosophical convention," was nevertheless sincere and significant trail blazing. It sustained the Tubman "open door policy" which clearly stipulates that American and other bona fide foreign enterprises are and will be welcomed by Liberia so long as they recognize the Republic's status as prime owner of its resources and accept common responsibilities for the nation's concern for the welfare of its people. Both in spirit and text the Stettinius statement of understanding was a mutual-trust replacement of the colonial-style exploitation, somewhat belatedly exemplified by the Christie concession, with an "enlightened developmental partnership between the Government of Liberia and Stettinius Associates–Liberia, Inc."

The specific proposals, as stated on September 3, 1947, were that Stettinius Associates–Liberia would directly establish The Liberia Company to promote and effect development of specific Liberian resources with due approval of the Liberian government and with 25 percent of capital stock issued directly to the Liberian government as prime compensation for the rights granted. Ten percent of the capital stock, again in hand or forthcoming, would be delivered to a nonprofit trust to be known as The Liberian Foundation, Inc., which would be devoted to appraising and advancing "the social aspects of the program for the development of Liberia."

The president of Liberia was authorized to appoint a "proper proportion of the directors of the said company or companies" and the Liberian government, at its discretion, would properly grant "comprehensive rights" for a specified period of years. In addition to the direct ownership grant of capital stock, Liberia would receive a fourth of all principal and incidental earnings.

The preamble of the statement of understanding proclaimed assuringly that the Liberian government and Stettinius Associates–Liberia "will jointly participate in a cooperative effort to bring to bear the advantages and benefits of private resources in capital and specialized knowledge from the United States and the natural resources of Liberia with a view to improving the levels of living of the people of Liberia and to enhance and expand their opportunities for economic and social advancement."

The statement further committed the Liberia Company to "shortly inaugurate" an impressive list of specific projects. These would include mining developments, lumbering operations, fisheries, "machinery for collecting, grading, processing, handling, and marketing of agricultural products," also subsidiary companies to import and export commodities and, "as permitted or required," to act as the official procurement agency for the Liberian government. Finally and even more grandiloquently, the Liberia Company proposed to inaugurate and make available "transportation and public services such as roads and bridges; light, power and water for public use; radio, telegraph and telephone. . . ." The understanding further stipulated that the ownership of all public-service type projects initiated by the Liberia Company would presently revert to the outright ownership by the government of Liberia when or as soon as the government (of Liberia) found itself in a position to assume financial and management responsibilities.

Patently the foregoing was a merging of ambitious planning, visionary ardor, and tall talking. Nine- or ten-digit capitalization was called for. As one amiable and Liberian-experienced onlooker, Harvey S. Firestone, noted, $100 million in capital stock would be a minimal opener, with at least ten times that amount on instantly available standby.

The first serious snag related to the sale of stock in the parent company; this was disconcertingly slow and in terms of indicated goals, infinitesimal; at the end of a year it was reportedly still below $1 million. Investors were staying away in multitudes. Stettinius began confronting a host of discomfiting financial realities. He had known and led or helped lead huge and prestigious companies with long-proved earning power. The proposed Liberia companies lacked such backlogs and purse-fattening histories. American foreign investment, still punchdrunk from the great war, was beset with caution. During the brief period of peace the predominant American urge was toward business at home, not abroad, and the appetite for reform and the thirst for doing good were simultaneously abated. Investors, even excepting those who used the names Liberia and Siberia interchangeably, tended to view Liberia as a quaint, dark blob of distant primitiveness.

Somewhat belatedly Stettinius turned to a facility which he had formerly received gratis and used adroitly—mass publicity. As public relations vice president of General Motors and "big" chairman of U.S. Steel, the former cheerleader had taken powerful support from two of the richest and most effusively publicized corporations which are also gargantuan buyers of advertising space and time. As a spotlighted New Dealer he had enjoyed or suffered the support of the most tremendous publicity works ever conceived by man and paid for by a tax-yielding public. Now that he was no longer in the hot bright lights of what protesters were terming "Potomac statism," Stettinius for the first time since his prep school years found himself obliged to set up or seek out his own figurative drum-and-bugle corps. It wasn't easy.

He turned to former Madison Avenue henchmen, who set up a

somewhat addled but persistent wheedling din. This took form in a fairly respectable midtown New York hotel, and featured a post-meridian Stettinius-attended open house for the working press. The coffee was appallingly bad, but the sandwiches were edible and the pleasantly extroverted presence of Edward R. Stettinius, Jr., was engaging. While munching the light refreshments featuring ham and cheese on rye, and shuddering down the pernicious coffee, the ink-stained wretches were invited to reflect on Liberia and the hopes and promises it brought of reward for Enlightened Developmental American Business Enterprise. The working press was generally sympathetic, but for the most part acutely short of available space. The shortage was caused by the fact that gimlet-eyed editors were less than enamored of the Negro republic and its validity as a solid news source. The Stettinius proposals were bubbly, appealing, dream-splashed, lacking in reportable attainments, and for all these reasons markedly vulnerable to the occupational cynicism of financial and other editors. And there was the persisting fact of journalistic life that practically any hard-working reporter is already laden with a hope chest of articles or other prose gems he has been waiting for months or years to sneak into type or air time, when and if ever he finds the boss in an acceptant mood.

It followed that publicly presenting the Stettinius enthusiasm was not easy to effect. There were editors and program directors who could not, even in fulfillment of an election bet, differentiate between Liberia, Nigeria, or Siberia. Even those who knew what and where Liberia is were inclined to disclaim their ability to understand exactly what Stettinius was getting at.

After all, the *World Almanac*, the *Encyclopaedia Britannica*, *Life* and the *New York Times* seemed pretty well agreed that Liberia had remained a jungle-edge, primitive never-never land where black men still sought to compromise with a most uncompromising environment. At best, which was very far from good enough, the basic economy of Liberia remained agricultural, but this meant subsistence farming geared to the needs and traditions of remote, hard-up tribal communities. An editor or, indeed, anyone else might ask how the Stettinius Associates proposed to exploit products that required bulk transportation. This intent was hampered by the fact that inland from its first port facility, then building at Monrovia,

Liberia was still lacking roads, railroads, or other means necessary for developing crops or other commodities for commercial export.

These and other primary needs prompted the Stettinius Associates to revise and reduce the original proposals, i.e., "statement of understanding," with the Liberian government. The subsequent (1949) "will do" list dropped all mention of public works and endeavors and emphasized: (1) the planting, processing and marketing of cacao, palm products and "incidental" agricultural products; (2) acting as official purchasing agent for the government of Liberia; (3) "extracting," buying and selling gold, diamonds, petroleum, and other metals and minerals excepting iron ore; and (4) "Such other suitable projects as may be incorporated into the revised Statement of Understanding by further agreements between the Parties. . . ."

For the most part the specific undertakings that ensued were small pickings, in several instances experimental projects doomed to early abandonment. But the intent or philosophy was destined to live on. The Christie iron concession, as instituted in 1945, was just another white man's exploitation of an internationally coveted mineral resource, i.e., exceptionally rich iron ore. Its directives, at least in the beginning, were readily comparable to those of a self-assured white boy who would inveigle a poor little black boy to hand over his most readily negotiable possession for a shiny nickel.

The Stettinius "approach" was one of mutual benefit. It permitted, indeed encouraged, the Liberian government to limit the terms and duration of concessions, to increase rentals (in the case of mineral concessions, to a minimum land rental of one dollar an acre), to share royalties or profits far more equitably, and, as already noted, to admit the nation to a sharing partnership in stockholdings.

The actual attainments were destined to be severely limited. Regrettably, during 1952 Edward Stettinius became fatally ill; his early death added to the handicaps and lapses, and no comparable "personality" was available to take over. Even so, the Stettinius Associates endured and boldly took to the exacting and ever perilous task of developing a primary agricultural export. The choice of cacao, known in Liberia as "coco," was not irrational, but it was and is destined to remain an extremely hard way. The "tree melon with giant seeds" is, of course, native to the American tropics and had gained first introduction to tropical Africa back in the 1890s. By 1920 no fewer than a million tribal Africans were growing and marketing the demanding crop, for the most part rather badly.

For African use cacao had demonstrated its primary advantage as a small-acreage crop readily adaptable to tribe-owned lands where tribeswomen can do most of the required work. The persisting disadvantages were and are that, in general, the "high-flavor" (and premium-priced) varieties of cacao do not thrive in Africa, the cacao disease hazards are severe and chronic, and the required processing is extremely exacting and frequently beyond the means of the small-acreage grower.

Beginning in the early 1920s Liberians, including the tribespeople, had gained firsthand experience at cacao growing. In some instances they had made astonishing advances in the demanding techniques of harvesting, fermenting, and otherwise readying the harvest for market. (The old Liberia routine of effectively protecting the dried "chocolate beans" from mold damage by varnishing them with a coating of fine clay was typical.)

In any case, the resident observers found the decision of the Stettinius Associates to gamble on cacao as its prime export product surprising and, as many believed, unfortunate. Some of the interested chiefs suggested that the American entrepreneurs, if hell-bent on cacao, could better serve and profit by installing up-to-date processing equipment and letting the tribespeople grow the raw product. But this was not the first-chosen procedure.

During 1948 the Associates began setting a first 2,000 acres of cacao plantings on a well-chosen concession site between Ganta and Sackripi. The wait for bearing required six years and the area actually planted was quite skimpy even for use as a pilot or testing plantation. But the pioneering work was admirable. It included the importation of superior seeds and budding material from highly successful cacao experiment centers in Turrialba, Costa Rica, and Lancetilla, Honduras, and the employment of an eminent cacao authority, Dr. Santiago Porcella of Costa Rica, as resident director. The Costa Rican cacao expert began to encourage independent

Liberian growers to adapt the crop. Hc supplied them with superior planting stock and gratis counsel and supervision when and as these were requested. Next Dr. Porcella and his colleagues began to correlate cacao growing with on-the-scene improvement of an even more valuable crop, the African oil palm.

This handsome, food-yielding palm is native to Equatorial Africa and had long been a wild-growing resource of much of hinterland Liberia. Its principal harvest is the large top-borne clusters (weighing anywhere from 50 to 100 pounds each) of reddish nut kernels. Both the nut kernels and their pericarps, or outer portions, provide well-flavored, edible, and nutrient-rich oils readily processable as cooking or salad oils or margarines. Both the kernel and pericarp oils are relatively easy to press out and transport. The per-acre yields are generous, up to a ton per acre. The palm usually reaches bearing age within five or six years, maximum yields at around fifteen years, with bearing life sometimes continuing for fifty years or longer. The horticulture is advantageous in several respects. The palm responds to systematic pruning and may be kept to convenient orchard size to facilitate easy harvest. The crop also responds readily to improvement by plant-breeding techniques, and its nursery requirements are exceptionally modest.

As the Stettinius Associates helped in demonstrating, the African oil palm, currently the fastest-gaining commercial crop of the American tropics as well as Equatorial Africa, offers its growers numerous advantages. The bearing groves can be used doubly as improved pastures for cattle, sheep, and other livestock. The plantings can be profitably intermixed with other grove or orchard crops, including cacao or coffee. (Liberian coffee, though never impressive in quantity, is markedly superior in quality and on that basis a valuable resource.)

The net result of the efforts of the Stettinius Associates to adapt and revise cacao as a principal commercial export were not successful. The severely limited working base could not overcome the many and formidable handicaps, including the huge, low-quality harvests that proliferate in other areas of tropical Africa. More recently the cacao plantings have been substantially replaced by Hevea rubber plantings. But the primary effort, like the underlying philosophy, has been proved valid and undeniably beneficial to

Liberia as a whole. The "company crop" which did not succeed has contributed valuably to citizen crops, such as oil palm and rubber, that are succeeding—widely and in part brilliantly. In all these and in other ways the weight of tangible evidence proves that Edward R. Stettinius, Jr., did not dream in vain.

15

RUBICON AT MID-CENTURY

THE TWENTIETH CENTURY had opened with a near deluge of mottoes, adages, taglines, and abbreviated generalities. William Jennings Bryan, the perennial candidate for president of the United States, released the sparkler that the twentieth century was predictably the unpredictable century. Dwight L. Moody, who was ending his mortal span as the most renowned of American evangelists, had predicted in 1899 that the twentieth century would be a great deal like the nineteenth, except "very, very different." Rudyard Kipling, who would learn of American ways from his turbulent and otherwise unhappy residence in Dummerston, Vermont, had readied for mass distribution the tagline, "The White Man's Burden," but his target was the United States. With the Spanish-American War the new power of the West had definitely joined in the inter-hemispheric fiesta of empire grabbing.

Although blessed with one of the most imaginative and distinctive folk cultures known anywhere, Liberia has never excelled at coining mottoes or taglines. But long before the twentieth century and its better known prophets began, Liberia had learned and proved a great deal about the Black Man's Burden. This remained vividly true during the 1930s when the United States was being swashed by still another figurative tidal wave of mottoes, adages, and taglines—in the greatest part from the prevailing ocean of New Deal politics and politicians.

One of the more successful of the Rooseveltian word jugglers was the longtime secretary of agriculture and one-term vice president of the United States, Henry Agard Wallace of Des Moines, who came up with the taking phrase, "Century of the Common Man." No sane person could list Wallace as a common man, but none could deny him credit for being one of the most able self-publicists of all time.

But for the most part official Monrovia did not redound with agreement with the century-of-the-common-man routine. The rather well-enunciated Liberian view was and is that every century is a century of the common man. In the Liberian capital of the latter 1930s one of the more diligent students of Roosevelt, Wallace, and the New Deal in general was a nimble-witted, hard-working, and controversially liberal senator from what had once been Maryland in Liberia.

The young and at times argumentative black man had acquired most of his knowledge of history from the Holy Bible, law books climaxed by an exceptionally successful tenure as an associate justice of the Liberia Supreme Court, and alert observation of his strongly contrasting and in part strongly opinionated fellow countrymen. The young Negro senator, who was usually identifiable by way of an oversize cigar and a succinct but emphatic point of view, insisted that all history is from its roots a chronicle of common people with uncommon problems and that the public servant's job is to identify and help solve the common man's problems and never mind the mottoes, taglines, and purple platitudes. In Monrovia, as in other capitals, such statements were construed by some as being heretical. It was commonly accepted that the young black senator, even while winning friends, particularly among the "lower strata," more specifically the tribespeople or "natives," was alienating important established names in government. The young senator's spirited remarks about the "self-invented, self-advertised, self-admitted, and self-propelled princes of privilege" were unquestionably quotable and entertaining to *hoi polloi*, but they were obnoxious to important sectors of the Monrovia establishment. The latter's consensus was that the inventive, meditative, and occasionally sparkling young blackman from Harper would eventually find out that his quips and puffs about "social justice" would get him nowhere beyond legislature's election to the Supreme Court.

At mid-century the excessively outspoken young black man from rustic Harper town was well along in his first eight-year term as president of Liberia. But William Vacanarat Shadrach Tubman still had a great deal to think, talk, and quip about. He was no longer the first officer of Africa's only republic. Other African republics were clearly in the borning. President Tubman could clearly foresee five and anticipated the incubation of at least twenty more by the end of the decade. As the senior black republic, Liberia was obligated to assume a degree of leadership—not as an American or any other kind of satellite but as a sovereign African nation and precedent-maker. All this was additional to the already formidable labors of self-development, including a government for all the people.

Liberia's first prerogative and mission could not be served or fulfilled merely on a basis of area, population, developed wealth or even of distinguished precedence. The second half of the twentieth century was finding Liberia still a comparatively poor country and a very small one; another decade would find it the fifth from the smallest of thirty-two independent and sovereign African states.

The fine old adage, "If you can't whup 'em jine 'em," could not be literally applied. Liberia is not and has never been a warring nation, and formal union with the yet unborn is rarely recommendable and practically never easy to accomplish. And the Liberian government, as any one could see, was almost frantically busy at caring for its own.

Nevertheless the oldest African republic, and by 1950, far and away the oldest continuing Negro republic, had great and sustained bases of validity and capacity to help others. It has survived as a constitutional republic and it remained essentially a bona fide African phenomenon. It was not a black American stepchild and had not been papped, repressed, and otherwise manipulated as just another colony.

In this there was strength and comfort and grounds for hope. But there were also paradoxes and grounds for severe challenge. As of 1950 Liberia still lacked what political scientists sometimes term the mystique of nationalism, what journalists frequently term the attainment of functional integration. At mid-century Liberia still had an official language (English), in which, so the United Nations investigatory team reported, only about 8 percent of the total population was formally literate. The United States dollar was its basic currency, but the functioning circulation of the dollar as measured by mass earning and buying power was punitively inadequate. The indigenous economy was not yet in position to absorb or gain effective correlation with exploitative investments of outside capital. Throughout most of Liberia and practically all of the hinterlands, prevailing wages remained at or near coolie levels; the average "tribesman's wage" was somewhere near 40 cents a day. Economically, Liberia was showing growth without proportionate development.

Stated another way, the African rootage, although present and alive, was not being adequately tilled; its deserved and necessary flowering and fruiting were not being attained. To a recognizable extent the same held for Liberian government. The Americo-Liberian political structure was most notable as a minor saga of survival. But it *had* survived.

Put another way, the African roots of Liberia, although surely present and alive, were still not being adequately tilled, and its deserved and necessary flowering and fruiting had not yet been adequately attained. To a recognizable degree, the same continued to hold for the Liberian government. An objective appraiser could not deny that the competence of the national government was steadily improving. But the so-called Americo-Liberian political hegemony was still not sufficiently assimilated. As a majority group the tribespeople had proved and continued to prove their will and competence to take part in national government. But as Tubman continued to point out, adequate "unification" required a much greater proportion of tribespeople in elective office. As of 1950, only three of the thirty-nine legislators were from the tribes. Nobody could describe that as an adequate balance and nobody could convincingly argue that it could be regarded as conducive to establishing a commendable example for the newer African republics to follow.

More equitable representation was very much needed, but as the already impressively long roster of tribespeople who had served the national government firmly indicated, equal representation could and would be more nearly approached. Subsequent years would also prove that although Liberia did not have a capable two-party system for other African republics to emulate, it was not surely limited to one party or imperiled by dictatorship. As we have already noted, except for one very brief lapse, Liberia had kept with constitutionally stipulated elections for more than a century.

William V. S. Tubman had already established his image as a strong-willed president without intentions of retiring from office by his own volition. But the Bible scholar and former senator and supreme court justice from Harper Village had won his first presidential election despite vigorous opposition of the conservative ranks of his own party (True Whig), and he was already faced with the task of winning reelection in what had to be spirited competition with a dissident wing of his own party. There was good evidence, too, that Tubman was pivoting a long, hard turn toward functioning democracy.

But the presidency of Liberia was not conducive to theorists' daydreaming. William Tubman had won office by—some said in spite of—his advocacy of "unification," i.e. bringing all Liberians into a government of, by, and for all the people. He was well aware that such a course would require greatly increased collection and expenditures of public monies. He admitted to being reminded of a minister in his hometown who had set forth on a lengthy and audacious missionary enterprise from which he returned to find his children gone hungry and his wife dying of the fevers. The moral, as Tubman noted, was that devotion to causes, however noble, can never wholly transcend responsibility to primary human needs.

Recognizing that his country was permeated by inescapable home needs, Tubman had boldly devised and openly announced Liberia's Open Door Policy toward and for foreign investors and developers. The responses were already extensive and in part encouraging, but the most immediate results were that American corporations were dominating the foreign-trade sector of the Liberian economy. At best this was not all good.

The Tubman administration was also obliged to accept and live with the fact that the so-called foreign aid tendered by the United States during the war years and the remainder of the 1940s had accomplished disappointingly little good, at least as Liberia is obliged to measure values. The eminent exception was the $19 million advance for building the Free Port of Monrovia, but Liberia had already assumed obligations for the systematic repayment of that loan.

Roberts Field had proved out well as a strategic international airport and Liberia had shared in its benefits. By contrast, the United States Army's brief orgy of roadbuilding had been abandoned too abruptly and prematurely; the Negro nation remained cripplingly lacking in roads.

Unfortunately the greater part of the American "aid" had turned out to be a regrettable potpourri of bureaucratic bumblings and fumblings, lacking experienced planning or competent administration. In instance after instance well-intentioned projects for helping the Liberian government expand public health services and improve its imperatively needed agriculture had become ensnarled with bureaucratic rivalries or back-stabbings initiated in war-disheveled Washington's deplorably indiscreet choices of personnel. The primarily conservative and acceptant administration of Edwin Barclay had endured with exquisite patience the earlier years of the improvised and repeatedly addled American bureaucracy, transplanted to Liberian shores. Beginning with its inauguration during January, 1944, the Tubman administration had graciously but in evident suffering followed suit, well aware that many crucial developmental needs were not being met or, indeed, perceptively identified, but unable for the time to effect remedy.

The resources in stoicism were further strained by several occurrences that were conspicuously avoidable. One especially painful example was the wretched and premature death of a scientific enterprise in which the then newly incumbent Liberian president had placed exceptional hope and confidence. This was the Liberian Institute (for international research in tropical medicine) of the American Foundation for Tropical Medicine.

The funds required for building and staffing the institute had been raised in the United States. The Liberian government eagerly granted the necessary concession and building site and accommodated with an official commitment (virtually unprecedented) to grant unqualified entry and exit permission to all scientific talent required by the Institute, to honor medical degrees from all nations and to permit opcn distribution of all findings to any and every nation. Significantly no other sovereign government in either hemisphere was willing to grant such permissions.

The facility was built and the nucleus of a staff was provided; Liberia was gracious and cooperative in every way. But the Foundation fell afoul of deplorable medical politics and personality clashings. A meddlesome corporation lawyer maneuvered his way into the picture and rang in a hand-picked kennel of experienced foundation nibblers. The U.S. Public Health Service attempted to rescue the research center, but following a muddled effort to revive and revise, tripped over its own red tape. The Tubman administration looked on politely and resignedly, perhaps too politely and too resignedly. The Liberian president's private reactions were simply stated: "We've taken another licking and relearned the essential lesson, namely, that Liberia must administer its own needs in its own way."

Tubman lighted an oversized cigar and puffed energetically. "Some beautiful someday," he continued, "I will very personally strike off a chrome-plated, hubcap-sized medal for bestowing on the Liberian public servant who has endured and survived the most and the stickiest of American nutsiness, be it of public or private bureaucracy."

But the Tubman prime concern was with the materializing growth and the necessary development of the living economy of his country. From a statistical standpoint the 1950s promptly began to take shape as years of impressive and unprecedented growth. The prime cause was the aggressive exploitation of natural resources, beginning with Liberian workers, iron ores, and rubber harvests. By 1952, the statistical advances were showing cloudburst proportions; the ensuing seven years would show the nation's money income quadrupled, labor earnings tripled, government revenue collections increased eightfold. By 1954 and continuing through 1960, Liberia, with the single exception of Japan, led the entire world in the growth rate of what census statisticians like to call the real gross national product.

In its May, 1962, issue the United Nations *Monthly Bulletin of Statistics* formally confirmed the foregoing—as it prevailed from 1955 through 1960. Using the 1950 national products estimates as a base of 100, the UN statisticians accorded the following relative scores for the six-year period 1955–1960:

Japan	180
Liberia	175
Ghana	160
Nigeria	150+
West Germany	150
Switzerland	131
Uganda	125
United States	121
United Kingdom	116
Congo	110
Ireland	104

Meanwhile, in a capable attempt to "cover" the entire decade of the 1950s in terms of Liberia, the Monrovia Port Management Company compiled the better-detailed summation of "economic growth" shown on the following page.

As usual there were noteworthy developments awaiting correlation with the prevailing statistics and tabulated summaries. To list only a few: the 1953 completion of a bridge over the St. Paul River was a first step in the long-delayed opening of the Western, or "wilderness," province. The same event epitomized an expansive policy in national financing. As of January, 1950, Liberia's external debt totaled $584,000, about 50 cents per capita, the lowest then reported by any sovereign nation. Then, as it confronted multiplying domestic needs, the Liberian government began to discard its earlier and largely extemporized debt limit. The first sizable move to raise that limit took form with the January, 1951, receipt of a $5 million loan from the United States for use in launching a road-building program.

This borrowing, which was punctually repaid, overtured a decade's total of $51 million in U.S. loans to Liberia; $28 million in participating grants for public works (in which Liberia paid somewhat more than half the total tabs), and about $30 million in direct foreign aid. Throughout the heyday of borrowing, Liberia's credit was being nurtured by impressive increases in gross domestic income.

The more grim, or certainly less ebullient, sides were still to be

Year	Gross Domestic Income (dollars)*	Government Revenue (dollars)	Rubber Exports (pounds)	Dry-cargo Imports (long tons)	Iron-ore Exports (long tons)	Tribal Net Money Income (dollars)	All-Weather Road Mileage
1950	35.8	3.9	66.7	120	—	1.8	230
1951	45.7	12.8	79.3	161	.2	2.2	—
1952	52.6	8.6	78.0	143	.9	2.7	250
1953	58.4	11.2	78.8	155	1.3	3.0	—
1954	60.5	11.9	82.8	165	1.2	3.4	—
1955	79.1	15.3	87.5	191	1.8	3.9	—
1956	89.7	17.9	88.5	213	2.0	4.5	470
1957	90.9	20.1	83.9	254	2.1	4.8	—
1958	97.1	18.1	94.8	241	2.1	5.5	—
1959	130.1	24.6	96.2	305	2.8	6.3	—
1960	154.7	32.4	95.4	396	2.9	7.3	1,150

* Figures are all in millions, either dollars, pounds, or long tons.

SOURCE: Port of Monrovia Authority, Annual Report VIII, Monrovia, 1963.

seen and felt. For one persistently discouraging item, Liberian agriculture, the prime economy of the tribespeople, continued to fall ever farther short of needs. Yet industrial employment was also dawdling. During 1951, for example, only 57,000 Liberians were on industrial payrolls; 62 percent of these were employed by Firestone Plantations, and industrial wages were apparently frozen at somewhat less than 50 cents a day. The skilled-labor population was being guessed at no more than 10,000, with average earnings below $900 per year.*

The plight of public education had remained dour. As of 1950 only 5 percent of the total government revenue was being appropriated for that purpose. After four years the Tubman administration had raised this to 12 percent, but even this increase had not altered the fact that as of 1954 only 9.5 percent of Liberia's school-age population was actually in school.

There were clearly visible improvements even so. One was that the national election of May, 1951 (here it may be noted that the present Liberian Constitution provides that the president and vice president serve first terms of eight years, but subsequent reelections are for only four years), Liberian women were permitted to vote for the first time. Full franchise was also provided tribespeople who owned huts or other property. As an encouraging result, participation in national elections climbed to about 70 percent of the estimated total of voting-age citizens, which was well above U.S. averages.

Another item of political significance was that although Tubman easily won reelection in 1951, he was not unopposed. A short-lived but highly audible tribespeople party challenged him. Four years later, Edwin Barclay, the Tubman predecessor, received the nomination of the "Independent" True Whig Party and vigorously opposed the incumbent.

Although Tubman won his second reelection (for the four-year "repeater" term) fairly decisively, the fact that Barclay centered his campaign on opposing the Open Door Policy (toward foreign investors) was notable. Barclay validly pointed out that as of 1955 the foreign-based concession holders were not adequately sharing their profits with the Liberian government. At the time the most flagrant instance of short changing was being committed by the Christie-led Liberia Mining Company, which was then paying only

*Northwestern University Panel, *Growth Without Development*, Evanston, 1966.

five cents per ton in excise on marketed iron ore. Fortunately, this leak was subsequently plugged by the Tubman administration and all exploiters of Liberian iron ore are currently paying 50 percent of their net profits to the government of Liberia.

In opposing the Tubman Internal Unification Plan (for extending rights and increased government participation to the tribespeople), Barclay virtually assured his own defeat. Somewhat inconsistently, too, the former president bypassed several of the more vulnerable faults or oversights of the first Tubman administration. For examples, one of Liberia's then two daily newspapers was government-owned; and the only radio station then effective was also government-owned, and this would shortly demand correction.

Furthermore the prevailing tax structure was erratic and otherwise faulty; a Liberian legislator told me: "God forgive us, this Liberian tax structure is almost as lousy as that of the United States. Your stacked tax mess is destroying your middle-class earners, handing ridiculous advantages to your wealthy people and corporate slickers, fattening your damnable 'military-industrial complex' and otherwise destroying you. Liberia's tax structure still penalizes our tribespeople, our unskilled labor, and our still too sparse professional classes. Our poor people, like yours, are very much too poor for the nation's good. Within our trying limits I think our government is doing more for its poor people than yours is—in terms of constructive legislation. But if I speak correctly, I must grant that we still aren't doing well enough."

Perhaps one of the better summations of the Liberian economy during the 1950s was offered in Volume XVI of Northwestern University's *African Studies*:

> Since 1950 . . . Liberia's economic growth has been: (1) exceptionally rapid; (2) very recent in origin; (3) stimulated primarily by foreign investments in mining and plantation agriculture; (4) dominated and largely directed by expatriate personnel; (5) fruitful in providing the government with developmental funds (directly through tax revenues as well as indirectly through loans and grants); (6) heavily oriented toward production for export; (7) concentrated in a small number of industries; and (8) ineffective in creating internal forces making for structural change in an industrial economy.

The socially consequential shortcomings included the displacement of tribes or tribespeople from lands that were being leased by foreign investors and their less than satisfactory resettlement in less desirable forest lands or bush sites. This added to the shortcomings of an already inadequate agriculture. The shortage or complete lack of health facilities also lingered. The per capita earnings of the tribespeople still lagged deplorably.

The respected estimates of the United Nations *Statistical Yearbook* continued to point out that even in terms of African averages Liberian annual per capita earnings were still painfully under par; during the so-called rapid-progress years 1957–59, they still averaged only $123. Several of the new African republics with comparable proportions of tribespeople were showing much higher averages; for example, Ghana was $187, the Federation of Rhodesia and Nyasaland, $152.

The potential and developing values of Liberian resources were as self-revealing as a country washday. But the impeding earning discrepancies were still working against the tribespeople. Many of the "aborigines" were receiving a bad break from the government tax collectors. However, this was being proved correctable. The more-damaging hurt was related to the failure of concessionaires to pay wages proportionate to earnings and profits and the continuing deterioration of subsistence agriculture.

The Tubman administration had recognized and acknowledged all the worst faults and lapses and renewed its pledge to correct them or, at least, to "sweat them down." The administration also kept with both its Open Door and National Unification policies. In his inaugural address of January 5, 1956, the president reiterated:

> We shall encourage foreign investments and the granting of foreign concessions where Liberians have not reached the position where they are capable to explore and exploit the potential resources of the country. . . .

The president was not obliged to reiterate that the number of concession-seekers was growing rapidly. As of 1950 the Liberian government had granted only two concessions—to the Firestone Plantations Company for natural rubber and the Liberia Mining

Company for iron ore. By the decade's end the list read:

Concession Holder	*Principal Product*	*Year of Agreement*	*Development Cost (millions of dollars)*	*Country**
Firestone	natural rubber	1925	32.0	U.S.
Liberia Mining	iron ore	1946	37.0	U.S.
Liberia Company	rubber	1947	2.1	U.S.
African Fruit	rubber	1952	4.5	German
Goodrich	rubber	1954	4.3	U.S.
Delimco	iron ore	1953	100.0	German
Lamco	iron ore	1953	215.0	Swedish
Monrovia Breweries	soft drinks, beer	1956	3.5	Swiss
National Iron Ore	iron ore	1958	30.0	U.S.
Liberia Independent Forest Co.	lumber	1958	.4	Spanish
Limpex Palm Oil	palm oil, pineapple	1958	.5	German
Munarriz Works	bricks, soap	1952	.2	Spanish
Le Tourneau of Liberia	lumber	1952	3.0	U.S.
Maryland Logging	lumber	1960	.5	English
Providence Mining	diamonds	1960	.05	English

* *Annual Report,* Free Port of Monrovia, 1969. (Not numbered.)

Natural rubber was gaining for three prevalent reasons; steady growth, if sometimes erratic, of international demands, strongly improved yields and, for Liberia, the widespread increase in citizen participation. By 1959 about 6,000 Liberians were owners of Hevea rubber groves and there was strong evidence that the number would presently double. Also four additional rubber-growing concessions were being developed by foreign rubber companies and two more by other concession-holders, including the Stettinius company, which was moving into rubber growing. Firestone had contributed most to improving the enduring tree crop and making it available to the country at large. But Liberia as a whole was contributing to sustaining Hevea rubber as a staple export commodity. The prime contributors were unchanging— suitable soils and climate, available lands, and, most important of all, a superior labor force— featuring the most exceptional manual skills of the tribal tappers.

But the most decisive innovation of the 1950s was iron; at a time when the United States, the world's predominant iron consumer, was running out of high-grade iron ores, Liberia was the center of the most impressive iron-ore bonanza the plundered planet had yet known. By 1957 the Bomi Hills center, operated by the Christie-maneuvered Liberia Mining Company, had opened the first substantial treasure trove of Liberian iron and was marketing about 3 million tons per year. The fact that Liberia Mining had already responded to Liberian government persuasion to the extent of sharing its profits at the rate of 35 percent with the promise of 50 percent beginning in 1958 was a particularly encouraging note for the future.

However, the beginning years of Liberian iron development had already demonstrated that the requirements for capital investments were very large—clearly beyond the means of citizen investors and, for that matter, of the Christie Company, which found itself hard-put to raise $37 million—a minimum for what was turning out to be one of the smaller iron-ore centers.

During 1954 a Swedish surveying party, astutely heeding the work trails of tribal blacksmiths, as well as successive government surveys, picked its way to Mount Nimba, a principal peak in the mountain range of that name—in the upper, Guinea frontiers of Liberia. First refining tests from shallow drillings taken in that area showed amazingly high iron contents, some averaging 70 percent of bulk. The probe showed multimillion-ton deposits overlaid by only two or three feet of surface matter. The total recovery average showed at least 20 percent more iron recovery than the best of the Mesabi Range of Michigan had shown.

Remoteness had to be considered. The Nimba Mountains are generously scattered through the forest and jungle Saniquellie area of Liberia and extend into the Republic of Guinea. The total ore lodes are estimated as high as a billion tons, much of it so rich that it requires very little preliminary processing or pelleting.

Even while the Nimba mine sites were being explored, several other large lodes or iron-ore centers were being discovered or reappraised—in the Bassa Hills southeast of Monrovia, in Putu in the Eastern Province, and along the Mano River and the Bong Hills. Never before has so small a country shown so vast and so accessible a supply of the most basic industrial metal. During September, 1953, for the first time in its history, the Liberian government awarded a distinctly businesslike concession, covering about 500 square miles, to the newly formed International African-American Corporation. IAAC readily agreed to a fifty-fifty profit-sharing with the Liberian government, but despite its substantial capitalization found itself unable to raise the necessary funds—no less than $200 million—for developing the center.

This led to the establishment, early in 1954, of a rather complex joint-venture enterprise, the Liberian American-Swedish Minerals Company (LAMCO). The ownership of this enterprise is equally divided between the Republic of Liberia and the original concessionaire, i.e., International African-American Company. This last-named includes shareholdings by Bethlehem Steel, the Swedish LAMCO syndicate, and at the present time some three hundred Liberian citizens. The Stockholm-based Granesbury Company, the world's largest exporter of ores, took over direct management of the enterprise, which is now far and away the largest industrial enterprise in Africa and handles more than 12 million tons per year of the international crude-iron supply.

The developmental maneuvers continued. During 1958 the German-Liberian Mining Company acquired a concession for iron-ore mining in the Bong Mountains centered about fifty miles northeast of Monrovia. The ore deposits here are describable as rich rather than ultrarich. But the estimated 200-million-ton lode justified building still another ore-carrying railroad and a $50 million "benefication" and ore-pelleting plant.

During the same year the National Iron Ore Company, Ltd., which is 90 percent owned by Liberian citizens, received a concession covering iron-ore deposits along the Mano River and in the Bie Mountains near the Sierra Leone boundary. At present the Liberian government owns 50 percent of the capital shares of National Iron Ore, with some 1,700 Liberian citizens and the Liberian Mining Company owning the rest.

The economic saga of Liberia's iron was only beginning as the 1950s ended; the social impacts were but dimly indicated. But the amazing mineral resources of the amazing little country were starting to sparkle like a barrelful of diamonds.

For early in 1957, beginning in the valley of the Lofa River and the Saniquellie jungle fringes, a real diamond rush began. By then deposits of other minerals, including gold, manganese, columbite, corundum, zinc, copper, and mercury, had also been identified.

The diamond treasure, like the vast iron resources, had first been uncovered by tribespeople. By mid-1957 the diamond finds were well beyond the stage of jungle-edge yarn spinning. Rubber tappers and mine workers were fading from their relentlessly underpaid posts to participate, and the gaily dressed, foot-free Mandingo tribesmen were moving in to find places as diamond buyers. At least a few would emerge with wallets too precious to be carried anywhere except in the clenched right hand.

The odds are that nobody knows or will ever know how many diamonds have been or will be carried out from the Lofa country. Export records show that by 1960 the Liberian diamond exports had reached a high of almost a million carats yearly, at that time some 6 percent of the burgeoning total of exports. By 1962 the Liberian-Swiss Mining Company had gained a government-approved diamond mining concession. By then the recorded finds were diminishing.

But the diamonds were, are, and will be taken at least in part on a finders-keepers basis, which this writer, for one, cordially approves. The Liberian diamond rush of the latter 1950s endures as a bright symbol of the aborigines' right of self-benefit.

The first devotion of William V. S. Tubman and his administration was for government. By 1953 the Liberian government was demonstrating marked improvements in administrative competence, particularly as regarded public works. It was effectively matching, in most instances better than matching, the grants of the U.S. Foreign Operations Administration and other "aid" agencies of Washington. The fact was noteworthy that other African countries were consistently receiving larger grants than was Liberia. Also, Liberia was demonstrating a degree of enterprise and self-direction which few so-called developing countries could rival. On its own volition and with its own funds, the Liberian government employed seventy-five generally well-qualified American technicians to join in planning and directing public-works programs. These included outstandingly sound projects in crop development, malaria control, mineral surveys, updated teacher training, and revivals of of roadbuilding, hydroelectric projects, and further contributions to public health and the national school system.

But the total of needs seemed to be permanently ahead of the potentials for fulfilling them. There was the inevitability of growing pains, and there were occasional flare-ups of unprecedented violence. On June 22, 1955, the Liberian president barely escaped an assassination attempt, a discomfiting reminder that being an African chief of state can no longer be listed as a completely safe occupation.

The Tubman administration continued to seek closer and more friendly ties with an epochally changing Africa. Its policy of Pan-Africanism began acquiring noteworthy substantiations. One significant omen was the presence of thirty-five official delegations at the third Tubman inauguration; twenty-eight were from African countries. Another was the first official exchanges of ambassadors or ministers with such far-aparts as Ethiopia, Israel, and the United Arab Republic. In April, 1958, the Liberian president personally led his country's delegation to the First Conference of Independent African States at Accra, capital of the new Republic of Ghana. The gathering clearly defined the Liberian willingness to champion the "Pan-Africanism" that veered toward identification with the West. It also marked the beginning of the move toward African "moral federation"—short of formal union. The "Tubman Pan-Africa Doctrine," presently to be formally recorded for the sixteenth session of the United Nations General Assembly,* was in essence:

> . . . We Africans must remember that what we seek is justice. There is no time for us to brood over the grievances and sufferings of the past. We must extend to the white man the hand of forgiveness and fellowship. We must invite him to join us in burying misunderstandings and in working for a better and happier world.

The might of coincidence was causing the white man's hands to reach toward Liberia more and more avidly. The epochal coincidence was the black republic's emergence as a world-influencing source of iron ores.

*Part 1, p. 90, Agenda Item No. 27, Monrovia, 1961.

16

THE SAGACIOUS SIXTIES

THE 1950s were Liberia's decade of unprecedented economic gains—at least as indicated by the run-of-the-mill statistics. As usual the statistics did not tell the entire story. But at least to a degree, they had indicated that the oldest African republic was gaining both economic and political status, and was a bellwether for a rapidly advancing or, at very least, a rapidly changing Africa.

The 1950s had also been a decade for observing Africa; for its part Liberia had received more news mention than it got during all thirteen of its previous decades. The 1960s promised more of such attention. One of the better reasons was that the now senior African republic was beginning to demonstrate impressive competence as a peace urger in a rambunctiously war-prone era. Africa as a vast whole had entered a period of more than usual belligerence. Beginning in the latter 1940s and continuing throughout the '50s, combative moods were more and more evident in principal areas of European settlement. The so-called De Gaulle War in and around Algeria had provided a significant overture. Throughout seven festering years Tunisia struggled to regain a seafront which would include the extremely strategic, French-developed port and naval base of Bizerte.

There had been serious border clashes between Ethiopian and Somalian forces. Morocco had challenged the sovereignty of Mauritania and aggressively opposed its right to endure. Throughout the 1950s the reach of African strife and controversies had grown and grown. The closing years of the mid-century decade had shown the total African situation changing for the worse.

In the magnificent but formidably complex Congo, Africans were also fighting Africans, and tribal dissension in Nigeria was already ominous. There were bitter Arab-black African clashes in Zanzibar, and inter-black warfare in Rwanda-Burundi—in 1960 a United Nations trust territory pending liberation from Belgium during 1962. United Nations troops were seeking perhaps more valiantly than wisely to rescue Belgian and other nationals who found themselves entrapped in a vast wonderland they had supposedly conquered. Katanga forces would fiercely resist the UN troops, charging unwarranted intervention in Congolese affairs. The great Dag Hammarskjold would lose his life while flying to meet and seek truce with the gifted and combative Moise Tshombe, who began moving into global prominence during 1960 with Belgium's hesitant agreement to "divest" itself of the Congo.

The beclouded African horizons showed other intermittent rays of light. In 1960 a brilliant, pacifistic Zulu chief, Albert John Luthuli, received the Nobel Peace Prize. On December 9, 1961, magnificent Tanganyika gained independence from the British Empire. On April 27 of the same year, Liberia's erstwhile contentious colonial neighbor, Sierra Leone, by then a sovereign republic, became the one hundredth member of the United Nations. Kenya was emerging as a republic, while Uganda, temporarily a British protectorate, had been promised sovereign status by October, 1962. Meanwhile, heavily peopled Nigeria, beginning in 1961, had boldly enacted the first social-security system in any African country. But the glad tidings were being countered by the dour. During 1961 television broadcasts materialized in Equatorial Africa, for the first time south of the Sahara. In Ghana the brilliant and audacious Kwame Nkrumah was duly ensconced as a president without limitation of tenure and with distinct prospects of emerging as the first career dictator of the new Africa.

But even if the times were not yet in joint, nobody could deny that they were exciting or that mighty Africa was awaking and moving. Liberia was cogently aware of this most essential fact of African life. Purposefully, the first African republic had been planning and moving accordingly. As a charter member of the United Nations and one of the more ably represented, during December, 1960, Liberia won and earned its place as the first black African member of the UN Security Council. Although the initial tenure was only for one year, the accreditation assured the black republic's position of prestige among the thirty-two African states which would shortly comprise the largest member group in the United Nations.

Liberia maneuvered deftly to keep in step. Beginning in 1953 the Liberian government had enacted far-sighted domestic legislation to prohibit or aggressively oppose racial discrimination in employment by concession-holders. The same government had foreseen that the United Nations would be made a world forum for the expression of African disapproval of imperialism both in and out of the black man's continent. It had also anticipated the African formation of indigenous blocs ranging from Soviet-friendly "neutralists" (presently to be exemplified by the Casablanca group—Algeria, Guinea, Mali, Morocco, United Arab Republic, and Ghana), to the West-leaning Brazzaville group (the Cameroon, Central African Republic, Chad, the Congo Republic, Gabon, Dahomey, Ivory Coast, Malagasy Republic, Senegal, Upper Volta, etc.). Well before 1960, Liberia, via the Tubman administration, had also recognized and begun to demonstrate its attainable advantages as an arbiter, counselor, and African friend-in-waiting.

The projected and already materializing role was one of exceptional self-dependency as well as cogency and courage. Liberia could not and did not count decisively on diplomatic Annie Oakleys from the United States; the African policy of the United States, if it could be called a policy, ranged from well-intentioned fuzziness to nonbenevolent evasiveness. That was all the more reason why the first African republic found itself in the confluence of diplomatic courses clearly in support of the Western powers and, simultaneously, of the rapidly emerging Pan-Africanism. Obviously Liberia could not welsh or withdraw from its position and stature as the only adult republic in the continent which abruptly was leading all continents in the number of existent republics.

Yet as fifth from the smallest of the new or hatching African states, and, from a standpoint of per capita earnings, still one of the poorer, Liberia was finding itself obliged to take its role of African leadership and justify that role by doing for its own people what it was necessarily obliged to urge other African states to do for theirs. While setting good examples for its host of neighbors, Liberia was essentially dependent on its own distinctively African resources, particularly its tribespeople and its two better-developed commercial resources, iron ore and rubber. No less requisite were the still unattained feats of improving agriculture and rapidly advancing public education and health.

The upbounding gross national product and the conspicuously improving trade balances (in 1960, $40.27 million in exports and $27.79 million in imports) were proof of impressive gains in iron-ore and rubber production. But the basic tribal industry, that of subsistence agriculture, continued to deteriorate; the country was still nowhere near self-sustaining in edible harvests. Furthermore, foreign trade was still not in distributive balance; again as of 1960, about 75 percent of all Liberian trade remained with the United States. Clearly, Western Europe was the best sphere for trade expansion, but except for West Germany the needed balances had not as yet materialized. Also severe isolation persisted. The corporately built and operated ore-carrying railroads were not common carriers. The country at large still endured a crippling shortage of roads; the sought-for national highway system was very far from being a reality.

In terms of effective merchant shipping Liberia also remained wanting. The fact that the first African republic led the world in the official chartering or flagging of merchant shipping merely told that an attainable revenue source had been ably exploited but without solid benefit to Liberian foreign trade as such. It was true enough that Lloyd's Shipping Registry for 1960 showed that 975 foreign-owned merchant vessels, representing a gross capacity of some 10.078 million tons, were paying registry tolls to the Liberian government. That was (still is) almost half of the world total of merchant shipping in international operation; it includes most of the registries of American-owned petroleum carriers, roughly 60 percent of all British-owned merchant shipping, and at least a third of that owned by governments or nationals of the Soviet-bloc nations—including Red China.

But the mass registration of merchant shipping was no real tribute to the black republic and no guarantee of its dependable shipping strength. The Liberian registry of commercial tonnage began as and remains a stratagem for bypassing shipping regulations which other nations, in all at least sixty-six, had enacted for the more capable protection of their merchant seamen, including just pay and working standards. Undeniably, Liberia's charter dodge benefits shipowners throughout half the world. It does not benefit the stature or integrity of legitimate merchant shipping. And it certainly does not brighten the escutcheons of the oldest Negro republic nor provide more than a very small percentage of revenue needs.

But Liberia's needs for public services were continuing to intensify. Inevitably the most demanding of the needs were in the ever-frustrating realm of public education. The truth was axiomatic that public education remained at the head of the most needed list. For purposes of expanding working skills, professional establishment, progress in unifying the population components, raising health levels, and shaping the bases for leadership in African growth—cultural, political, and economic—public education is hardly less necessary than breathing. Yet the sardonic if not really exceptional truth persisted that the harder the Liberian government toiled to improve education, the more obstacles it seemed to meet.

The statistics-fattened 1950s had gone their way without a corresponding upturn in public education. At very best the overall literacy in English was hardly more than 20 percent; some estimated it as less. The 1959 records showed elementary school enrollment holding at about 47,000, but the bottleneck in secondary schooling (only 2,600 pupils in regular attendance) remained virtually unyielding, while the three colleges together had fewer than 500 students. There were some noteworthy gains in numbers; by 1959 the total of operative schools had increased to 366 government "elementaries," 147 mission schools, and 68 private schools. But the countable enrollments still dragged, with hardly more than about 15 percent of the elementary grade-school population actually in school attendance.

As before, the great stymie was in the tribe country. During 1961–62 the Liberian government gamely resumed its corner turn-ings by building 200 additional schoolhouses and making room for 30,000 additional pupils, practically all in comparatively isolated tribal areas. The effort featured notable innovations, such as portable kilns for use in making building brick directly from clay subsoils present in a given community; also turning to the then newly organized U.S. Peace Corps for teaching help. To effect the latter the Liberian government requested the assignment of seventy volunteer Peace Corps schoolteachers and placed them on its payroll for well-deserved bonus compensations.

The school problem remained worrisome. Even so, by 1965 the total enrollment had reached 60,000; the number of government-kept schools had grown to 658, and although the prospects were tangibly improving, the Liberian government was reminded again that developing a public school system, like furnishing a home, is an interminable labor that, along with patience, money, and stubborness, establishes an unwaning demand for communications. In a more or less correlated move the government arranged with Radio Corporation of America to supervise the installation of telephone exchanges and to plan and originate a first public radio broadcasting system and presently a first television facility.

"Public education and public communications go together like faith and charity," President Tubman mused, adding that the same holds for domestic legislation and administration and what the school books call foreign policy. He could only add that in the case of Liberia the all-essential breath and blood of any sufficing foreign policy has to include African policy—by 1960 the going designation was "Pan-Africanism."

And that, as anyone could see, is much more easily said than done. The mighty continent that had so long been darkened by colonialism would not be instantly brightened by the death or senility of colonialism. Furthermore, Liberia's position in African affairs had to be one of moral persuader. Out of respect for more urgent citizen needs it could not afford an extensive military establishment nor permit a military-industrial complex.

By way of acceptance, during September, 1959, the Liberian government had announced its entry into a "defense agreement" with the United States—not a formal military treaty, but rather a casual memorandum of agreement which promises only "mutual consultation" with regard to "U.S. military assistance for Liberia in the event of aggression or threat of aggression against Liberia."

In a period when the United States was sowing military-aid commitments broadside, the Liberian memorandum was graciously modest, yet conspicuously motivated. Anarchistic or Socialist-inspired violence was flaring on both sides of the Sahara. New governments were openly declaiming that a formal union of "Free Africa" was mandatory. From Monrovia the Tubman administration declined discreetly to subscribe to that point of view. Instead it continued to build what it termed a policy of thoughtful flexibility in African relations.

Still in 1959 the Liberian government proposed the formation of a "neighborly association" of independent African nations to be known as the Associated States of Africa. As a first move toward implementation, leaders of Liberia, Guinea, and Ghana gathered in Monrovia during June, 1959. When Ghana's Kwame Nkrumah eloquently proposed the creation of a "formal union of sovereign African republics," the Tubman delegation discreetly deferred but managed to use the Monrovia Conference as a way-opener for a first gathering of the then fourteen African states which indicated their willingness to "advance and correlate technical and political developments" then in progress.

Stated simply, the Liberian position was that inasmuch as continental Africa was by then the most prolific mother of new independent states that the world has ever known, Liberia was willing and eager to serve as midwife, or baby sitter, or otherwise as a friendly and helpful neighbor for any or all of the new African nations inviting such services or associations. Meanwhile, and as also becomes a good neighbor, Liberia would continue to do its absolute best to keep its own house in order.

In the same mood and general text, in his New Year's Day (1960) address at his fifth inauguration, President Tubman announced that Liberia was in position to assume a more active role in the advancement of Pan-Africanism. He proposed establishing a common market for the West African republics; he urged all African people to "avoid excessive nationalism, class hatreds and racial bigotry." He pledged that his country would increase its endeavors to advance African needs both in Africa and in the growing folds of the United Nations.

Liberia's admission to the United Nations Security Council (in

December, 1960) marked a strong resurgence of the country's role in Pan-Africanism. A particularly tantalizing target was the lingering, politically amplified apartheid segregation in the Republic of South Africa. As leader of the Liberian delegation to the second conference of African states at Addis Ababa, Liberia's Tubman recommended that all the *bona fide* African states sever trade with the Union of South Africa. He next moved to set up an African *triparte* of Liberia, Guinea, and Ghana to deal cooperatively with economic, educational, cultural, health, and nutritional problems common to Equatorial Africa as a whole. A paralleling move was centered on arranging transportation concessions that would serve to benefit Africa as a whole, or in principal part. This included making Liberia's Roberts Field available to Scandinavian Airlines in the latter's extension of plane services to Africa and South America. Accompanying moves included granting of concessions for agricultural developments by firms based in Germany, Spain, and Italy. The additional implementations of Liberian iron and rubber concessions served to strengthen and expand trade ties with the West.

The correlation between domestic policy, trade expansion, and international affairs continued to show improved effectiveness. During May, 1962, Liberia served as host for the Monrovia Conference of Fifteen African Nations, a meeting which again advocated the African federation in principle but short of formal political union. The Tubman advocacy of responsible Pan-Africanism beginning within home boundaries began to gain stronger following. The outcome included renewed proselytizing for the resumption of improvements of schools, public health, agriculture, and communications within the respective countries.

The Tubman administration again expanded enterprises in experimental farming and livestock growing, public schools and health facilities, and supplemented the homeland endeavors with additional ventures in Pan-Africanism. One fairly typical innovation was the Accra Conference on Legal Education in Africa. Others included Liberia's very active participation in the United Nations Africa Economic Mission and the Geneva Disarmament Conference. Although Liberia's army was only a two-battalion militia force, the senior African republic contributed two fully manned companies of United Nations troops for active duty in the Congo. At the 1961 Lagos Conference of African Governments, Liberia resumed its endeavors to strengthen Pan-African cooperation in economic, cultural, and political fields.

As Liberian prestige continued to gain so did its foreign-trade patterns. Rubber exports rose in volume, market range, and placement as a citizens' crop. Even so, by 1962 rubber accounted for only 40 percent of the country's exports, while iron ore moved surely and permanently to first place.

Early in 1963 the senior black republic was made a member of the United Nations Trusteeship Council. Next it showed prominently in the Third World Congress of the Afro-Asian Peoples' Solidarity Organization. Next, and nearer home, Liberia joined a group of fourteen former African colonies in forming the Lagos Pact, a mutual defense and security covenant of West and Central African republics. At the Addis Ababa Conference of 1963, where thirty-one African states joined in founding the Organization of African Unity, Liberia's influence and determined stand for "moral cooperation" rather than political union proved brilliantly successful.

In its roles as special prophet for the new Pan-Africanism the Tubman administration encountered its most trying difficulties on home grounds. Among these tribulations were exceptionally severe strains on treasury reserves and credit responsibilities.

The costs of public works, particularly health services and public school expansions, began to race ahead of estimates as inflationary price rises afflicted more and more of the indispensable imports. These were aggravated by almost simultaneous declines in world prices of the principal exports, iron ore and natural rubber. Government revenues, heavily dependent upon excises and concession profits, sagged markedly even though export volumes continued to rise. Stoppages in roadbuilding, in the development of public water supplies and in similar facilities proved painfully expensive.

The Tubman administration chose to push on with the most-needed construction and offset with an austerity program in all other departments of government. In his inaugural address of January 6, 1964, the Liberian president noted matter of factly that his country, unlike the United States of America, could not endure an indefinite succession of fiscal deficits and arbitrary raising of debt ceilings.

Liberia's veteran chief executive next brought together what he termed and promptly proved a "purposefully economizing cabinet of fourteen patriotic Liberians who can read anything except the placement of clock hands that tell it's quitting time." In a like mood the national legislature joined in sharply reducing all administrative budgets and departmental appropriations, and gave the quick-freeze to the salaries of all government employees—including the legislators'.

During November, 1965, William Tubman found his seventieth birthday impressively commemorated with a new executive mansion replacing the weatherworn, long-moldering White House, and a new (and first) military academy. Less than elatedly, Africa's senior elected official accepted the "presents" on behalf of his country. He did not publicly reiterate two items of common knowledge: (1) he had spent most of his official tenure as the resident of an extremely modest beachside bungalow which remained perhaps the world's humblest executive mansion, and (2) his nation has sustained one of the smallest military budgets ever recorded by any sovereign nation.

The Tubman warnings against the "wrong kinds of economies" were also coming home to roost. The most obnoxious entry here was the coolie-level wages from which most of the tribespeople suffered. Without adequate exceptions concession-holders and citizen employers alike had not remedied the submarginal labor wages that had lingered and afflicted through the generations.

A revealing protest materialized early in 1966 when about 12,000 Firestone rubber plantation workers (at the time about half of the Firestone force), went on strike demanding cash wages of 15 cents an hour—about $1.20 a day. At the time a Firestone tappers' wage was 65 cents a day plus rice issues of from eight to sixteen pounds per week, and minimal shelter in labor camps or villages. It was pointed out that since their establishment back in the 1920s, the tappers' wages had been raised from 16 cents per day to the munificent 65 cents then prevailing. The evidence of labor exploitation was discomfiting.

For almost a quarter-century the Firestone rubber operations had shown consistent profits. Regardless of the recurring down trends in world rubber prices the steadily improving yields and value-adding processing methods, such as replacing baled rubber with liquid latex, justified better wages for the tappers. The darker side of the rubber coin, to speak metaphorically, was that the international and sometimes very elastic price structures for natural rubber had been built on outrageously low wages for the tappers; the world average for 1966 was barely 49 cents per day.

Firestone's management negotiated promptly, limited the strike to only five days, approximately doubled the base wage for tappers, increased the rice issues, accelerated the improvement of housing, accredited employee seniority and yielded various other fringe benefits. As gauged by procedures in the United States, the negotiations were entirely routine. But the situation in Liberia was markedly different. The "great tappers strike" was the first major strike the country had known. Labor statutes and precedents for government negotiations were lacking. There were other causes for concern; the most instant and audible were expressed, in some part clamorously, by the citizen rubber growers who were understandably concerned about the immediate future of their groves. Most of the citizen-owned Hevea plantings were still young and yielding only "small-small."

There was every reason to believe that all growers, including the small independents, would shortly be obliged to raise tapper's wages to or near the Firestone level. As the old Liberian expression goes, the "little ones didn't wish to be humbugged one time," i.e., bothered immediately.

Port and excise records, in any case, showed 1966 a better than average rubber year, at least for Liberia, with profits very near par for the 1960s. Grade and quality improvements tended to counterbalance the rise in tapping costs.

But the government opposed the strikers and their cause aggressively and almost instantly. While reaffirming his opposition to the exploitation of Liberian workers, President Tubman insisted with vehemence that the tappers' strike had been originated by alien troublemakers. He branded these in toto as "despicable persons entering the country with the intention of creating terror and subversion designed to disrupt Liberian peace and stability."

The assertion may have touched some fringes of truth. Resident personnel on the Firestone plantations agreed that some few apparent organizers had moved in from beyond boundaries, but for the most part the strike had been legitimately organized and peacefully executed. However, following the Tubman temper tantrum, which was unprecedented at least in terms of official records, the national legislature overreacted by granting the president a twelve-month tenure of "emergency powers." These included the authority to double the strength of the 2,500-man national guard, mobilize a "citizen defense force" and appoint special policemen to guard against "foreign invasion or internal revolt," and even more regrettably, to "create special tribunals to try the accused parties."

Most fortunately and to his enduring credit Tubman did not actively invoke any of the emergency powers. Most unfortunately he did order troops into the strike area, thereby projecting himself into the role of partisan strikebreaker—for a labor altercation that had in effect already been settled—rather than ex officio arbiter. He dispatched a national guard unit to the scene with specific orders to subdue violence and prevent arson; reportedly one striker had been killed and two injured, but later investigations did not so confirm. Several small fires had been set, but the resulting damage was trivial.

By no means surprisingly, and as this writer believes, entirely justifiably, Tubman was criticized sharply from several sides and by respected groups, including prominent members of his own administration. When tempers had cooled somewhat, the president—perhaps belatedly—pointed out that his actions had been motivated in greater part by the perils of so-called mob invasions to which a prolonged labor disorder might have made the country vulnerable.

At the time, and this was confirmed by various United Nations and other responsible reports, principal areas of West Africa were being threatened by throngs of transients, presumably Africans, who had chosen to abandon all former home associations and set forth to forage over as much of the continent as they chose. United Nations observers had already reported that the total number of the "swarmers" could have exceeded that of the entire population of Liberia. The mass migrancy continues, at least as this is written, and the Tubman forebodings were subsequently substantiated by UN observers who agree that Liberia or any other African country with no more than minimal frontier guards or police force might, indeed, be swept under or overwhelmed by the mass tide of migrants. Evidence to date has not widely sustained the charges or dread of criminality among the wanderers. But fanatic leaders have repeatedly been cited. The Tubman insistence that a small African country with minimal military or police forces is obliged to keep with precautionary actions that are not obligatory to a larger power is beyond easy denial. As Tubman philosophizes, "The working denominator is one of sagacity. Public servants, particularly when under great stress, can meet shortages of sagacity. We are, after all, just fallible people and our mistakes, great or small, are subject to almost infinite magnification. And like my stonemason father used to say, 'Excuses don't excuse after the mortar dries.' "

Regardless of the tappers' strike and its regrettable aftermaths, 1966 turned out to be a pivotal year for a changing Liberia.

The country's trade balance—$142 million in exports to $117 million in imports—remained favorable and growing. Excessive dependence on the United States as decisive buyer and supplier of Liberian goods began to abate. During 1966 only 39 percent of Liberian exports went to the United States. Germany received 32 percent, the United Kingdom 10 percent. The remainder was widely divided among smaller buyers in West European and Scandinavian countires. Rubber, although still gaining in tonnage (roughly 20,000 tons a year were being grown by private citizens and 30,000 tons by concessionaires), had waned in comparative value to 20 percent of the country's total exports. Thanks in greatest part to sharing iron ore profits, Liberia's revenue collections for 1966 totaled $46 million—by impressive contrast to the $700,000 in revenue collections for 1944, the first year of the Tubman presidency.

But the absolute needs of providing domestic services and other citizens' needs and for maintaining a convincing party-of-the-first-part basis for African leadership had placed the senior Negro republic in the quandary of practically all family heads everywhere: the more one earned, the more he *had* to have. Liberia was holding status as a superior bill payer; but it wasn't easy. By the end of 1966, 22 percent of all net revenue receipts were committed to debt services. President Tubman fondled his oversize cigar and recalled solemnly:

> Back in my childhood I used to get lickings when the teacher caught me spelling debt "d-e-t," money "m-o-n-i-e" and water with two t's. Sixty-five years later I get another kind of licking because—he spelled out the words correctly and with extreme care—"money" goes like "water." But bear in mind that just because the Liberian government pays its debts instead of just raising our debt ceiling does not mean that we are trying to be "un-American." For a small country like ours, placed as we are in a vast and troubled continent, keeping our government solvent is an obligation—prime and absolute. . . .

The obligation is also grim and enormously difficult. Government services commitments were plunging ahead of available revenue collections. Ore exports had zoomed from 3.4 million tons in 1961 to 15.5 million in 1966, with 20 million virtually assured for 1970 and 30 million tons probable for 1980. But the industrial importance of superior iron ore, although ever increasing and ever more global, could not offset the even more crucial needs of the enduring tribal or hinterland economy of Liberia which unlike the sleepy wet air, the sweeping silvery rains and the recurring rainbows is not, as yet, self-sustaining or naturally provided.

A tribewoman spins, dyes, and weaves a "skirt wrap" of cloth for herself or her mother, sister, or daughter. Priced competitively with commercial loom work the skirt wrap is worth perhaps four dollars, but is also a work of loving care that comprises several weeks or months of her life. The fiercely hot pod pepper which the tribal wife carries to the native market may be worth barely forty cents in official money, but she has put in several hours at growing, picking, and stringing the pepper and a full day at selling it.

All this is self-evident repetition of the prime rudiment that folk crafts simply cannot compete economically with technically mechanized manufactures. The still folkish agriculture of the predominantly agrarian tribes has implicit merits and weaknesses but, along with these, a profound indispensability as an irreplaceable food supplier. The tribal "ways" deserve and demand respect and complement. To that end Liberia's government during the 1960s again strove to develop a better-fitting agriculture for the tribespeople.

Typical enterprises included importing and distributing cattle and poultry especially bred for tropics needs, and improved rice production, featuring hardier and higher yielding wetland varieties suitable for planting in formerly useless mangrove swamps recently converted to floodable rice paddies. The government also joined individual tribes in building ponds and small lakes and stocking them with edible fishes.

There were numerous failures but fortunately there were successes to report even during a particularly disappointing year for Black Man's destinies. For Africa at large 1966 was a bad year; for the ghetto-bound American Negro it was even worse. The heartbreaking Biafran tragedy and the hardly less heartbreaking tragedy of Watts in California provided black and historic contrast to what many saw as Liberia's most progressive year.

On May 2, 1967, William V. S. Tubman, then seventy-two, was reelected president of Liberia for the sixth time, with a third vice-presidential replacement, William Tobert. Once again a renovated Tubman administration plowed into formidable labors. By then a third part of all revenue collections were committed to debt payment, and the third was destined to increase to half by 1970. The civil needs continued to multiply. With revenue collections again sagging as a result of recurrently lagging world prices for iron ore and rubber, Liberia renewed its austerity program. For the first time in its history the Negro republic imposed an "education tax" on all the larger personal incomes, and enacted legislation to severely limit credit enterprises. Not wholly coincidentally, for the first time in its history about half of the national legislature, eighteen of the thirty-one members of the House of Representatives and three of the twelve senators, was composed of tribespeople. For the first time, too, tribal votes accounted for more than 70 percent of all ballots cast.

Government operations as a whole showed undeniable improvement. The primary disappointment was an intensifying shortage of food production, which saw food imports abruptly doubled, i.e., from about $32 million in 1960 to $66.5 million in 1967.

The refurbished Tubman administration moved swiftly to commission an international grain company to import and mill rice, the basic grain of the tribespeoples' diet. Next the government contracted with one of its more recent rubber concessionaires (U.S. Royal) to develop an experimental and demonstration farming center in the Grand Bassa area north of Monrovia, with the particular goal of introducing, proving (or disproving), and helping to make available to citizen farmers more and better food crops, including tropics-adapted cattle, soybeans, rice, cassava, and beans.

In Liberia as elsewhere, the introduction or restoration of major food crops rarely comes easily or promptly. The Grand Bassa venture proved as much; a good deal of its work must be listed as preparatory for the twenty-first century.

The same difficulties obtain no less for an important and symbolic attack on the most crucial of all Liberian needs. During 1967 AID (the U.S. Agency for International Development) served as medium for a grant of $17 million to be used in building at Monrovia a prime health facility now named the John F. Kennedy Memorial Hospital. This center succeeds the National Training Institute for Medical Arts, which was first established in 1946 as a training center for "para-medical workers," principally nurses, practical nurses, and midwives (the respective totals were 108, 49, and 41). The Kennedy Center includes the basic facilities for training young Liberians in medical and health sciences as well as providing a pivotal national hospital.

The health center was soundly conceived and powerfully motivated. During 1960 the World Health Organization had compiled and published a preliminary survey of tuberculosis and found infection ratios as high as 70 to 80 percent of the population above thirty years of age. "Infection ratio" is not synonymous with developed infection, but the figures were alarming.

Another WHO survey made in 1960 suggested that at least 2.2 percent of the entire population of Liberia suffered from one form or another of leprosy. The so-called prevalence rate for yaws had reached a high of 19 percent in various hinterland areas; active infections ran above 2 percent. Until 1965, when mass vaccination was applied to at least 95 percent of the population, Liberia had suffered grievously from smallpox. Malaria is still a dogging and menacing health problem, and a prime reason for the extremely slow increase of the population.

In its rededication to satisfying public-health needs, Liberia encountered two contributory factors that recur on every side. One is the lack of small community hospitals which can serve as clinics and obstetrical, sanitation, and preventive centers for the various hinterland communities. (However, Liberia is better supplied with small clinics than many African nations.)

The other factor is the need for continued improvement of public education. In 1962 the Tubman-appointed education commissioner, Dr. John Payne Mitchell, had bluntly reported that after a century of legislation sustaining "compulsory education" hardly more than 15 percent of the nation's school-age children were actually enrolled in school.

With absolute candor Mitchell exhorted and demanded that his country cease and desist from imitating or mimicking public school procedures of other countries, particularly those of larger and richer ones, and build its own "saga of self-redemption" in public education. The Mitchell thesis is that Liberia cannot endure merely as a black miniature of the United States or any other nation outside or inside Africa. It must walk on its own feet, with its own stride, casting its own shadow.

On New Year's Day, 1968, William Tubman, the oldest president of the oldest Negro republic, once more took his oath of office, and speaking in the distinctive cadence of the African-born and African-descended, began his seventh inaugural address:

> . . . We, the non-nuclear nations, must learn how to settle disputes without risking the intervention of nuclear powers. . . . We, of peace-loving Africa, must accept the role of peacemaker . . . for all the world. . . .

A tired, slightly stooped, obviously aging black man was gazing at his listeners and beyond them at the mute, kneeling noonday shadows. But Liberia was not kneeling; as its aging president spoke, Liberia was standing tall.

17

SHADOWS ON BENDED KNEES

> In the history of this new Africa which has just come into the world, Liberia has a preeminent place because she has been for each of our peoples the living proof that our liberty was possible. And nobody can ignore the fact that the star which marks the Liberian national emblem has been hanging for more than a century—the sole star that illuminated our night of dominated peoples.
>
> SEKOU TOURÉ, president of Guinea,
> Liberia Independence Day Address
> (July 26, 1960).

IN MUCH of the tribe country of Liberia a person's shadow is believed to be one of his souls. In several of the tribe languages (specific reference here is to Kpelle), "shadow on bended knees" is an idiom signifying the act of peering thoughtfully into the future.

In the tribesman's believing mood of taking guidance from shadows on bended knees, one who views and studies Liberia will see wall writing, earth writing, and other auguries in the process of changing from forecast to fact. Many others are taking recognizable forms on Liberian horizons.

What follows is either proved or in advanced phases of becoming fact, or solidly predictable. In some part it is based on Liberian history, in greater part on the current beliefs and testimonies of perceptive and present Liberians—rich and poor, tribal and non-tribal, in government and out.

The shapes of consensus tend to include the following:

Liberia will keep with its gaining position as a bellwether for peace in Africa and the world beyond. This acceptance is based on the convinced testimony of cogent residents—from transient hunters to the president. The support factors include prevailing domestic and diplomatic records of the Liberian government and diverse works of the United Nations—including its Security Council, of which a Liberian tribeswoman, Mrs. Angie Brooks, is currently president.

Liberia will retain its status and continue to gain stature as a sovereign nation. As such it will remain a benefiting friend of the United States, a dependable advocate of the Western Powers, and a most valuable doorway into a most significant continent. At the same time Liberia will remain an especially effective advocate of Pan-Africanism.

But Liberia will not join any absolute union of African states. This position was very strongly confirmed throughout the 1950s and the early 1960s when the opportunities and motivations for joining, even leading, a United States of West Africa were rife and enticing. Liberia responded and continues to respond with reiteration of willingness to join informal associations or fraternities of African states to the end of improving neighborly and inter-African relations and effecting better confrontations with common problems.

But Liberia has chosen to remain sovereign and independent. This choice, which is cogent and, from all appearances irrevocable, accepts a continued status of geographical minuteness—of being one of the smaller African nations, without possibility of territorial aggrandizement or any apparent likelihood of substantial population increase. Liberia is definitely not a confluence of immigration. Although its citizenship is attainable by black people of any national origin, the prevailing immigration and emigration are very slight. Property ownership and suffrage remain exclusively for persons of African descent, but there is currently no cause for anticipating any substantial immigration from any source. Accordingly, the likelihood of census increase rests on the already resident population, and quite apparently on reducing markedly the prevailing and excessive infant and young-child mortalities; and the consistent improvement of public health, agriculture, and education—or, as we Americans like to say, standard of living.

These and similar statements sustain the no less insistent generality that the responsibilities of Liberian government, already extremely heavy for any nation of its size, will inevitably grow heavier. Liberia is, and will remain, obliged to work very hard and move very rapidly in order to sustain its domestic gains already effected; to continue moving ahead it must work still harder, run still faster, leap even higher.

In this mandatory acceleration Liberia's tribe-peopled frontiers (hinterlands) are more and more definitive, but they must now be accepted as vertical rather than conventionally horizontal frontiers.

There is no convincing prospect of an easy or immediate shift to an industrial economy as such. The preponderant tribespeople remain basically agricultural, and they must farm better in order to endure. Any reasonably perceptive student of tropical agriculture can recognize that this is possible, although certainly not simple or easy.

The prevailing per capita income of Liberia, at the moment estimated at about $185 per year, is not likely to sink lower, on the principle that when one is so very near the floor he cannot fall far. But one can accept that the prevailing economic floor, built on the two already developed and increasing exports of iron and natural rubber, is very likely to endure. The exportable outputs of both commodities are upward bound, at least by decade averages, and the increases seem almost certain to continue throughout the 1970s and very probably the 1980s.

Fortunately, too, the production of "raw" rubber and basic iron are trending toward a much higher proportion of direct citizen participation. Also, as pertains to iron ore, toward more generous profit-sharing at least partially supplemented by increases in citizen ownership of corporate stocks of some of the concession-holders.

Yet, granting that both of the basic exports are showing more gracious correlations with Liberian needs, they cannot of themselves assure a balanced national treasury. Particularly since 1960 Liberian government expense loads have risen rapidly and inalterably; as already noted, 1970 found approximately half of all collectible government revenues committed to the repaying or servicing of the national debt. The burden here is not necessarily an unending attrition, but it cannot be expected to diminish quickly or soon.

Herein a profound and obvious irony is involved: in order to sustain solvency a small, poor nation must attend and amortize its indebtedness with promptness and consistency, whereas the world's wealthiest nation, the United States, does not and shows no convincing intentions of ever paying its stupendous accrual of national debt. By impressive contrast, and despite past implications to the contrary, Liberia is and has long been one of the better credit risks in all the family of nations.

Noble as it is, this fact of life and national morality does not remove Liberia from the ranks of debtor nations or alleviate the hunger for credit that characterizes the economics of developing nations.

Valid and impressive as they are, Liberia's gaining exports of iron and rubber cannot singly or combinedly alleviate the essentially healthy hunger for credit any more than they can pay the tabs for all the burgeoning needs for government services and the laborious raising of living standards. Stated bluntly, both iron and rubber are minimal-value supplying enterprises, subordinate to and dependent on perennially changing, giant, and complexly entangled industries of fabricating. The "mineside" value of iron ore rarely exceeds two percent of the consumer's price of the manufactured products and is usually less than the primary shipping costs. The supplier of the primary ingredients remains at the farthest end of the paying line.

Substantially the same holds for rubber. On a tonnage basis the prevailing grower's price of raw rubber is less than one-tenth of the going price of the auto tire or other bulk manufactures. Furthermore, despite its splendid natural advantages, Liberia is not a dominant world source of either iron or rubber. The developable sites for rubber growing still include tens of billions of tropical acres; the synthetic sources include multibillion dollar industrial plants already working or readily adaptable.

As for iron, it is a geologist's adage that a twentieth part of the earth's mass is ferrous and that each decade unveils at least one more advantageous source of commercial iron ores. As this is written Australia looms as the most probable locale of the oncoming iron rush. Successive and responsible surveys indicate that Liberia has other encouraging possibilities for developing mineral resources, including gold, diamonds, copper, platinum, lead, chrome, aluminum, and no doubt others. But these and comparable possibilities prevail in many African lands and certainly in the comparatively recent past, the exploitations have not extensively helped African peoples.

Not long ago a tribe elder from Kakata favored me with a graphic recounting of how, back in the 1940s, his native "half town" became a casualty of the "gold fever." While a dutiful new wife was cleaning her master's hut she scrubbed a base sector of the wall and found in her diligent young hands genuine flakes of gold. As a dutiful bride should, she reported the find to her husband and together they swashed down and panned what had been the walls of her hut. By the time they had recovered several ounces of flake gold, neighbors joined in "watering away" their own hand-built residences. The gold fever kept spreading until the half town was virtually devastated. But the entire recovery of flake gold barely repaid the labor and the miscellaneous costs of building new huts. The elder reflected that had the labor required for the "humbug" (folly) of watering away the huts been spent constructively at farming, the half-towners would have been very much better off. "Gold folly makes bad medicine," he concluded. "Farming makes proper medicine."

His wisdom was evident. Now as through the years Liberia's number two resource, agriculture (inevitably its people are its number one resource), has continued to lag. Granting this is particularly apropos of the majority tribespeople, for the nation as a whole the food deficits are steadily and worrisomely increasing. Since the 1940s much of the tropical earth has enjoyed impressive gains in tropical agriculture. For the most part the very widespread advances are based on the developments of more effective plant genetics and livestock husbandry. These join in facilitating better adaptations to temperate-zone food crops, beginning with rice, corn, barley, and other people-sustaining grains, but including potatoes, beans, peanuts, sweet corn, and various other staple vegetables, as well as livestock-supporting forage grasses and soil-enriching legumes.

For the most part Liberia, particularly hinterland Liberia, has not succeeded in keeping pace with other tropical areas, including such developing tropical nations as the Sudan Republic, the Philippines, Indonesia, Ecuador, and many others. Almost any long-time student or practitioner of tropical agriculture will testify that drastically improved agriculture is readily attainable in Liberia. But this conviction does not bypass the need for dedicated, untiring, and perceptive effort.

There are undeniable needs for more and better localized research and experimentation, for much better appraisals of the implicit merits of traditional tribal farming, and for the purposeful development of more expert agricultural teachers and leaders among the tribespeople.

The present Liberian government is making increasing, admirable efforts to help with developing an indigenous farm leadership. But there are various primary needs such as better surveys of cultivable tribal lands and better adaptation of commercial forestry methods (a crucial area in which Liberia is still regrettably lacking), that are not yet adequately confronted.

As one career student of tropical agriculture, the writer is deeply disappointed by the persisting evasion of the food-supply needs by the iron exploiters and some of the principal rubber growers. The truth is that food-crops research and propagation are definitely compatible with the routine planning and operation of rubber groves. There is no invincible reason why rubber workers cannot be provided suitable lands and, as need be, guidance for making their own gardens and oil-palm groves, and for growing their own fruit, particularly citrus and bananas, which in most of Liberia can be grown effectively and easily. Just as certainly there is no divine decree prohibiting the establishment of pastures in or around the rubber groves and providing meat and milk animals to graze them.

There is need for better enforcement of legislation which requires the iron-mine concessionaires to cover the earth scars that result from strip or open-drill mining with methodical plantings of useful forest trees and grasses.

The fact that the United States and the white man's world at large have such deplorable records as polluters and despoilers (granting, as one must, that other races are also reprehensible for plundering) only stresses that Liberia is now confronted with its own formidable conservation problems. However, as President Tubman thoughtfully points out, Liberia has the undeniable advantages and heritage of an aboriginal tradition for conservation. Through the generations tribal subsistence farming has directed that a member shall clear a field, plant it, and after several years of cropping permit the cultivation to return to forest (small bush), meanwhile making a new clearing. The evident sense here is the methodical continuity abetted by natural replacement.

One evident lesson is that when and as its agriculture is upgraded, Liberia's traditional food-growing rationales will retain validity. Because of the exceptionally heavy rainfall the literal adoption of temperate-zone plowing routines would lead in great part to ruinous erosion losses. The traditional Liberian woman with the hoe and man with the ax or bolo (an oversize work knife) symbolize conservation practices that will not be invalidated. They reiterate that successful Liberian agriculture is surely committed to correlating some of the new with much of the old.

The conservation of natural resources and the integration of the premier resource—people—are mutually disposed to advance or languish together as what some Liberians term soul mates.

Despite some undeniable flaws and lapses, Liberia's score for effecting integration of its people is impressively better than that of the United States and, so it seems to me, of most of the other Americas.

This book, which seeks to be a kind of biography of the first African republic, has cited some conspicuous failures to attain integration while at least indicating a gaining tide of successes. In a mood of summation I find myself recalling a particularly revealing evening spent at listening to and reviewing some of the plans for the centennial celebration then being arranged for the hundredth birthday year, 1947. The host was Gabriel Dennis, then Liberia's secretary of state. Having favored his guests with a particularly delightful sequence of Liberian country chop and an impromptu piano recital featuring the works of Beethoven and Liszt, the cabinet officer encored with a very perceptive précis of his estimates of some of the more notable omissions in the centennial plans.

The secretary's first point was that the planners and commentators alike were failing to note adequately the number of tribal Liberians who had already held or were then holding important posts in their government. By 1947 about 200 tribespeople had proved themselves capable elective officials and for the small-personnel government that was indeed an impressive number.

Moreover, the roster included members of thirteen different tribes. The Greboes, for example, had already provided a vice president, two Supreme Court judges, an attorney general, nine members of the national legislature, and a particularly revered circuit judge. The Bassas had contributed a secretary of public instruction and, for the nation at large, at least four outstanding church leaders. The Vai had given a brilliantly capable postmaster general (with the engaging name of Momolu Massaquoi), and two exceptionally able legislators. And so on down an already memorable list.

The black secretary of state did not regard the obtaining participation of tribespeople as adequate, but he held that the degree of political integration already attained was not only impressive but could be epochal. He noted thoughtfully that the United States had not granted any status of citizenship to the Indians ("American aborigines") until 1924 and that the Indians' subsequent participation in national government was almost nil. As for American Negroes, it was common knowledge that this largest American minority was still not being admitted to citizen rights, and that the Negro's participation in federal government was still substantially limited to message running, serving as maids or janitors, or, in the higher positions, as window washers.

In 1947 as at present, anyone could see that politically as well as socially and economically and "integrationally" Liberia had a great deal of growing yet to do. Fully as evident was, and is, the fact that Liberia must attain the integration of its exceptional diversity of black people in its own distinctive ways. Certainly during its first century the black republic had demonstrated most convincingly that it cannot endure as a little black satellite of the United States; as Gabriel Dennis stated, Liberia had endured and would live on only as a "self-sustaining protoplasm" of and in Africa.

Gabriel Dennis excelled as a prophet, as secretaries of state are expected to. After the passing of most of another quarter-century, Liberia is even more convincingly African than it was at the centennial. Scratch a Liberian and an African bleeds; shake his hand and there is a better than even chance that he will respond with the spontaneously playful, profoundly African "finger-snapping" handshake.

The spiritual and tangible, almost genetic immersion in Africa continues to produce or relate to an unending variety of ambiences that cannot be surely classified either as causes or effects. Inevitably many of these encompassing forces are political. One entry which has proved baffling to passing commentators and resident analysts alike is the persistence of a one-party government. As this book has noted in considerable detail, in all its one hundred and twenty-five years as a republic Liberia has had only two enduring political parties. Throughout most of the past century one, the still incumbent True Whig Party, has been in power; ballot competition, when offered, has been mostly from highly temporary dissident groups within the party. This continuing fact of life and history invites such opprobriums as "contrived monopoly" or "government by collusion."

Currently one notes that most—at this writing at least twenty-eight—of the new African republics or recognizable facsimiles of republics have one-party governments. Undeniably, and properly, Liberia is a bellwether for the newer Africa and quite properly it is being emulated and imitated. But here again there are bound to be root causes—much more compelling than the normal mimicry of the very young. Probing for causes, always one of the more satisfying and rewarding of mortal pursuits, gains exceptional moment and pertinency as regards Africa's very special heritage of political life.

One who would use Liberia as his study desk, or laboratory table, finds immediate cause to accept that part of the cause for the one-party system is routinely financial and organizational. Whatever the country, it takes money and immense quantities of work to keep any political party alive and functioning. To keep two alive requires much more than twice as much money and work; the out party being very much more of a care and feeding problem than the in. Liberia remains a comparatively poor country. Its prevailing ranges of public-servant salaries are minuscule by contrast to those of the United States. Emoluments are not keeping pace with the rapidly rising standards of competence; there is no lush overage for feeding even the in party.

At about this point explanatory efforts shift farther toward the negative pole. One cannot deduce factually that the Liberia one-party system comprises a passkey to dictatorship. Liberia has never been a dictatorship; recurrency of strong presidents has not changed this fact, nor effectively stifled divergent viewpoints within an administration. In this there is no visible or incipient likelihood of change. Liberia has no military-industrial complex; it has never known a *coup d'état*; it has never had an actual civil war or even more than a few weeks of junta rule. The records and prospects of military dictatorship balance at zero.

But Liberia's one-party system, now a precedent for most of contemporary Africa, has many revelations to offer. Its prime reason for being is lack of sufficient motivation for a rival party or parties.

As we have already noted, Liberia's incumbent True Whig Party took root as the True Black Man's Africa-for-Africans Party, standing opposed to the alleged élite of immigrant brown men, the long-demised Republican Party. Under its banners, which unabashedly stressed degrees of blackness, the True Whigs sought and eventually won a following principally of farmers, outlying homesteaders and tribespeople who chose to join the Negro settlers from abroad. The passing years had increased the scope and variety of members, and in time removed or at least greatly diminished the accentuation on shades of skin pigmentation.

For almost a century the rootage for an effective and self-perpetuating rival party or parties had not been sustained. The prevalent—in most of the white man's world the inevitable—labor party, which usually attracts not only "labor" or blue collars (in most of Africa, no collars), but white collars including teachers, professional people, and others, has remained absent. Like practically all of the new African states, Liberia does not as yet have enough available membership to effectively sustain a labor party.

The necessary fusion has been tardy. A primary reason is the implicit opposition of tribal life and tradition. As recent African history has shown so unhappily, the phenomenon of a political party made up of a given tribe or tribal bloc can lead to absolute disaster. Similarly, the direct association of African political parties with specific religions is a perilous business. Liberia's Africa-typical status as a nation made up preponderantly of tribes with its elected president necessarily a chief of chiefs acknowledges tribal precedents and procedures, including those that commit all tribe workers to obedience to their chiefs and to sustaining the tribe. Inevitably, compliance with the traditional ways and mandates of the tribe remains at cross furrows with prevailing Western concepts of liberal labor legislation and the cause and progress of labor unions.

The signs here point out that in a world of accelerated change the tribe is not and cannot be wholly unchanging. Public schooling, advancement of more and more young men and women into professional and government services, and multiplying pressures on tribal leadership are in the fore ranks of the guarantors of change. So, inevitably, is the proliferation of communications, including radio and television—in Liberia no real cause for celebration—and road-building, which at this writing is still nothing to get excited about or to entice the motoring tourist.

But the strongly improving, more convincingly professional Liberian government is inevitably a force of change—for the better. All these forces and developments and quite possibly others are relevant to the certainty of changes that will eventually make way for a labor, or liberal party and for more farsighted and needs-conscious labor legislation in Liberia. The first factor of assurance and significance here is the absolute that Liberia has endured and shaped survival patterns primarily by virtue of perceiving and attending—if belatedly, not fatally so—to the really vital needs of its people. It is Liberian diamonds to Liberian foofoo balls (dumplings) that Africa's first black republic will keep on showing the way to political survival by means of dealing more good to more and more of its people.

A person, practically any person, who has spent his or her lifetime or best years in the tropics, whether as teacher, preacher, or some other kind of developer, or even as an occasionally celebrating tropical tramp, grows irrevocably aware that tropical governments can endure only by giving their people substantially more than they take from them. This is one of the comparatively few absolutes of tropics environment, a particularly demanding environment that accentuates and magnifies the essentiality of the prime human needs for food, shelter, and health, and if at all possible, access to neighbor settlements.

The hard essence here stems from man's inability to stand alone against the voracious, conquering jungle which appears to be too busy at propagating to find time or space for dying. In Liberia, as in tropical Africa as a whole, and for that matter, most other "deep," Equatorial tropics, any enduring government is obliged to accommodate the elemental survival needs by means of very special calibers and reaches of services to resident peoples. Through its dark years and its verdant years Liberia exemplified and accommodated the obligations very well.

If a white-haired, sun-seared *tropico* may again briefly indulge in the first person: During my earlier years of tropical work (there are those who contend that "employment" should be substituted for "work"), the most weighty questions and topics for gin-and-bitters debate were: How much (how little) is the tropics government giving the native, and how little or how much is it taking back from the native? In gab marathons usually punctuated with mosquito slapping and elbow lifting, in locations ranging from back-bush palaver houses to manacca-shack pubs to the somewhat more ornate capital verandas, the prime tropical thesis of "government" *vs.* "native" was practically insatiable as well as perennial.

Particularly in African capitals, Monrovia included, the colonial-offices crowd, including the British, French, Belgian, Portuguese, Spanish, or whichever was there first, were inveterate participants. Their standby thesis and near consensus was unchanging—colonies and colonial government had endured because, directly or indirectly, they put more into the palms of the chiefs or in the bellies of the commoners than would otherwise obtain. Most tropics colonies would therefore endure, and kindly whistle for yet another round of drinks.

In those generally unmourned years—special reference here is to *circa* 1935 to 1945—Liberia was the stock example, in Africa the only example, of the dismal futility and the impending, pitiable doom of a black republic, perish the thought, in Black Africa. Liberia, so the gabbing went, was by far the most "primitive" sliver of the African tropics. It had the least to give the natives—laughably less than the colonial governments were giving, and almost necessarily, the most to take. Therefore, Liberia would inevitably sink and molder away while the African colonies, however insolently maligned, besplattered and aggravated, would endure.

I never really believed a damned word they were saying. My heretic doubts and usually unspoken denials were supported by neither clairvoyance, inherent intelligence, Reuters, nor Winston Churchill. But in my plodding, snail-brained way I had looked on and listened to most of Liberia and prior to that I had marked or served time in better than a dozen other deep-tropics countries. I did not believe many or any of the colonies would endure primarily because their governments took too much, gave too little, and knew too little. Even I could see that poor, maligned, little Liberia was even then doing more for its people and taking less from them than was any colonial government I had encountered.

Being the sporting type I left the judges' decision to history—which, I am told, is the classic attitude of almost any befuddled snail. Once more history came across. Liberia endures. Most of colonial Africa has faded away, much like a very large bad smell. There is strengthening reason to believe that the remnants of African colonies will do likewise, most probably within the present century.

Meanwhile, in more and more areas of giving and doing—public schools, health and sanitation services, agricultural research and revivals, professional training and scholarships, and so ever on, Liberia is providing more than averagely well for more and more of its people, even while pace-setting with increasing competence for more and more of the newer Africa about it.

Liberia moves forward, in greatest part on its own power and for its own people, but increasingly as a way shower for the oversize wonderlands of an awakening continent. Meanwhile, the black republic, Africa's oldest, is most engagingly tridentated; it is yesterday, today and tomorrow clasping hands and pressing ahead with happy, ground-gaining and distinctly African dance steps.

APPENDIX

The Presidents of Liberia	*Dates of Tenure*
1. Joseph Jenkins Roberts	1847–1856
2. Stephen Allen Benson	1856–1864
3. Daniel B. Warner	1864–1868
4. James Sprigg Payne	1868–1870
5. Edward James Roye	1870–1871
6. James S. Smith	1871–1872
7. Joseph Jenkins Roberts	1872–1876
8. James Sprigg Payne	1876–1878
9. Anthony W. Gardiner	1878–1883
10. Alfred H. Russell	1883–1884
11. Hiliary R. W. Johnson	1884–1892
12. Joseph J. Cheeseman	1892–1896
13. William D. Coleman	1896–1900
14. Garrett W. Gibson	1900–1904
15. Arthur Barclay	1904–1912
16. Daniel E. Howard	1912–1920
17. Charles D. B. King	1920–1930
18. Edwin Barclay	1930–1944
19. William V. S. Tubman	1944–1970

NOTE: Actually only seventeen men have been presidents of Liberia. Both Roberts and Payne were returned to the presidency following interim periods as private citizens.

BIBLIOGRAPHY: RECOMMENDED AREAS FOR READING

THE AMERICAN COLONIZATION SOCIETY

The varied publications of the American Colonization Society remain one of the better reservoirs of background information regarding Liberia. Fortunately a substantial portion of this vast accumulation of diverse material is now available on microfilm. Of the very diverse total, the following entries may be mentioned as particularly worthy of listing here:

American Colonization Society, *Annual Reports*, 1818 through 1910, Washington, D.C. Of these ninety-one volumes or brochures, Numbers 1, 22, and 26 are listed under the Society's original name, The American Society for Colonizing Free People of Colour of the States. In all, sixty-eight of the volumes have been reproduced in photostats by University Microfilms of Ann Arbor, Mich.

The official journal of the American Colonization Society, *The African Repository* (and *The Colonial Journal*) 1825–1910, was compiled and published in 1910 by Way & Gedeon, Washington, D.C. Beginning in 1948, University Microfilms, Ann Arbor, Mich., has made film copies of this material, continuous from 1825 through 1892.

In addition more than a hundred special publications by or for the American Colonization Society have been transmitted to the Library of Congress or distributed publicly by the Society. These publications are particularly helpful in terms of their delineations of the various periods of the Colonial Society's long and ever-changing life span. Some especially revealing instances are:

A Few Facts Respecting the American Colonization Society, Way & Gedeon, Washington, D.C., 1829.

Address of Francis Scott Key at the Middle Dutch Church, Protestant Episcopal Press, New York, 1829.

Mathew Carey, *Letters on the Colonization Society*, "stereotyped" by L. John, Philadelphia, 1828.

———*More Letters on the American Colonization Society*, Carey & Hart, Philadelphia, 1935. This publication is especially interesting because it provides a review of legislation by the various states as well as the national government with respect to the colonization of free slaves and an enlightening back section entitled "A Report by Joseph Jones, a Coloured Man Lately Sent to Liberia by the Kentucky Colonial Society to Ascertain the True State of the Colony."

Connecticut Colonization Society, *Annual Report of the Managers*, New Haven, 1841.

Hall, James, *An Address to the Free People of Colour of the State of Maryland*, Maryland Colonization Society, Baltimore, 1819 and 1835.

Lugenbeel, James W., *Sketches of Liberia: A Brief Sketch of the History of Liberia and a Succinct Account of the Geography, Climate, Products and Diseases and the Customs and Superstitions of the Contiguous Native Tribes*, C. Alexander, Washington, 1850.

Roberts, Joseph Jenkins, *First President of Liberia*, Hail, 1869; and Sunderland, Byron, *Liberia's Next Friend*, Annual Discourse delivered at the sixty-ninth annual meeting of the American Colonization Society, January 17, 1886.

Warren, George W., *The Duty of Strengthening Liberia*, Sixty-third Annual Meeting of the American Colonization Society, Washington, D.C., 1880.

Latrobe, John H. B., *Liberia: Its Origin, Rise, Progress and Renewal*, American Colonization Society, Washington, D.C., 1880.

OFFICIAL OR QUASI-OFFICIAL PUBLICATIONS

Republic of Liberia, *Liberian Code of Laws*, by Authority of the Legislature of Liberia, Cornell University Press, Ithaca, N.Y., 1956.

Dassen, J. J., and L. A. Grimes, *Cases Decided in the Supreme Court of Liberia*, esp. Vol. 1, 1861–1907; Vol. IX, 1945, 1947; Vol. X, 1948–1950. Law Reports Digest, New York, 1968.

Cole, H. B., *The Liberian Year Book*, Diplomatic Press and Publishing Company, London.

Tubman, William V. S., *President Tubman of Liberia Speaks*, Consolidated Publishing Company, London, 1959.

Solomon, M. D., with W. L. d' Azevedo, *A General Bibliography of the Republic of Liberia*, Northwestern University Press, Evanston, Ill., 1962.

SPECIAL STUDIES

Brawley, Benjamin G., *A Social History of the American Negro*, Macmillan, New York, 1921.

Duryee, William Rankin, *The Present Success of Liberia*, American Colonial Society, Washington, D.C., 1882.

American University, *Area Handbook for Liberia*, Superintendent of Documents, U.S. Government Printing Office, Washington, D.C., 1964.

Reeve, Henry Fenwick, *The Black Republic, Liberia: Its Political and Social Conditions*, Negro University Press, New York, 1969.

Strong, Richard P., Editor, Harvard African Expedition, 1926–1927, Harvard University Press, Cambridge, Mass., 1930.

Huberich, Charles Henry, *The Political and Legislative History of Liberia*, Central Book Company, New York, 1947.

Miller, Armistead, *Liberia Described: A Discourse Embracing a Description of the Climate, Soil, Agriculture, Missionary Works, Improvements, Etc. by a Citizen of Monrovia*, John M. Wilson, Philadelphia, 1859.

Massachusetts Colonization Society, *The Colony at Liberia*, Pierce & Parker, Boston, 1831.

Taylor, Wayne C., *The Firestone Operations in Liberia*, National Planning Association, Washington, D.C., 1956.

Cloward, Robert W., with R. P. Armstrong and Others, *Growth Without Development, an Economic Survey of Liberia*, Northwestern University Press, Evanston, Ill., 1966.

Johnston, Sir Harry Hamilton, *Liberia, in Geographical Journal*, Vol. XXVI, No. 2., August, 1905, London; also Smithsonian Institution Publication 126, Washington, D.C., 1906.

McLaughlin, Russell, *Foreign Investment and Development in Liberia*, Praeger, New York, 1966.

Foote, Commander Andrew H., *Africa and the American Flag*, D. Appleton, New York, 1854.

Sumner, Senator Charles, *Independence of Hayti and Liberia: A Speech on the Bill to Authorize the Appointment of Diplomatic Representatives*, United States Senate, April 23 and 24, 1862, Congressional Globe, Washington, D.C., 1862.

Padmore, George, *American Imperialism in Liberia*, Centrizdat, Monrovia, 1931.

Burroughs, W. L., *Remarks on the Colonization of the Western Coast of Africa by the Free Negroes of the United States*, W. L. Burroughs Steampower Press, New York, 1850.

Constant, Victors N., *Salut, Frères de la lointaine Afrique*, Imp. de L' Estat, Port-au-Prince, 1959.

International Court of Justice, the Hague, *An Official Account of the Contentions and Proceedings on South West Africa Before the International*

Court of Justice, 1960–1966, The Hague, 1968.
African Study Center, *Liberian Studies Journal*, Vol. 1, 1968, DePauw University, Greencastle, Ind.
Price, Frederick A., *Liberian Odyssey by Hammock and Surfboat,* Pageant Press, New York, 1954.
Henries, A. Doris Banks, *Liberian Folklore, A Compilation of 99 Folk Tales*, Macmillan, London, 1961.
Hale, Sarah J. B., *Liberia, or Mr. Peyton's Experiment*, Harper & Brothers, New York, 1853; University Microfilms, Ann Arbor, Mich., 1960
U.S. Public Health Service, *Health Missions in Liberia*, Vol. 63, No. 42, October, 1948, Washington, D.C.
Schwab, George, *Tribes of the Liberian Hinterland*, edited by George W. Harley, M.D., Peabody Museum, Cambridge, Mass., 1947.

GENERAL

Anderson, Robert Earle, *Liberia: America's African Friend*, University of North Carolina Press, Chapel Hill, N.C., 1952.
Buell, Raymond Leslie, *Liberia Century of Survival*. University of Pennsylvania Press, Philadelphia, 1947.
Greene, Graham, *Journey Without Maps*, Doubleday, Doran & Company, Garden City, N.Y., 1936.
Furbay, Elizabeth Jane, *Top Hats and Tom-Toms*, Ziff-Davis, Chicago, 1943.
Henries, Richard and Doris, *Liberia, the West African Republic*, F.R. Brun, New York, 1950.
McPherson, John Hanson Thomas, *History of Liberia*, Johns Hopkins Press, Baltimore, 1891.
Mills, Lady Dorothy R. M. W., *Through Liberia*, Duckwood, London, 1926.
Richardson, Nathaniel R., *Liberia, Past and Present*, Diplomatic Press and Publishing Company, London, 1959.
Shufeldt, Robert W., *The American Navy and Liberia*, American Colonization Society, Washington, D.C., 1876.
Tolson, Melvin, B., *Libretto for the Republic of Liberia*, Twayne, New York, 1953.
Warner, Esther S., *The Crossing Fee: A Story of Life in Liberia*, Houghton Mifflin, Boston. By the same author, *New Song in a Strange Land*, V. Gollancz, London, 1948.
Welch, Galbraith, *The Jet Lighthouse*, Museum Press, London, 1960.
Wilkeson, Samuel, *A Concise History of the Commencement, Progress and Present Condition of the American Colonies in Liberia*, Madisonian Office, Washington, D.C., 1839.
Young, James C., *Liberia Rediscovered*, Doubleday, Doran & Company, Garden City, N.Y., 1934.

INDEX

71 72 73 10 9 8 7 6 5 4 3 2 1